Through the Bible

Through the Bible
Workbook

Patricia J. David

ISBN-13: 978-0-89827-130-0
ISBN-10: 0-89827-130-4

CONTENTS

ACKNOWLEDGMENTS

In September of 1989, I embarked on a journey that was both exhilarating and frightening at the same time — a year-long study through the entire Bible with the congregation at Our Savior's Wesleyan Church in Mukwonago, Wisconsin. I am grateful to those who attended our weekly Bible study that year. Their eagerness to learn and their patience with my nervousness (and stammering) was a great encouragement and an incentive for me to study harder and to work even more diligently to make the Bible clear to them.

I am also deeply indebted to my husband, Dan, and our two children, Jonathan and Rebecca. Without such an understanding and affirming family, this entire study would have been impossible.

I also would like to thank my father, Hugh Hackney. Since Dad gave his life to Christ late in 1978, he has always had an intense desire for truth and is an ardent student of the Scriptures. His commitment to God's Word undoubtedly has influenced me. Many times, he acted as a sounding board for my ideas and offered me resources to help in my study.

Thanks are also extended to Dr. Joe Seaborn for reading through the manuscript soon after it was written in 1991. His kind and affirming words were an encouragement to me and a confirmation that perhaps this study could be useful in the church at large.

Lastly, I would like to thank God for providing the most wonderful Book in the world. I am thankful that He opened my eyes and allowed me to discover the exciting truths of Bible books which I had considered uninteresting before. I know that God helped me every day as I sought His guidance and a proper understanding of His Word in order to complete this study. To Him be all the glory!

INTRODUCTION

Without question, the Holy Bible is the most wondrous book ever to be written. Every year over thirty million copies are sold in more than eleven hundred languages and dialects, an obvious indication of a popularity that transcends language, culture and time. Any credible literary scholar would be inclined to agree that the Bible is without equal among writings through the ages; it is a literary masterpiece.

— Bible Project

One historian is often quoted as saying that most people's understanding of history is like a graduated string of pearls, but without the string. What do you think this statement means?

Wisdom comes from the fear of the Lord.

The purpose of this study is to help supply the "string" for the events of the Bible, to enable you to examine every passage from the perspective of the Bible as a whole.

If you are like most people, just the thought of having to study through the whole Bible is overwhelming. Where will you ever find the time to read the entire Bible?

G. Campbell Morgan once told a local congregation that the entire Bible could be read from beginning to end, from Genesis 1 to Revelation 22, in only seventy-eight hours at pulpit speed. A lawyer in the group challenged Morgan, but, to his amazement, found he was able to read the entire Bible himself in just eighty hours. Even a slow reader devoted to reading only thirty minutes a day should be able to complete the whole Bible three times in one year.

What are the major hindrances to reading and understanding the Bible?

1. *Lack of commitment*

2. *Lack of time*

3. _____

If you were to ask forty authors today to write on the subjects of law, history, philosophy, ethics and prophecy, there would undoubtedly be very little unity, if any, among them. There would be no general consensus of opinion among them on even one subject, even if they all had similar educational, political and religious backgrounds.

But consider the Bible: It was written by more than forty authors from all walks of life — kings, farmers, shepherds, fishermen, prophets, a physician and philosophers — from different lands and cultures, spanning some fifteen hundred years. The topics they covered ranged from philosophy and theology to law and government. And yet the Bible is a cohesive unit with a central theme and unity of thought throughout. There is no contradiction or dispute. Indeed, it was fashioned by one Mind, for "no prophecy of Scripture came about by the prophet's own interpretation. For prophecy never had its origin in the will of man, but men spoke from God as they were carried along by the Holy Spirit" (2 Peter 1:20b-21).

Men may have been the vehicles through which the words were written, but the finger of God is on every page. No human effort could have produced such a masterpiece of revelation. The Bible is not of human origin; it is the divinely inspired Word of God, completely inerrant in the original autographs. It is truly the most amazing book in the world.

What is the predominant theme that runs throughout the Bible, and where does it begin?

God Seeking Man

Sin/Fall

The Bible is divided into two major sections, the Old and New Testaments. "Testament" means "covenant" or "agreement." What is the relationship between the Old and New Testaments?

Before we begin to study the first and foundational book of the Old Testament, it is helpful to note the major divisions of the Old and New Testaments and what information you can expect to find there. (See the charts at the end of the lesson for the arrangements of the books of the Bible.)

Now that you are familiar with the divisions of your Bible, you are ready to begin studying it. Secure a good, accurate translation of the Bible from which to study. Then, read each book of the Bible before each class, and pray for God's guidance as you study. Together, we are about to embark on a fantastic journey as we see how God's plan is unfolded through His Word.

For personal reflection:

1) How much time do you spend reading the Bible right now?

2) How much time do you think you could set aside for reading the Bible in preparation for this class?

3) In what ways do you think your life could benefit from a better, broader understanding of God's Word?

4) Have you made a commitment to attend every class you possibly can?

5) Pray this week that God will help you to persevere, even through the difficult weeks of the not-so-exciting books of the Bible.

For the next lesson . . .

Read all of Genesis, or at least the following:
- Genesis 1:1–3:24
- Genesis 4:1–5:32
- Genesis 6:1–8:22
- Genesis 9:1-17; 11:1-8
- Genesis 12:1–13:18; 15:1-21
- Genesis 22:1-19; 28:10-22; 32:22-32
- Genesis 37:1-36; 39:1–45:28

The Old Testament Bookshelf

The word "testament" means "will" or "covenant." The term "Old Testament," therefore, refers first to God's covenant or promise-law to bless mankind through the Jewish nation. It has also come to refer to the *writings about* the Old Covenant, although, strictly speaking, these ancient books are the Old Covenant *Scriptures.*

Purpose/Theme:
The Scriptures of the Old Testament record the story of God's chosen people, Israel, and their relationship to His covenant to bless all nations through them.

The Books of Law

Genesis · Exodus · Leviticus · Numbers · Deuteronomy

The Books of History

Joshua · Judges · Ruth · First Samuel · Second Samuel · First Kings · Second Kings · First Chronicles · Second Chronicles · Ezra · Nehemiah · Esther

The Books of Poetry

Job · Psalms · Proverbs · Ecclesiastes · Song of Songs

The Books of Major Prophets

Isaiah · Jeremiah · Lamentations · Ezekiel · Daniel

The Books of Minor Prophets

Hosea · Joel · Amos · Obadiah · Jonah · Micah · Nahum · Habakkuk · Zephaniah · Haggai · Zechariah · Malachi

The New Testament Bookshelf

The term "New Testament" refers first to the covenant God made with all people to save them through His Son, Jesus Christ. It has also come to refer to the *writings about* that promise-law.

Purpose/Theme:
The Scriptures of the New Testament show how God's Old Covenant is fulfilled in Jesus Christ. It describes how the early Christians became the Church, and how to live in the light of the risen presence of Christ.

The Gospels

Matthew | Mark | Luke | John

History

Acts

Letters by Paul

Romans | First Corinthians | Second Corinthians | Galatians | Ephesians | Philippians | Colossians | First Thessalonians | Second Thessalonians | First Timothy | Second Timothy | Titus | Phileomon

General Letters

Hebrews | James | First Peter | Second Peter | First John | Second John | Third John | Jude

Prophecy

Revelation

Reprinted from *The Bible Visual Resource Book*, © 1989 by Gospel Light Publications, Regal Books, Ventura, CA 93003. Used by permission.

GENESIS

"Genesis" comes from the Greek word that means "beginnings," and that name defines for us both the scope and the limits of the book. Genesis is a book of beginnings.

What are some of the beginnings described in the book of Genesis?

Physical

Tim

People

_____

_____

In the time span recorded in Genesis, we learn more about the character of God than in any other single book in the Bible. Genesis shows us a sovereign God in control of a world He created. It describes how He interacts with His people — how He walks with them, talks with them, and brings them into a covenant relationship with Him. His grace and judgment are both revealed, as are His requirements of man.

It is in Genesis that we see the oldest and most profound definition of faith (15:6). In fact, more than half of Hebrews 11, the great faith chapter of the New Testament, refers to characters found in the book of Genesis. Turn to Hebrews 11:1-22 and list these characters:

Abram believed

_____

_____

_____

Much like the first chapter in any good book, Genesis provides portents of what is to come. It sets the stage for the rest of Scripture. Indeed, it is virtually impossible to understand the meaning and necessity of the New Testament without the foundation laid by the book of Genesis.

GENERATION

The most profound proclamation of all time appears in the first verse of Genesis: "In the beginning God created. . . ." The Bible nowhere attempts to prove or defend the existence of God. It was considered to be self-evident that God exists and considered foolish to believe otherwise. In the beginning, this God created — also a logical conclusion based on what we see.

Why is it so important that we believe the first chapter of the Bible — that God created everything that is?

Foundation

In Genesis 1:31, God looked over all that He had made (plant life, fish, birds, animals and man) and saw that it was very good. But by the time we reach chapter 6, God is grieved that He even made man and decides to destroy all but a handful of His creation.

What happened between chapters 1 and 6?

Sin — turned away from God

DEGENERATION

Read Genesis 3:1-19.

List four of the tragic results of the fall of Adam and Eve:

1. _Death_

2. _Separation between God & Man_

3. _____

4. _____

How was God's grace evident, even in the midst of punishment?

2nd chance

Write out Genesis 3:15.

_____

_____

_____

This principle is foundational in the Bible: Where there is sin, there is always judgment and the shedding of blood. We see this in the Old Testament with the sacrificial system of Israel, where animals are sacrificed to atone for the sins of the people, and throughout the New Testament, where we find Jesus Christ, the perfect Lamb of God, shedding His blood as the atonement for man's sin. Romans 6:23 declares, "For the wages of sin is death," and this principle becomes unequivocally clear to Adam and Eve.

By the time we read the story of Cain and Abel in Genesis 4, we have seen the rapid progression of sin: from the eating of forbidden fruit to the jealousy and hatred that result in murdering a family member. By chapter 6, ". . . every inclination of the thoughts of [man's] heart was only evil all the time" (6:5). Adam and Eve succumbed to an outward temptation, but now the temptation is from within. Man's heart has become thoroughly evil.

Chapters 6 through 9 record God's judgment on mankind. Yet even after the Flood, men still refuse to obey the God who created them. But chapter 12 initiates a new phase in God's plan.

REGENERATION

REDEMPTION is the theme that runs through the entire Bible, and now we begin to see God inaugurating His plan. He calls Abram, from Ur of the Chaldeans (or Babylonians), to go to the Land of Canaan, the "Promised Land." God chooses Abram to be the father of His chosen people, through whom the promised Redeemer would come, and God establishes a covenant with Abram that is critical to our understanding of Israelite history.

List the conditions, promises and sign of God's covenant with Abram (12:1-3):

_____

_____

_____

_____

_____

The remainder of Genesis is an account of patriarchal history, the beginnings of the nation of Israel, and the further unfolding of God's plan of redemption. In short, Abraham (formerly Abram) and Sarah have a son (born to them in their old age), Isaac, who marries Rebekah, and they have twin boys named Jacob and Esau. Esau sells his birthright to his brother for a bowl of stew, and Jacob receives Isaac's blessing. Jacob (who is renamed "Israel" in Genesis 32:28) becomes the father of twelve sons, who become the heads of the twelve "tribes" of Israel. One of these sons, Joseph, is sold into slavery by his brothers, but becomes second in command over all of Egypt and eventually saves his family from famine. The family of Jacob, seventy in all, then comes to settle in the land of Goshen, as a family favored by all of Egypt. This takes us right up to chapter 50 in Genesis.

List the twelve sons of Jacob/Israel (35:22-26):

_____

_____

_____

What foreshadowing do we see in Genesis of God's promise of a Redeemer?

_____

_____

_____

_____

_____

What do we learn about the character of God in Genesis?

_____

_____

_____

_____

_____

_____

For personal reflection:

1) Do you have trouble believing that God created the world and everything in it? If so, why do you think that is so?

2) Have you ever noticed in your own life the effects of original sin that have plagued the human race since Adam?

3) What do you think the world would be like if Adam and Eve had never sinned?

4) Do you think your fellowship with God is still broken if you sin? Does God still require punishment and the "shedding of blood" as the penalty for sin?

5) Pray this week that God would help you to see why mankind needs a Redeemer and to begin to understand the uniqueness of God's plan of redemption.

For the next lesson . . .

Read all of Exodus, or at least the following:
- Exodus 1:1–3:22
- Exodus 7:14–11:10
- Exodus 12:1-51; 13:20–14:31
- Exodus 16:1-35
- Exodus 19:1–20:21
- Exodus 24:1-18; 31:12-18
- Exodus 32:1–34:35; 40:34-38

EXODUS

E xodus stands in relation to Genesis much the same as the New Testament stands in relation to the Old Testament. Genesis revealed man's failure under every condition: a perfect environment, the rule of conscience, and patriarchal rule. But with Exodus comes divine deliverance; God steps into history and rescues His people from bondage.

Each book in the Bible seems to have a predominant theme which buttresses the overall theme of redemption. In Genesis, it was man's failure; in Exodus, it is revelation. We must keep in mind that the early Israelites did not have the luxury of owning a completed and printed Bible. Theology and knowledge of God were at the beginning stages. In Exodus, God begins to teach man about himself — to reveal His person and His nature to those who would serve Him.

GOD REVEALS HIS PERSON.

In Exodus 3, God appears to Moses from the midst of a burning bush. What is the significance of the name God revealed to Moses?

I am has sent me (Moses) to you.
(-eternal power, unchangeable character)
Yahweh - derived from hebrew term for I am

Right from the outset, God reveals His name, because He wants His people to begin to learn who He is. Most of the "revelations" in Exodus describe and define that name.

GOD REVEALS HIS POWER.

In chapters 7 through 12, God sends a series of plagues upon the Egyptians. What is the purpose of these plagues?

1. They are the culmination of a promise.
2. They are a revelation of a Person.
3. They are a demonstration of power.

Each plague reveals God as the almighty God who is more powerful than the Egyptian deities — deities such as Khnum, the guardian of the Nile, and Hapi, the spirit of the Nile; Heqt, a god in the form of a frog, revered as the god of resurrection; Hathor, the mother-goddess in the form of a cow; Apis, the bull of the god Ptah and a symbol of fertility;

Imhotep, the god of medicine; Isis, the goddess of life; Re, Aten, Atum and Horus, all sun gods; Pharaoh, who was worshiped by the people as a deity; and Osiris, the giver of life.

The Israelites now have lived in a foreign land for over four hundred years and undoubtedly have been exposed to the Egyptian religions. God wants all the world to know that He is the one true God and that none of the "gods" of man's creation are any match for His power.

GOD REVEALS HIS PROVISION.

GOD REVEALS HIS PROTECTION.

GOD REVEALS HIS PRECEPTS.

Now, three months after they left Egypt, the Israelites arrive at the Sinai Desert and camp at the base of the mountain (chapter 19). Up to this point, God has been dealing with them in grace and mercy, but now a new order begins in the lives of the Israelites as God reveals to them their part of the covenant; God begins to unfold His law — His moral law, the way to holy living.

Why did God give the Israelites the Ten Commandments?

Giving the Law and covenant

What were they (chapter 20)?

Pertaining to God, respecting:

God's person _No other go_

God's worship _____

Literal God's name God's name _not misuse → Matt 5-34_

God's day _Made for man_

Pertaining to others, respecting:

Parents _honor_

Life _murder_

Purity _____

Honesty _Steal_

Truth _False testimony_

Covetousness _Do not covet_

God's people understand that this is a conditional covenant, contingent on their continued obedience to the law of God: "Now if you obey me fully and keep my covenant, then out of all nations you will be my treasured possession. Although the whole earth is mine, you will be for me a kingdom of priests and a holy nation" (19:5-6).

GOD REVEALS HIS PRESENCE.

What was the purpose of the Tabernacle (25:8)?

To serve as a sanctuary of God

The Tabernacle is God's tangible way of teaching Israel that He is indeed actively present among them.

GOD REVEALS HIS PLAN.

Nothing is done by accident in Exodus. Every incident and every command is designed by God to reveal who He is and what He expects from His people. And everything points toward a future fulfillment. Through the events in Exodus, God slowly unfolds His plan, which won't be realized fully until the coming of Christ. We see God's master plan revealed in two passages at the heart of Exodus:

A. THE PASSOVER (12:1-30)

In the Passover, the Israelites were delivered from the angel of death (a harbinger of God's judgment), but through the work of Christ, they would be saved from eternal death. The Israelites were to celebrate the Passover annually, in order that they would be so ingrained with God's way of redemption that they easily would see and understand when fulfillment came.

B. THE TABERNACLE (chapters 25–27, 30)

As was the Passover, so is the Tabernacle also a shadow for the Israelites, a symbol of the Christian life yet to come. The arrangement of articles in the Tabernacle was designed purposely to point Israel to the way of redemption.

To come to Christ, we must first CONFESS our sins, and then be CLEANSED by His atoning sacrifice. We also CONSECRATE ourselves to God — we fully commit ourselves to following His will. It is only when we have "come through the Tabernacle" in this way that we can truly come into the presence of God and experience COMMUNION with Him.

The Tabernacle was a temporary shadow of the reality that was to come through Jesus Christ. Read Hebrews 9 to gain a better understanding of the significance of the Tabernacle.

Genesis began with God and ended with death. Exodus begins in slavery, but ends with the glory of the Lord filling the Tabernacle (40:34). In Genesis, man was cut off from God and cast from His presence; in Exodus, God reaches down to man, revealing himself and His plan so that man can know Him and can experience communion with Him once again. What a wonderful foreshadowing of the redemption of God through Jesus Christ!

For personal reflection:

1) In what ways does God still reveal himself to us today?

2) Why does God want us to know Him?

3) Do you think God still requires obedience to a covenant, or have things changed? Must we still follow the Ten Commandments?

4) What are some of the "gods" people worship today?

For the next lesson . . .

Read all of Leviticus, or at least the following:
- Leviticus 1:1–3:17
- Leviticus 4:1-35; 5:1-19
- Leviticus 10:1-10; 11:1-47
- Leviticus 16:1-34; 17:11-12
- Leviticus 20:1-27
- Leviticus 23:1-44; 25:1-55
- Leviticus 26:1-46

The Exodus

The exodus and conquest narratives form the classic historical and spiritual drama of OT times. Subsequent ages looked back to this period as one of obedient and victorious living under divine guidance. Close examination of the environment and circumstances also reveals the strenuous exertions, human sin and bloody conflicts of the era.

Miles 0 20 40 60 80 100
Kms 0 50 100 150

Marah—Oasis
Rameses—City or settlement
Trade routes
Israelite route

Sea of Kinnereth

CANAAN Jordan R. AMMON

Rabbah

Jericho Heshbon

Ashdod Mt. Nebo

Lachish
Gaza Hebron

PHILISTIA Salt Sea

Beersheba

Lake Menzaleh

Way of the Land of the Philistines

DESERT OF ZIN

AMALEKITES

Rameses

Migdol DESERT OF SHUR

Punon

GOSHEN Way to Shur

Wadi of Egypt Kadesh Barnea EDOM

Pithom • Succoth

SHASU NOMADS

On

Exact crossing place through the Biblical "Yam Suph" is unknown.

Trade route

DESERT OF PARAN

Memphis •

EGYPT Way of the Land of the Red Sea

Ezion Geber

MIDIAN

Marah

Elim

Nile R.

Red Sea DESERT OF SIN

Dophkah

Hazeroth

The Israelite tribes fled past the Egyptian system of border posts, through the Red Sea and into the desert, where they avoided the main military and trade routes leading across northern Sinai. The less frequently traveled "Way of the Sea" led to the remote turquoise and copper mining region northwest of Mt. Sinai.

Rephidim Mt. Sinai

DESERT OF SINAI

Red Sea

It was necessary for Moses to take refuge in Midian where the Egyptian authorities could not reach him. The decades spent on "the far side of the desert" were an important formative part of his life.

Red Sea

In historical terms, the exodus from Egypt was ignored by Egyptian scribes and recorders. No definitive monuments mention the event itself, but a stele of Pharaoh Merneptah (c. 1225 B.C.) claims that a people called Israel were encountered by Egyptian troops somewhere in northern Canaan.

Finding precise geographical and chronological details of the period is problematic, but new information has emerged from vast amounts of fragmentary archaeological and inscriptional evidence. Hittite cuneiform documents parallel the ancient covenant formula governing Israel's "national contract" with God at Mount Sinai.

The Late Bronze Age (c. 1550-1200 B.C.) was a time of major social migrations. Egyptian control over the Semites in the eastern Nile delta was harsh, with a system of brickmaking quotas imposed on the labor force, often the landless, low-class "Apiru." Numerous

Canaanite towns were violently destroyed. New populations, including the "Sea Peoples," made their presence felt in Anatolia, Egypt, Palestine, Transjordan, and elsewhere in the eastern Mediterranean.

Correspondence from Canaanite town rulers to the Egyptian court in the time of Akhenaten (c. 1375 B.C.) reveals a weak structure of alliances, with an intermittent Egyptian military presence and an ominous fear of people called "Habiru" ("Apiru").

Exodus 12:31—Deuteronomy 34:12
(Summary: Numbers 33:1-48)

Reprinted from *The Bible Visual Resource Book*, © 1989 by Gospel Light Publications, Regal Books, Ventura, CA 93003. Used by permission.

The Tabernacle

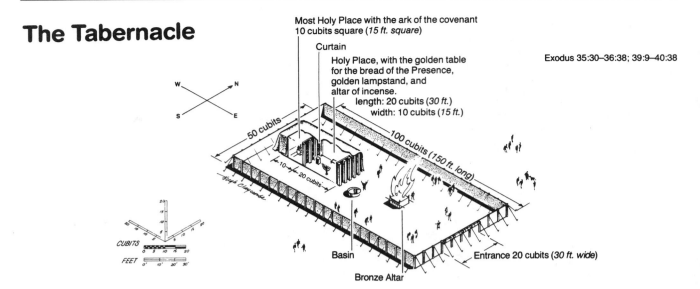

Most Holy Place with the ark of the covenant
10 cubits square (*15 ft. square*)

Curtain

Holy Place, with the golden table
for the bread of the Presence,
golden lampstand, and
altar of incense.

length: 20 cubits (*30 ft.*)
width: 10 cubits (*15 ft.*)

Exodus 35:30–36:38; 39:9–40:38

50 cubits

100 cubits (*150 ft. long*)

10 — 20 cubits

CUBITS

FEET

Basin

Bronze Altar

Entrance 20 cubits (*30 ft. wide*)

The new religious observances taught by Moses in the desert centered on rituals connected with the tabernacle, and amplified Israel's sense of separateness, purity and oneness under the Lordship of Yahweh.

A few desert shrines have been found in Sinai, notably at Serabit el-Khadem and at Timnah in the Negev, and show marked Egyptian influence.

Specific cultural antecedents to portable shrines carried on poles and covered with thin sheets of gold can be found in ancient Egypt as early as the Old Kingdom (2800-2250 B.C.), but were especially prominent in the 18th and 19th dynasties (1570-1180). The best examples come from the fabulous tomb of Tutankhamun, c. 1350.

Comparisons of construction details in the text of Ex 25-40 with the frames, shrines, poles, sheathing, draped fabric covers, gilt rosettes, and winged protective figures from the shrine of Tutankhamun are instructive. The period, the Late Bronze Age, is equivalent in all dating systems to the era of Moses and the exodus.

© Hugh Claycombe 1981

The Tabernacle Furnishings

Exodus 37–38:8

The symbolism of God's redemptive covenant was preserved in the tabernacle, making each element an object lesson for the worshiper. The Levitical priests, including some with Egyptian names and perhaps Egyptian training, gave meticulous attention to facts about the shrine. Reconstruction of the furnishings is possible because of extremely detailed descriptions and precise measurements recorded in Ex 25-40.

The ark of the Testimony compares with the roughly contemporary shrine and funerary furniture of King Tutankhamun (c. 1350 B.C.), which, along with the Nimrud and Samaria ivories from a later period, have been used to guide the graphic interpretation of the text. Both sources show the conventional way of depicting extreme reverence, with facing winged guardians shielding a sacred place.

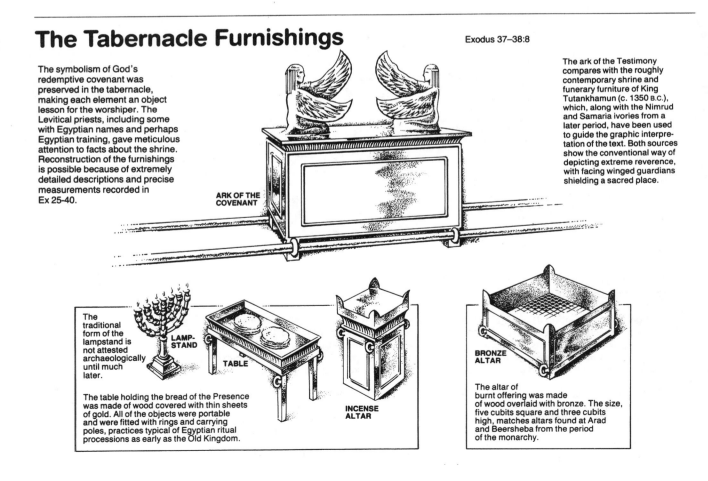

ARK OF THE COVENANT

LAMP-STAND

The traditional form of the lampstand is not attested archaeologically until much later.

The table holding the bread of the Presence was made of wood covered with thin sheets of gold. All of the objects were portable and were fitted with rings and carrying poles, practices typical of Egyptian ritual processions as early as the Old Kingdom.

TABLE

INCENSE ALTAR

BRONZE ALTAR

The altar of burnt offering was made of wood overlaid with bronze. The size, five cubits square and three cubits high, matches altars found at Arad and Beersheba from the period of the monarchy.

LEVITICUS

In Exodus 20 through 23, God gave to Israel the moral law, the Ten Commandments. This was His ideal and His righteous requirement for mankind. But because of sin, it was impossible for man to live up to that law. So now, in Leviticus, God gives the ceremonial law — the provisions for atonement (restoring fellowship and satisfying God's justice) when man would break God's moral law.

The instructions in Leviticus were given to Moses during the month and twenty days between the setting up of the Tabernacle (see Exodus 40:17) and the departure of the people from Mt. Sinai (see Numbers 10:11). "Leviticus" means "pertaining to the Levites" (who served God as priests) and often was referred to as the "Book of Atonement."

Some of the key words in the book give us a clue to its purpose: "sacrifice" is used 42 times; "atonement," 45 times; "blood," 86 times; "holy," 87 times; and "priest," 189 times. The key to atonement with God was to be found in the sacrifice and the shedding of blood performed by the priest. God's people were then called to live holy and pure lives before Him.

Look up these New Testament examples of Leviticus terminology: Romans 3:25; John 1:29; 1 Peter 1:19; Romans 8:3; 1 John 1:7; Ephesians 5:2; and Hebrews 7–8.

It is virtually impossible to understand the significance of Christ's shed blood without an understanding of Leviticus. The sacrifices described here were performed by the Israelites year after year for twelve to fourteen hundred years before Christ came, and the terminology and significance of the sacrifice were ingrained in the Israelites from birth.

THE WAY TO GOD: SACRIFICE (1:1–10:20)

Sacrifice always had been an integral part of religion and was a part of the pagan cultures at this time. But the sacrificial system described in Leviticus is different because it was authored by God. It was part of His plan of redemption. As we examine the sacrifices, it should soon become clear how these sacrifices were preparing God's people to understand His plan of salvation. There were basically five kinds of sacrifices or offerings presented to God:

A. THE BURNT OFFERING: DEDICATION (chapter 1)

The burnt offering was a voluntary offering of a male domesticated animal or two birds without defect. The distinctive feature of the burnt offering was the burning of the entire animal, signifying total dedication and complete surrender to God (cf. Rom. 12:1).

B. THE GRAIN OFFERING: DEVOTION (chapter 2)

The grain offering, referred to in some translations as a cereal, meat or meal offering, was a voluntary offering consisting of grain, flour, olive oil, incense, baked bread or salt. It is expressly noted in Leviticus 2 that no yeast or honey was to be a part of this offering. Some think that perhaps this was because of the use of these items in brewing beer or their prevalence in Canaanite rituals. In the New Testament, yeast becomes a metaphor for sin, and the Jews would readily perceive the correlation with the grain offering.

The purpose of the grain offering was to acknowledge God's goodness and provisions; it was an expression of homage, thankfulness and devotion (cf. Heb. 13:15).

C. THE FELLOWSHIP OFFERING: COMMUNION (chapter 3)

The fellowship offering, or "peace offering," was voluntary and consisted of any animal without defect from the herd or flock and a variety of breads. It symbolized peace between God and man, as well as the inward peace or wholeness that resulted.

One peculiar characteristic set this offering apart from the others: it was meant to be shared. The fat was burned, but the priest and the family of the offerer ate the rest. The Israelites considered this offering an expression of communion and fellowship and a way of expressing thanks to God. It was an indication of a desire to maintain and demonstrate right relations between God, man and neighbor (cf. Eph. 2:14).

D. THE SIN OFFERING: PROPITIATION (chapter 4)

The sin offering was a mandatory offering to bring atonement for a specific unintentional sin when the offender became aware of that sin. The offering involved the confession of sin by laying hands on the head of the sacrifice, transferring the guilt to the animal. In this way, the offerer recognized that the animal's life was being taken as a substitute for his own, since sin was punishable by death. In His mercy, God accepted a substitute life, and His justice was satisfied (cf. Rom. 8:3).

E. THE GUILT OFFERING: RESTITUTION (5:14-19)

The guilt offering, like the sin offering, was a mandatory atonement. It was prescribed for those offenses which required restitution. A ram or lamb was to be slaughtered and restitution was to be paid, including a 20% fine. The guilt offering brought cleansing of the conscience.

What was the usual order for the offering of the sacrifices, and how was that order significant (Lev. 9)?

bull calf for sin off & ram for burnt offering
fellowship

Christ was the final sacrifice, offered once and for all for our atonement (see 1 John 4:10). He died in our place for our sin — He was the perfect atoning sacrifice! Christ's death takes on new meaning in light of Leviticus:

> This is an illustration for the present time, indicating that the gifts and sacrifices being offered were not able to clear the conscience of the worshiper. They are only a matter of food and drink and various ceremonial washings — external regulations APPLYING UNTIL THE TIME OF THE NEW ORDER (Heb. 9:9-10, emphasis added).

God was preparing His people so that they would have the fullest possible understanding of the significance of the work of Christ.

Leviticus continues in chapters 6 and 7 by giving various laws pertaining to offerings, and then addresses the priesthood in chapters 8 through 10. Aaron's family was designated to serve the function of priests, and the Levites as a tribe were set apart to care for the Tabernacle and were given the tithes of the people for their sustenance. The deaths of Nadab and Abihu, Aaron's sons, for offering unauthorized fire before the Lord (chapter 10) may seem unusually harsh, but Israel had to understand from the outset that God demanded complete obedience.

THE WALK WITH GOD: SEPARATION (11:1–27:34)

The overwhelming message of the remainder of Leviticus is that God is holy and demands holiness in His presence. The call to "be holy" is found in Leviticus 11:44-45; 19:1; and 20:7, 26. In fact, the word "holy" appears more times in Leviticus than in any other book of the Bible. Israel was to be totally consecrated to God, which was to be expressed in every aspect of her life, to the extent that all of life had a certain "ceremonial" quality.

Part of the priest's responsibility was to "distinguish between the HOLY and the common, between the unclean and the clean" (10:10, emphasis added). Every aspect of daily life was governed by God's law and required constant consideration of what was clean or unclean.

What was the purpose of the Day of Atonement, and what was its significance (chapter 16)?

10th day 7th month

— Handed Aaron's

— deny yourselves — no work

Chapters 18 through 20 contain various ethical and moral laws forbidding practices unimaginable to most of us, but which were commonly practiced by the pagan nations around Israel (18:3).

Suzanne Joy

The various feasts that the Israelites were required to celebrate are described in chapters 23 through 25 (see the chart at the end of this lesson). These feasts helped to preserve Israel's identity as God's chosen people and to remind them continually of God's goodness to them. The sacrifices were a reminder of Israel's sin, but the feasts were a reminder of God's grace.

Leviticus closes with the pronouncement that God rewards obedience (26:3-6, 9, 11-12) but that disobedience would bring certain punishment (26:14-39). Notice especially Leviticus 26:27-35, a graphic prophecy of the judgment which Israel eventually did invoke on herself in 722 and 586 B.C.

The way to God was by sacrifice. In the Old Testament, the only way man could be reconciled to God was through the substitutionary death of an animal, which provided only temporary atonement. The sacrifices were performed endlessly, day after day, year after year. The festivals came and went. Through it all, Israel constantly was reminded of the sin which cut them off from God's presence. But they also were reminded that God, in His mercy and compassion, was willing to accept a substitute — the death of an animal instead of the offender. God was revealing His purposes so that, in the fullness of time, Israel would recognize and appreciate the atoning work of Christ.

Leviticus also shows us that the walk with God is one of separation. God taught the Israelites early what He expected from His chosen people. He demanded complete obedience, separation, consecration, sanctification — in a word, holiness.

For personal reflection:

1) For the Israelites, there was no sacrifice for deliberate, defiant sin. Do you think God is still intolerant of willful disobedience?

2) How does Christ's sacrifice on the cross provide atonement for sin?

3) Does God still expect holiness from His people today? Does that mean we're supposed to be ritualistic and legalistic?

4) Pray that God would convict you of any sin in your own life and help you to realize the price that was paid for your redemption.

For the next lesson . . .

Read all of Numbers, or at least the following:
- Numbers 5:1–6:27
- Numbers 8:5–9:14
- Numbers 11:1–12:16
- Numbers 13:1–14:45
- Numbers 16:1–17:13
- Numbers 20:1-13; 21:4-9; 22:1-41
- Numbers 27:12-23; 33:50-56

Leviticus

Old Testament Feasts and Other Sacred Days

NAME	OT REFERENCES	OT TIME	MODERN EQUIVALENT	DESCRIPTION	PURPOSE	NT REFERENCES
Sabbath	Ex 20:8–11; 31:12–17; Lev 23:3; Dt 5:12–15	7th day	Same	Day of rest; no work	Rest for people and animals	Mt 12:1–14; 28:1; Lk 4:16; Jn 5:9; Ac 13:42; Col 2:16; Heb 4:1–11
Sabbath Year	Ex 23:10–11; Lev 25:1–7	7th year	Same	Year of rest; fallow fields	Rest for land	
Year of Jubilee	Lev 25:8–55; 27:17–24; Nu 36:4	50th year	Same	Canceled debts; liberation of slaves and indentured servants; land returned to original family owners	Help for poor; stabilize society	
Passover	Ex 12:1–14; Lev 23:5; Nu 9:1–14; 28:16; Dt 16:1–3a, 4b–7	1st month (Abib) 14	Mar.-Apr.	Slaying and eating a lamb, together with bitter herbs and bread made without yeast, in every household	Remember Israel's deliverance from Egypt	Mt 26:17; Mk 14:12–26; Jn 2:13; 11:55; 1Co 5:7; Heb 11:28
Unleavened Bread	Ex 12:15–20; 13:3–10; 23:15; 34:18; Lev 23:6–8; Nu 28:17–25; Dt 16:3b, 4a, 8	1st month (Abib) 15–21	Mar.-Apr.	Eating bread made without yeast; holding several assemblies; making designated offerings	Remember how the Lord brought the Israelites out of Egypt in haste	Mk 14:1,12; Ac 12:3; 1Co 5:6–8
Firstfruits	Lev 23:9–14	1st month (Abib) 16	Mar.-Apr.	Presenting a sheaf of the first of the barley harvest as a wave offering; making a burnt offering and a grain offering	Recognize the Lord's bounty in the land	Ro 8:23; 1Co 15:20–23
Weeks (Pentecost) (Harvest)	Ex 23:16a; 34:22a; Lev 23:15–21; Nu 28:26–31; Dt 16:9–12	3rd month (Sivan) 6	May–June	A festival of joy; mandatory and voluntary offerings, including the firstfruits of the wheat harvest	Show joy and thankfulness for the Lord's blessing of harvest	Ac 2:1–4; 20:16; 1Co 16:8
Trumpets (Later: Rosh Hashanah—New Year's Day)	Lev 23:23–25; Nu 29:1–6	7th month (Tishri) 1	Sept.-Oct.	An assembly on a day of rest commemorated with trumpet blasts and sacrifices	Present Israel before the Lord for his favor	
Day of Atonement (Yom Kippur)	Lev 16; 23:26–32 Nu 29:7–11	7th month (Tishri) 10	Sept.-Oct.	A day of rest, fasting and sacrifices of atonement for priests and people and atonement for the tabernacle and altar	Cleanse priests and people from their sins and purify the Holy Place	Ro 3:24–26; Heb 9:7; 10:3, 19–22
Tabernacles (Booths) (Ingathering)	Ex 23:16b; 34:22b; Lev 23:33–36a, 39–43; Nu 29:12–34; Dt 16:13–15; Zec 14:16–19	7th month (Tishri) 15–21	Sept.-Oct.	A week of celebration for the harvest; living in booths and offering sacrifices	Memorialize the journey from Egypt to Canaan; give thanks for the productivity of Canaan	Jn 7:2,37
Sacred Assembly	Lev 23:36b; Nu 29:35–38	7th month (Tishri) 22	Sept.-Oct.	A day of convocation, rest and offering sacrifices	Commemorate the closing of the cycle of feasts	
Purim	Est 9:18–32	12th month (Adar) 14,15	Feb.-Mar.	A day of joy and feasting and giving presents	Remind the Israelites of their national deliverance in the time of Esther	

On Kislev 25 (mid-December) Hanukkah, the feast of dedication or festival of lights, commemorated the purification of the temple and altar in the Maccabean period (165/4 B.C.). This feast is mentioned in Jn 10:22.

© 1989 by Gospel Light Publications. Permission granted to purchaser to reproduce this Sheet for class purposes only.

Reprinted from *The Bible Visual Resource Book*, © 1989 by Gospel Light Publications, Regal Books, Ventura, CA 93003. Used by permission.

NUMBERS

Numbers is a fascinating, though disappointing, look at God's chosen people. It might more aptly be called "The Book of Murmurings," for the Israelites are characterized throughout Numbers as grumblers and complainers.

The theme that runs throughout the Bible is redemption, but each book contains its own sub-theme. In Leviticus it was that God is holy and demands holiness; in Numbers, God is faithful and demands faithfulness. This theme is punctuated by recounting, almost endlessly, the unfaithfulness of the Israelites and their leaders, and their subsequent punishment by God.

Numbers 1 through 9 begin the book with an overwhelming display of Israel's obedience to every command of God. Each of these chapters seems to build in its anticipation of complete compliance and heightened obedience on the part of the Israelites. The climax comes in Numbers 7:89, when communion is established between God and prophet when the Lord speaks to Moses from between the cherubim on the ark of the covenant. It is now clear to all of Israel that it is God himself, Yahweh, who is dwelling in the midst of their camp and is speaking through Moses, His prophet.

Finally, in chapter 10, Israel sets out, only a few weeks' journey from the Promised Land. But, only three days into their journey, Israel's lack of faith surfaces, as evidenced by grumbling and disobedience. The same thing happened a year earlier, when, just three days after the parting of the Red Sea, they began to complain.

The pattern is always the same, and it is illustrated over and over in the book of Numbers: A lack of faith, coupled with a distorted perspective, leads to grumbling, which in turn gives rise to rebellion. But, despite their grumbling, God proves time and again that He is faithful.

GOD IS FAITHFUL TO SUPPLY THEIR NEEDS.
(chapter 11)

GOD IS FAITHFUL TO SUPPORT HIS CHOSEN LEADERS.

Chapter 11 — God gives Moses seventy elders to help carry the burden of the people.

Chapter 12 — Miriam and Aaron oppose Moses and are rebuked by God.

Chapter 16 — Korah, Dathan, Abiram and 250 leaders rise up against Moses and Aaron. Again, God punishes those who oppose His chosen leaders. The ground opens up and swallows Korah, Dathan and

Abiram, along with their households. The other 250 are consumed by fire (16:31-35).

Chapter 17 — God confirms His choice of priests through the budding of Aaron's staff.

Why was it so important that God show support for His chosen leaders?

_____

_____

_____

_____

_____

_____

GOD IS FAITHFUL TO SECURE THE VICTORY.
(chapters 13–14)

At this point in their journey, Israel is ready to enter Canaan. Twelve spies, one from each tribe, are sent into the Promised Land to assess the situation. After this forty-day excursion, all twelve spies come back with the report that indeed, "it does flow with milk and honey!" (13:27). But notice the different perspectives on the situation in Canaan:

— Joshua and Caleb confidently exclaim, "We should go up and take possession of the land, for we can certainly do it" (13:30b).

— The other ten spies reply, "We seemed like grasshoppers in our own eyes, and we looked the same to them" (13:33b).

The difference between the two accounts is that Joshua and Caleb believe that God will be faithful to secure the victory: "And do not be afraid of the people of the land, because we will swallow them up. Their protection is gone, but THE LORD IS WITH US. Do not be afraid of them" (14:9b, emphasis added).

But the Israelites' distorted perspective gives rise to rebellion, and they refuse to possess the land God has provided for them. Again we see Moses interceding on behalf of the people, and God relents from His anger and forgives them (14:20). But He still punishes them. He condemns them to wander in the wilderness for forty years, until everyone twenty years old and older dies — these would never have the privilege of entering the Promised Land, though their children would.

GOD IS FAITHFUL TO SATISFY THEIR THIRSTING.

Chapter 20 begins "in the first month" of the fortieth year after the Exodus, when most of the old generation has died. The past forty years have been spent wandering in the desert, the events of which we have almost no record. The Israelites are now brought back to Kadesh-Barnea. They've come full circle, and the Land of Promise lies before them once again.

It is a new generation facing a new opportunity. But this new generation is just as bad as the old, and they begin the "let's go back to Egypt" refrain they have learned from their parents (20:3-5). Despite their grumbling and complaining, God provides water from a rock to satisfy their thirsting.

What was Moses' sin, and why did God punish him so severely (20:7-12)?

_____

_____

_____

_____

_____

_____

_____

GOD IS FAITHFUL TO SEND HEALING.

Chapter 21 recounts Israel's first victory over the Canaanite king of Arad. God gives them complete victory. But with the very next breath, they are impatient, and they grumble against God and Moses. Here, we read of their most flagrant attack on manna yet: "We detest this miserable food!" (21:5b).

And so God punishes them once again, this time with venomous snakes. Though many die, God is faithful to send healing. Moses is told to put a bronze serpent on a pole. If those who were bitten would look to the pole, they would live.

What is the New Testament significance of this act (see John 3:14-15)?

_____

_____

_____

_____

_____

_____

GOD IS FAITHFUL TO SUMMON FORTH BLESSINGS FOR HIS PEOPLE.

In Numbers 22 through 24, we read the curious account of the blessing of Balaam. Balak, the King of Moab, summons Balaam, a pagan diviner, to curse the Israelites. God knows that Balaam's original intention is to curse the Israelites, but only blessings come from Balaam's mouth. This story teaches us that no one is outside of God's control. And no one can thwart His purposes or His promises. God is faithful to summon forth blessings for His people, even from a pagan prophet whose greed tempts him to curse them.

GOD IS FAITHFUL TO SEAL HIS PROMISE.

What significance does Numbers have for us today (see 1 Corinthians 10:6-12 and Romans 15:4)?

_____

_____

_____

_____

_____

_____

_____

For personal reflection:

1) Have you ever been guilty of grumbling and complaining in spite of God's faithfulness?
2) Does God still punish disobedience in His people, or is everything "covered" by grace? Explain.
3) How has God shown His faithfulness to meet your needs?

For the next lesson . . .

Read all of Deuteronomy, or at least the following:

- Deuteronomy 4:1-40; 5:1-33
- Deuteronomy 6:1–7:26
- Deuteronomy 8:1–9:6
- Deuteronomy 10:12–11:32; 13:1-4
- Deuteronomy 18:9-22; 26:1-19
- Deuteronomy 28:1–29:29
- Deuteronomy 30:1-20; 34:1-12

DEUTERONOMY

Deuteronomy is Moses' farewell address to the nation of Israel. His style is very different than in the first four books of the Pentateuch — these are the final words of a man soon to die. He is sharing everything on his heart. For this reason, events mentioned are not always in chronological order, and there is often much repetition (sometimes whole verses or groups of verses are repeated).

Deuteronomy is written in the standard form of a **suzerain-vassal** treaty, which was a legal contract between an overlord and his subject people. These covenants were common at this time and typically included the following:

I.   Preamble (1:1-5)

II. Historical prologue (1:6–4:43)

III. Stipulations of the covenant (4:44–26:19)

IV. Curses and blessings (chapters 27–30)

V.   Succession arrangements and provisions for public reading (chapters 31–34)

LOOKING UP — LOVE

In essence, Deuteronomy is a covenant of love, and chapter 7 describes the nature of this covenant:

> Know therefore that the Lord your God is God; he is the faithful God, keeping his COVENANT OF LOVE to a thousand generations of those who love him and keep his commands (Deut. 7:9, emphasis added).

> The Lord your God will keep his COVENANT OF LOVE with you, as he swore to your forefathers (Deut. 7:12b, emphasis added).

Genesis portrayed God as the Creator.

Exodus showed Him as the Deliverer.

Leviticus emphasized His holiness;

Numbers, His faithfulness.

Deuteronomy shows that He is also a God of love (4:37; 7:7-8, 13; 10:15; 23:5).

Deuteronomy shows that God loves us and expects love in return. This is the essence of this covenant agreement: God declares His love for His people, and they are expected to return that love. The expectation is cited again and again: LOVE THE LORD YOUR GOD (6:5; 10:12; 11:1, 13, 22; 13:3; 19:9; 30:6, 16, 20).

What are some of the things that the Israelites' love for God would influence?

_____

_____

_____

_____

_____

_____

By giving them practical illustrations of the law in this covenant, God teaches them that LOVE is the true fulfillment of the law. Romans 13:8-10 and Matthew 22:37-40 reaffirm that all the commandments are summed up in loving God and neighbor, "therefore love is the fulfillment of the law" (Rom. 13:10).

The sign of this "covenant of love" is circumcision of the heart. "A man is not a Jew if he is only one outwardly, nor is circumcision merely outward and physical. No, a man is a Jew if he is one inwardly; and circumcision is circumcision of the heart, by the Spirit, not by the written code" (Rom. 2:28-29).

LOOKING <u>BACK</u> — REMEMBER

Moses recounts what has happened during the past forty years in the historical prologue. His focus is on God's love and care for His people. Remembering the past would bring encouragement and renewed faithfulness for the present (Deut. 4:9).

What were some of the things the Israelites were to remember when they entered the Promised Land, and why was it important to remember them (chapters 4–11)?

_____

_____

_____

_____

_____

_____

Remembering the past would keep them faithful, humble and obedient.

Deuteronomy 6:4-8 — the Shema — became the Jewish "confession of faith" and was recited daily by pious Jews. Everything they did was to remind them of God's commands, which they were to teach faithfully and deliberately to their children.

LOOKING <u>AHEAD</u> — OBEY

A standard section of all suzerain-vassal covenants was the "curses and blessings," in which the consequences for obedience and disobedience were stated clearly (chapters 27–28). Almost every chapter of Deuteronomy contains the command to obey — not because God delights in giving orders, but because He wants His people to prosper. He loves them and knows what is best, and He wants them to demonstrate their love for Him by obedience. The same is true for us today. In obedience to God, we find ultimate fulfillment and meaning for our lives.

Israel had a choice, just as we do, but God let them know what the consequences of their choice would be. The curses found in Deuteronomy 28:15-68 are horrible and terrifying; yet they are fulfilled later when Israel is sent into exile for her persistent disobedience and flagrant disregard for God's commands (see 2 Kings and Lamentations).

So Moses calls the nation to a new commitment. This is his final appeal — he pleads (Deut. 29:2-15), warns (29:16-28), encourages (30:1-14), and confronts them with choices (30:15-20). The key word in this section is OBEY, for to obey is the true test of fulfilling the covenant of love: "This is love for God: to obey His commands" (1 John 5:3a, see also John 14:15).

Finally, we read of the death and burial of Moses. It seems like an ending, but it's only the beginning. Deuteronomy is a book of transition to a new generation, a new possession, a new experience, and a new revelation of God as a God of love. Its influence as a covenant of love is far-reaching:

— 2 Kings 22 tells us that under King Josiah (the last godly king in the Davidic line prior to exile) the "Book of the Law," or "Book of the Covenant," is found. Reading Deuteronomy leads to a renewal of the covenant and spiritual revival.

— In the New Testament, Deuteronomy is quoted and alluded to more than any other Old Testament book — about one hundred times. Jesus quotes almost invariably from Deuteronomy, most notably while being tempted in the wilderness (see Matthew 4:1-11).

— Deuteronomy has value for us today. It enhances our understanding of the "covenant" concept, so when Christ is described as the mediator of a "new covenant" in the New Testament, we understand what is involved.

Deuteronomy records the death of Moses, gives the most extensive list of pagan practices in the Bible (chapter 18), and offers a test for prophets which foreshadows Christ (18:14-22). But the key to understanding the book of Deuteronomy is remembering that it was written in the standard form of a covenant, which was readily apparent to the people of Israel. It was a covenant of love. God loved His people, but He expected wholehearted love and obedience from them.

For personal reflection:

1) How are the old and new covenants alike? How are they different?

2) Why does God establish covenants with His people? Have you entered into His new covenant?

3) Do you love God with all your heart, soul and strength, or are there still areas where you need to love God more? Why should we love God with all our heart, soul and strength?

4) "Remember," "love" and "obey" are three key words in Deuteronomy. How can these words help change your life?

For the next lesson . . .

Read all of Joshua, or at least the following:
- Joshua 1:1–2:24
- Joshua 3:1–4:24
- Joshua 5:13–7:26
- Joshua 9:1–10:15
- Joshua 21:43–22:34
- Joshua 23:1-16
- Joshua 24:1-33

JOSHUA

In the Hebrew Bible, Joshua initiates a division called "The Former Prophets," which includes Joshua, Judges, 1 and 2 Samuel, and 1 and 2 Kings. This division is a recognition that, though these books are historical in content, they were written from a prophetic standpoint. They give us more than just a record of Israel's history; they show how God's message was fulfilled in the life of the nation. The writers of these books also hint that God's working in Israel pointed to some future, greater fulfillment.

Deuteronomy concluded with the death of Moses, the great leader of Israel who had been an instrument of deliverance from Egyptian bondage and who had led Israel through forty years of wilderness wanderings. Now Joshua — who has been appointed as Moses' successor (see Deuteronomy 34:9 and Joshua 1:1-2) — is alone, no doubt uncertain and a little afraid. So, right from the outset of Joshua's leadership, God sets the precedent for Joshua's success (Josh. 1:6-9).

SALVATION IS CONTINGENT UPON OBEDIENCE.

"Obey all the law . . . do not turn from it to the right or to the left" (1:7b). God requires of Israel complete obedience to all the law, with no room for variance. The New Testament equivalent is found in Matthew 7:13-14, where Jesus cautions us to enter through the narrow gate, since the way is broad that leads to destruction.

The precedent set here in the Old Testament continues through the New Testament: Salvation is contingent upon full obedience to the will of God. Jesus said, "Not everyone who says to me, 'Lord, Lord,' will enter the kingdom of heaven, but only he who does the will of my Father who is in heaven" (Matt. 7:21).

In Joshua 2, we find a practical illustration of this concept in the story of Rahab. Her faith must be coupled with obedience in order for Rahab and her household to be saved. When the Israelite army comes to destroy the city, Rahab has to tie a scarlet cord in the window of her home and gather her entire family inside. The early Christian church later would view the scarlet cord as a representation of Christ's atonement, just as the Passover was.

James exhorts us in the New Testament to couple our faith with works, because what we *do* is an indication of what we *believe* (see James 2:14-26).

Chapters 3 and 4 of the book of Joshua record the crossing of the Jordan. Faith is necessary, but the Israelites must obey before they will see the miracle — they have to step in the water before the Jordan actually will stop flowing. Why is this crossing of the Jordan significant?

1. _____

2. _____

_____

3. _____

_____

CONSECRATION IS THE RESPONSE TO DELIVERANCE.

The Israelites' response to God's deliverance from Egypt was circumcision and celebration of the Passover, neither of which were observed during the forty years in the wilderness. For the Israelite, circumcision (the sign of the covenant) signified that the Lord alone would be his God, whom he would trust and serve. It was an act of total consecration. Once circumcised, the Israelite could observe the Passover, the celebration of God's deliverance from Egypt ("Egypt" being a New Testament metaphor for sin).

In light of the New Testament (especially Romans 2:28-29), what is the significance of circumcision and the subsequent celebration?

_____

_____

_____

_____

_____

_____

_____

POSSESSION NECESSITATES CLEANSING.

How do we reconcile God's command to kill all the inhabitants in the pagan cities with our idea of a loving and merciful God? There are several factors to keep in mind:

  1. God's command here is **not a precedent** for future generations to follow.

  2. The book of Joshua should be understood in light of the unfolding of **God's plan of redemption** and the revelation of **His grace and judgment.** Genesis 15:16 reveals that God told Abraham that his descendants would return to Canaan when the sin of the Amorites had reached its full measure. In this light, these holy wars are an act of redemption for Israel and a judgment on the sin of Canaan. They give notice of the outcome of history and the destiny of mankind and creation.

  3. Since the strength of the nation is attributed to the strength of her deity, it is necessary for God to reveal himself as the **one and only God** who is in control of the land.

The cleansing that God requires is not limited to the outward inhabitants of the land; it also applies to the inward condition of the nation — a cleansing of Israel herself. After the fall of Jericho in Joshua 6, we find the account of Achan's sin in chapter 7. This one sin within the camp brings defeat (by Ai). Possession of the land occupied by Ai would necessitate cleansing of the Israelite nation; the sin within Israel's own camp would have to be purged. And so Achan and his family are stoned to death.

How is the account of Achan an illustration of how we should deal with sin?

_____

_____

_____

_____

_____

_____

_____

_____

Chapter 8 confirms that Israel indeed will have victory once the sin is purged from among them — their army is victorious over Ai.

PROVISION FOR THE BATTLE IS FROM GOD.

God's supernatural deliverance of Israel from the Amorites in chapter 10 reveals to Israel that it is not their own power that gives them victory.

How do these New Testament verses shed light on the victory that we can have today: Philippians 4:13; Romans 8:37; 1 John 4:4; and Hebrews 13:21?

_____

_____

_____

_____

_____

_____

COMPLETION OF GOD'S PROMISE IS SURE.

So the Lord gave Israel all the land he had sworn to give their forefathers, and they took possession of it and settled there. The Lord gave them rest on every side, just as he had sworn to their forefathers. Not one of their enemies withstood them; the Lord handed all their enemies over to them. Not one of all the Lord's good promises to the house of Israel failed; every one was fulfilled (Josh. 21:43-45).

What is the significance of the idea of "rest" in the book of Joshua?

_____

_____

_____

In chapter 24, God's covenant with Israel is renewed, and Joshua presents the choice before Israel, just as the choice is before us daily:

But if serving the Lord seems undesirable to you, then choose for yourselves this day whom you will serve, whether the gods your forefathers served beyond the River, or the gods of the Amorites, in whose land you are living. But as for me and my household, we will serve the Lord (Josh. 24:15).

For personal reflection:

1) Are you living a life of careful obedience, or are you trying to see how wide a road you can travel and still "make it"?

2) What kind of a response to salvation does God expect from His people today? Are you living that kind of life?

3) Do you have trouble accepting the fact that a loving and merciful God could act seemingly so cruelly toward the pagan nations? How does this help you understand God's attitude toward sin?

4) Complete this sentence: "As for me and my house, we will serve

_____."

For the next lesson . . .

Read all of Judges and Ruth, or at least the following:

- Judges 1:1–3:6
- Judges 4:1-24
- Judges 6:1–7:25
- Judges 10:6–11:40
- Judges 13:1–14:20
- Judges 15:1–16:31
- Ruth 1:1–4:22

Conquest of Canaan

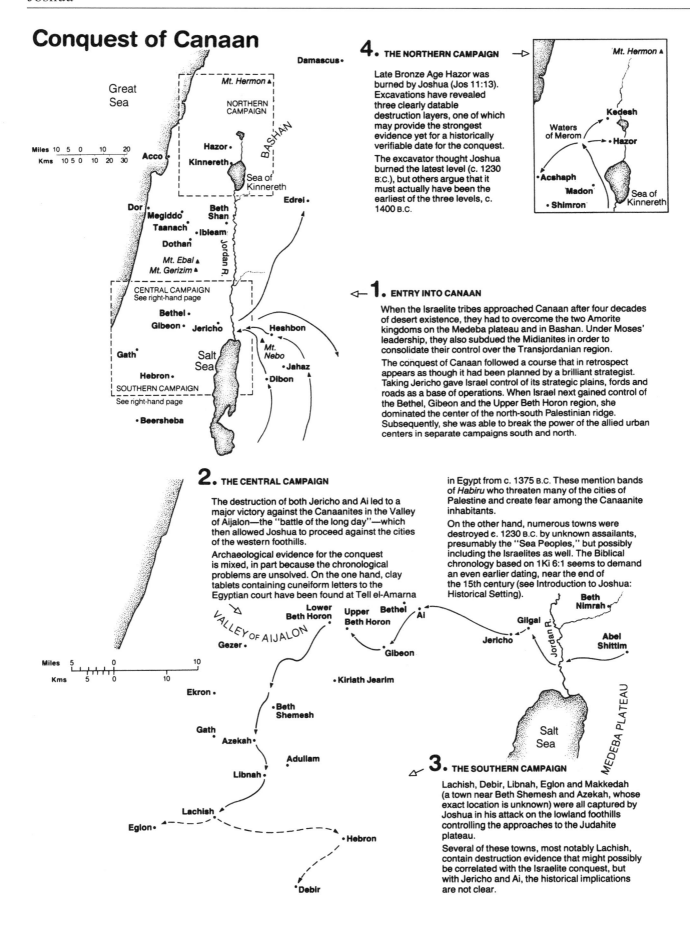

4. THE NORTHERN CAMPAIGN

Late Bronze Age Hazor was burned by Joshua (Jos 11:13). Excavations have revealed three clearly datable destruction layers, one of which may provide the strongest evidence yet for a historically verifiable date for the conquest.

The excavator thought Joshua burned the latest level (c. 1230 B.C.), but others argue that it must actually have been the earliest of the three levels, c. 1400 B.C.

1. ENTRY INTO CANAAN

When the Israelite tribes approached Canaan after four decades of desert existence, they had to overcome the two Amorite kingdoms on the Medeba plateau and in Bashan. Under Moses' leadership, they also subdued the Midianites in order to consolidate their control over the Transjordanian region.

The conquest of Canaan followed a course that in retrospect appears as though it had been planned by a brilliant strategist. Taking Jericho gave Israel control of its strategic plains, fords and roads as a base of operations. When Israel next gained control of the Bethel, Gibeon and the Upper Beth Horon region, she dominated the center of the north-south Palestinian ridge. Subsequently, she was able to break the power of the allied urban centers in separate campaigns south and north.

2. THE CENTRAL CAMPAIGN

The destruction of both Jericho and Ai led to a major victory against the Canaanites in the Valley of Aijalon—the "battle of the long day"—which then allowed Joshua to proceed against the cities of the western foothills.

Archaeological evidence for the conquest is mixed, in part because the chronological problems are unsolved. On the one hand, clay tablets containing cuneiform letters to the Egyptian court have been found at Tell el-Amarna in Egypt from c. 1375 B.C. These mention bands of *Habiru* who threaten many of the cities of Palestine and create fear among the Canaanite inhabitants.

On the other hand, numerous towns were destroyed c. 1230 B.C. by unknown assailants, presumably the "Sea Peoples," but possibly including the Israelites as well. The Biblical chronology based on 1 Ki 6:1 seems to demand an even earlier dating, near the end of the 15th century (see Introduction to Joshua: Historical Setting).

3. THE SOUTHERN CAMPAIGN

Lachish, Debir, Libnah, Eglon and Makkedah (a town near Beth Shemesh and Azekah, whose exact location is unknown) were all captured by Joshua in his attack on the lowland foothills controlling the approaches to the Judahite plateau.

Several of these towns, most notably Lachish, contain destruction evidence that might possibly be correlated with the Israelite conquest, but with Jericho and Ai, the historical implications are not clear.

JUDGES & RUTH

The book of Judges covers the history of Israel during their first 480 years in the Promised Land. (Depending on one's dating system and the possibility of overlap, some believe it could be as few as two hundred years.) Judges unfolds for us how God's people are expected to live once they've entered Canaan — from both historical and spiritual perspectives.

Tradition holds that the book of Judges was compiled by Samuel, though we have no way of knowing for sure. It is certain that the book was written during the monarchy, as evidenced by the repeated phrase, "In those days Israel had no king" (17:6; 18:1; 19:1; 21:25). During this period of Israelite history, there was no centralized government as such. Israel was to be a theocracy — obedient to the God who had chosen her — not subject to the dictates of man. Yet, God intermittently raised up leaders, or "judges," to lead His people and to deliver them from their enemies, hence the book's descriptive title, "Judges."

What factor, emphasized in chapters 1 through 3, accounted for Israel's dismal failure recorded in chapter 2?

_____

_____

_____

The main body of the book of Judges (3:7–16:31) was written in "cycles" built around the major judges: Othniel, Ehud, Deborah, Gideon, Jephthah and Samson. All six accounts have the same four components:

A. SIN

Each cycle begins with, "Then Israel did evil in the eyes of the Lord" (3:7, 12; 4:1; 6:1; 10:6; 13:1). These periods are characterized by apostasy — the worship of other gods and an association with the detestable practices of the Canaanite pagan religion.

B. SUFFERING

In each cycle, the Lord brings judgment on His sinful people by "giving," "selling" or "delivering" them into the hands of their enemies (3:8, 12; 4:2; 6:1; 10:7; 13:1). God allows them to pay the consequences for their sin, just as He stated in the "curses and blessings" of His covenant with them (see Deuteronomy 28).

C. SUPPLICATION

Each time, after years of oppression, Israel finally cries out to God. And God proves himself to be patient, long-suffering and merciful. He never fails to bring to them . . .

D. SALVATION

There are six major judges described in the book of Judges. If the account of Othniel (3:7-11) serves as the model for each successive story, then the remaining five cycles could be diagrammed like this:

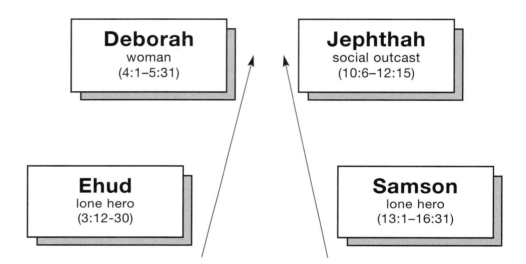

The structure of Judges focuses attention on the crucial issue of the period: Israel's attraction to the Baals of Canaan (shown by Abimelech) versus the Lord's kingship over His people (encouraged by Gideon). Israel is to be a theocracy, with the Lord God as her King, yet it is a time when Israel has "no king."

God is faithful to raise up deliverers to save His people from their oppressions when they call out to Him. However, serious questions arise concerning the morality of the people God uses: Jael breaks all the sacred laws of hospitality; Ehud stoops to assassination; Jephthah sacrifices his daughter to God; Samson leads a life of sexual promiscuity; and Israel herself is a nation that gloats over acts of cruel revenge against her enemies. How do we account for the fact that God used seemingly such sinful people to accomplish His purposes, and then commended them for their obedience?

_____

_____

_____

_____

Now let's look at the major judges, noting some of the highlights from their periods of leadership:

— **Othniel** is the first judge.

— **Ehud** assassinates the fat king of Eglon.

— In the account of **Deborah,** Jael kills Sisera, the commander of Jabin's army, by driving a tent peg through his head.

— **Gideon** is called by an angel of the Lord to His mission. But, like Moses, Gideon asks for a sign — the proverbial "fleece" used to determine God's will. God whittles down Gideon's army to three hundred men for defeating the Midianites, "In order that Israel may not boast against me that her own strength has saved her" (7:2b). The battle is won with trumpets, empty jars, and torches. Gideon states a fact that no one else seemed to realize: "The Lord will rule over you" (8:23b). And, because it was God who sold them to their enemies and raised up the judges, He is ultimately their Judge and Deliverer.

— **Abimelech** tries to set himself up like a Canaanite city-king with the help of Baal (9:4). He stands in sharp contrast to Gideon (Jerub-Baal) who attacked Baal worship and insisted on the Lord's rule over Israel. Abimelech suffers ultimate disgrace in the ancient Middle East as he is killed by a woman, who drops a millstone on him, cracking his skull.

— **Jephthah** is victorious over the Ammonites, but has to sacrifice his daughter because of a hasty and foolish vow he has made to God. This act reveals to us how little understanding the Israelites at this time have of their Lord.

— In looking at the account of **Samson,** explain how Samson's life typifies the nation of Israel.

_____

_____

_____

_____

The epilogue (chapters 17–21) turns the focus from the heroes to the immorality of the times. Israel's religious life, moral life and national life are in a state of decay.

The final verse recaps the key theme: "In those days Israel had no king, everyone did as he saw fit" (21:25). God tries to teach them that, in order to survive in the Promised Land, they have to submit to God's reign.

How does the New Testament continue the theme of lordship?

_____

_____

_____

_____

_____

The book of Judges offers a bleak picture of Israel during this period. But, in the midst of failure in the period of judges, we find a ray of hope in the book of **RUTH.** REDEMPTION is a key concept in Ruth, occurring twenty-three times in various forms in the Hebrew language in which it was written.

What three themes are important in the book of Ruth?

1. _____

2. _____

3. _____

The key truths to remember are these: In the book of Judges, the structure points to the lordship of Yahweh versus the continual apostasy of Israel, evidenced by their worship of Baal. The book of Ruth proclaims that even in the midst of decadence, God's purposes still are moving forward. God still works to fulfill His promises; He does not forsake His people.

Sometimes we despair over the moral decline of our society, wondering if God has abandoned us thoroughly. The answer is a resounding, "No!" God continually is preserving a faithful remnant through whom His purposes in this world will be fulfilled. He did it during the turbulent time of the judges, and He still is doing it today. The key to breaking the cycle of sin, suffering, supplication and salvation in society, as well as in our own lives, is making Christ Lord and giving Him His rightful throne. This is the overwhelming message of Judges and Ruth.

For personal reflection:

1) Have you ever stumbled because of "little sins" you either excused or neglected to surrender to God?
2) Have you made God the ruler of your life, or are you simply doing "as you see fit"?
3) Will you seriously pray this week that God will help you to give Him the throne in your heart?
4) Do you ever feel like a "Ruth" in the midst of our decadent society ? How does the book of Ruth give you hope as you stand firm for God?

For the next lesson . . .

Read all of 1 Samuel, or at least the following:
- 1 Samuel 1:1-28; 2:12–3:21
- 1 Samuel 4:1–6:12
- 1 Samuel 8:1–10:27
- 1 Samuel 13:1-15; 15:1-35
- 1 Samuel 16:1–17:58
- 1 Samuel 18:1-12; 20:1-42
- 1 Samuel 28:1-19; 31:1-13

1 SAMUEL

First Samuel is an exciting and suspense-filled look into the lives of three men: Samuel, Saul and David. The story begins in the time of the judges, the "Dark Ages" of Israel's history — a time when "Israel had no king" and "everyone did as he saw fit" (Judges 21:25).

We are introduced in chapter 1 to Hannah, a barren woman tormented by her husband's other wife. In desperation, Hannah cries out to the Lord and makes a vow: If God will give her a son, she will give her son back to the Lord for His service. This woman gives birth to Samuel, the last and greatest of all the judges over Israel. Hannah takes him to Shiloh after he has been weaned to live in the presence of the Lord and in service to Him at the Tabernacle.

SAMUEL: THE FAITHFUL PROPHET

Samuel is not tarnished by the times, unlike the judges we read about in the book of Judges. This could be the dawning of a new day for Israel — God once again is revealing His word through a prophet, the first great prophet since Moses.

How did Samuel's life contrast with the lives of Eli's sons (1 Sam. 2–3)?

_____

_____

_____

_____

_____

_____

What great disaster occurred, as recorded in chapter 4?

_____

_____

_____

_____

_____

The Israelites soon realize that *the ark* of God is a poor substitute for the *God* of the ark.

For the benefit of both the Philistines and Israel, God shows unmistakably that He cannot be "stolen" as a war trophy like the idols of the day. If Israel ever has wondered about the power of God in their midst, this demonstration should confirm that power. The narratives about the ark in chapters 4 through 6 offer undeniable proof of God's power and presence in Israel.

Finally, in chapter 7, Israel is mourning and seeking after the Lord, and for the first time in many years, revival comes to Israel. Samuel gives them the "recipe" for revival: ". . . If you are returning to the Lord with all your hearts, then rid yourselves of the foreign gods and the Ashtoreths and commit yourselves to the Lord and serve him only . . ." (7:3).

What were the ingredients in Samuel's "recipe" for revival?

1. _____

2. _____

3. _____

Israel responds by putting away their idols and serving God only (7:4). They fast and confess their sins (7:6). And God is faithful. The Philistines attack Israel, but are defeated soundly because of God's intervention.

However, the Israelites are not fully satisfied to have God alone as their King. What is the significance of Israel's request for an earthly king in chapter 8 (8:7; 10:19; and 12:12, 17, 19-20)?

_____

_____

_____

_____

_____

_____

God's plan was for a theocracy, not a monarchy. In essence, Israel is breaking their covenant with God, rejecting His kingship, and desiring to be just like all the other nations (8:19-20).

SAUL: THE FALLEN KING

God eventually gives the people what they have asked for, but He establishes the kingship in the context of covenant renewal, elevating Israel's monarchy to a different plane than that of the surrounding nations. Israel's king is not to be autonomous in authority and power, but subject to the law of the Lord and the word of the prophet (10:25; 12:23). God is the ultimate Sovereign. Then, God leads the people to choose Saul, "an impressive young man without equal among the

Israelites — a head taller than any of the others" (9:2b). By men's standards, Saul is the best candidate for Israel's king.

Saul, Israel's first king, begins his reign with great promise. But, despite being a man of great potential (not unlike Samson), he ends in utter failure. Already —almost from the outset — in chapter 13, he begins to fall from God's standard for a king.

A. Impatience

Saul is supposed to wait seven days for Samuel to come to Gilgal. But, unable to wait until the end of the seventh day, Saul sacrifices the burnt offering himself (13:8-9). The ultimate result is tragic: Saul's kingdom will not endure. God anoints another King.

B. Insubordination

God commands Saul, "Do not spare [the Amalekites]; put to death men and women, children and infants, cattle and sheep, camels and donkeys" (15:3b). Saul's direct disobedience is recorded in 1 Samuel 15:9, and yet Saul insists that he has obeyed God (15:13, 20). Saul fails to realize that partial obedience is total disobedience.

C. Indignation

This is Saul's response to David's show of courage in his confrontation with Goliath, the nine-foot-tall Philistine who issues a challenge to the Israelite army (chapter 17). While the Israelites quiver in fear, David displays the courage and strength that come from confidence in the Lord (17:26, 37, 47).

The women's song, "Saul has slain his thousands, and David his tens of thousands" (18:7b), evoke within Saul jealousy, anger (18:8), suspicion (18:9) and fear (18:12, 15), until he finally schemes to kill David.

D. Imprudence

Saul makes a rash and very foolish decision (chapter 28) when he consults the witch at Endor — an act strictly forbidden in Deuteronomy 18. Samuel "speaks" to Saul from the grave, prophesying imminent defeat by the Philistines and the death of Saul and his sons.

The next day, while David is leading his army to victory over the Amalekites (1 Sam. 30), Saul and his sons are meeting their deaths at the hands of the Philistines (chapter 31).

What contrasts do we see between Israel's first king, Saul, and Israel's final king, Jesus Christ?

_____

_____

_____

_____

_____

_____

_____

First Samuel covers a relatively brief period of approximately 115 years in the life of the nation of Israel, but this period forever changes the course of her history. The period of judges ceases and the monarchy is established. In 2 Samuel, we'll see the kingdom of David, the forerunner of the Christ to come. God's plan of redemption comes one step closer to fulfillment.

For personal reflection:

1) Who or what is "king" of your life right now?

2) Are there any areas in your life where you are practicing partial obedience? What might be the consequences if you continue?

3) What character flaw of Saul do you think was most instrumental in bringing about his downfall?

4) How does Saul's life portray bondage to sin? Are there any sins in your life that have begun to control you?

For the next lesson . . .

Read all of 2 Samuel, or at least the following:
- 2 Samuel 1:1-27
- 2 Samuel 5:1-16; 6:1–7:29
- 2 Samuel 9:1-13; 11:1–12:31
- 2 Samuel 13:1–14:23
- 2 Samuel 15:1-37; 18:1-33
- 2 Samuel 22:1–23:7
- 2 Samuel 24:1-25

2 SAMUEL

The continuous theme through the books of Judges and 1 Samuel was the lordship, or kingship, of God over His chosen people, and this theme logically continues in 2 Samuel, since 1 and 2 Samuel were originally one book.

Saul served as a negative example. His pride, self-will and partial obedience were contrary to all that God demanded of Israel's kings. But David is a prime example of the theocratic king. First Samuel 13:14 and Acts 13:22 testify that David was a "man after God's own heart."

So far, we've seen David as a shepherd boy, a court musician, a soldier, a true friend, an outcast and a fugitive. Now, in 2 Samuel, we find him a king. He is not perfect, and yet there is something about his spirit, his devotion to God, and his love for his Rock and Fortress that is pleasing to God and stands in sharp contrast to his predecessor, Saul.

THE STORY

At the beginning of 2 Samuel, an Amalekite brings the news of Saul's death to David, obviously fabricating a story in the hope of receiving a reward for killing David's enemy. David displays no personal satisfaction over Saul's death and condemns to death the one he believes to be Saul's murderer. The second half of chapter 1 is a beautiful lament for Saul and Jonathan, recounting all that was favorable in Saul's character: ". . . in life they were loved and gracious . . . . swifter than eagles, they were stronger than lions" (1:23).

David exemplifies the **SPIRIT OF FORGIVENESS.** His heart is truly filled with remorse, and all the cruelty Saul had shown to him in attempting to take his life is forgiven. How unlike Saul, who couldn't forget David's rise to honor in the kingdom and relentlessly pursued the one who was so faithful to him!

In chapter 2, God tells David to go to Hebron, where he is anointed king over the tribe of Judah. After the deaths of Abner (chapter 3) and Ish-Bosheth — Saul's son, who had been declared king over Israel (chapter 4) — David becomes king over a united Israel (chapter 5). David is thirty years old when he becomes king (5:4). But he was anointed by Samuel as king over Israel when he was only about eighteen years old; so he has waited twelve long years to see the fulfillment of that promise.

He could have killed Saul and taken the throne that was rightfully his, but David is controlled by a **SPIRIT OF PATIENCE,** allowing God to bring His promise to fruition in His own timing. What a contrast to Saul, who couldn't even wait until the end of the seventh day for Samuel to come to Gilgal to offer the burnt offering before the battle!

Following his coronation over the kingdom, David immediately conquers Jerusalem as his royal city. Why was Jerusalem a strategic acquisition for David?

_____

_____

_____

_____

_____

"And David knew that the Lord had established him as king over Israel and had exalted his kingdom for the sake of his people Israel" (5:12). David understands that God is in control and that his becoming king and acquiring Jerusalem is an integral part of God's continuing plan of redemption for Israel. In chapter 6, the ark is brought to Jerusalem. By returning the ark to a place of prominence in the nation, David, as a true theocratic king, acknowledges the Lord's kingship and rule over both himself and the people.

Chapter 7 is the most significant chapter in the entire book of 2 Samuel. What did God promise to David in this chapter, and why is this covenant significant in our understanding of God's plan of redemption?

_____

_____

_____

_____

_____

David's moving prayer of thanksgiving in 2 Samuel 7:18-29 expresses his **SPIRIT OF SUBMISSION** to his "Sovereign Lord" (a phrase used seven times in these twelve verses). David's spirit of submission, recognizing God's sovereignty, stands in sharp contrast to Saul's spirit of self-will and rebellion.

David's conquests are recorded in chapters 8 through 10. Here, we see God's faithfulness to give David victory over his adversaries. David exemplifies a **SPIRIT OF OBEDIENCE** in all his conquests: "David reigned over all Israel, doing what was just and right for all his people" (8:15). What a contrast to Saul, who feared the people, put his troops in danger by requiring a fast during battle, and was overtly disobedient to God's commands.

Of special consideration is David's **SPIRIT OF COMPASSION,** noted in chapter 9, where David shows kindness to Mephibosheth, the crippled son of Jonathan.

Up to this point, David's reign has been ideal. How we wish the story could end right here. But chapter 11 is included for a purpose. No matter how close we are to the heart of God, we are not immune to sin. Chapter 11 serves as a warning: Sin is not inevitable, but temptation is, and we must guard ourselves against it! Here we find King David guilty of adultery and conspiracy to commit murder.

Chapter 12 shows what distinguishes David from others in the Old Testament, and especially from Saul. When David is confronted by Nathan with his sin, he displays a **SPIRIT OF REPENTANCE.** Remember Saul's response to Samuel's accusation of disobedience (see 1 Samuel 15)? Saul denied it twice, saying, "But I did obey the Lord." When he did confess, he shifted the blame to the people. Saul was more interested in men's honor than in God's displeasure.

But David takes full responsibility for his sin and admits it. Psalms 32 and 51 give us greater insight into David's remorse and how his heart cries out to God for forgiveness.

The consequences of David's sin are great: three of his children are killed, and one is left desolate for the rest of her life. What a terrible price to pay for a moment of sinful "pleasure." David grieves bitterly over the loss of his son, Absalom, in 2 Samuel 18 and 19, showing a **SPIRIT OF BROKENNESS.**

In the two songs in the appendix (chapters 21–24), David beautifully relays the faithfulness and strength of the God he loves and serves. David shows once and for all his **SPIRIT OF TRUST** in God alone. Saul had trusted only in self and had desired his own honor above God's. But David trusts God as his shield and fortress, his strength and deliverer. David completely trusts God to bring His covenant promise to fruition (23:5). This leads us to . . .

THE SIGNIFICANCE

How does 2 Samuel fit into the Bible as a whole?

A. FROM A HISTORICAL PERSPECTIVE

_____

_____

_____

B. FROM A PERSONAL PERSPECTIVE

_____

_____

_____

C. FROM AN ETERNAL PERSPECTIVE

_____

_____

_____

For personal reflection:

1) Why do you think God was so hard on Saul when he sinned but so forgiving of David? Is God fair?

2) Are you sometimes impatient while waiting for God to fulfill His promises? How can David's example help you to find the strength to wait?

3) What impresses you most about David's spirit? In what ways would you like to become a little more like him?

4) Take some time to read several of David's Psalms this week. See how David tended to dwell on God instead of self. How can keeping a proper perspective help you stay faithful to the Lord?

For the next lesson . . .

Read all of 1 Kings, or at least the following:

■ 1 Kings 1:11–2:46
■ 1 Kings 3:1-28; 4:29-34
■ 1 Kings 6:1-38; 8:1-61
■ 1 Kings 8:62–9:9; 10:1-9, 14-29
■ 1 Kings 11:1-13, 26-43; 12:25-33
■ 1 Kings 17:1-24; 18:16–19:21
■ 1 Kings 21:1-29; 22:41-53

David's Conquests

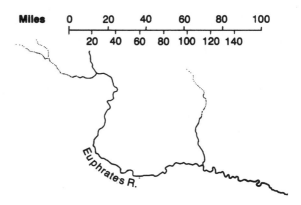

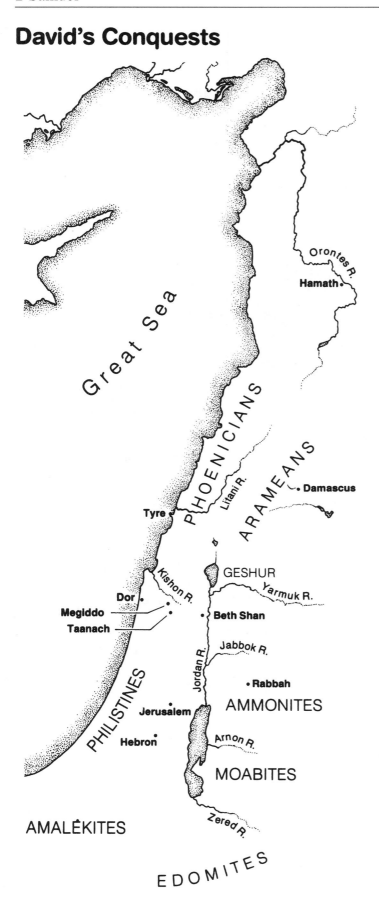

Once he had become king over all Israel (2Sa 5:1-5), David:

1. Conquered the Jebusite citadel of Zion/Jerusalem and made it his royal city (2Sa 5:6-10);

2. Received the recognition of and assurance of friendship from Hiram of Tyre, king of the Phoenicians (2Sa 5:11-12);

3. Decisively defeated the Philistines so that their hold on Israelite territory was broken and their threat to Israel eliminated (2Sa 5:17-25; 8:1);

4. Defeated the Moabites and imposed his authority over them (2Sa 8:2);

5. Crushed the Aramean kingdoms of Hadadezer (king of Zobah), Damascus and Maacah and put them under tribute (2Sa 8:3-8; 10:6-19). Talmai, the Aramean king of Geshur, apparently had made peace with David while he was still reigning in Hebron and sealed the alliance by giving his daughter in marriage to David (2Sa 3:3; see 1Ch 2:23);

6. Subdued Edom and incorporated it into his empire (2Sa 8:13-14);

7. Defeated the Ammonites and brought them into subjection (2Sa 12:19-31);

8. Subjugated the remaining Canaanite cities that had previously maintained their independence from and hostility toward Israel, such as Beth Shan, Megiddo, Taanach and Dor.

Since David had earlier crushed the Amalekites (1Sa 30:17), his wars thus completed the conquest begun by Joshua and secured all the borders of Israel. His empire (united Israel plus the subjugated kingdoms) reached from Ezion Geber on the eastern arm of the Red Sea to the Euphrates River.

1. The City of the Jebusites and
2. David's Jerusalem

Substantial historical evidence, both Biblical and extra-Biblical, places the temple of Herod (and before it the temples of Zerubbabel and of Solomon) on the holy spot where King David built an altar to the Lord. David had purchased the land from Araunah the Jebusite, who was using the exposed bedrock as a threshing floor (2Sa 24:18-25). Tradition claims a much older sanctity for the site, associating it with the altar of Abraham on Mount Moriah (Ge 22:1-19). The writer of Genesis equates Moriah with "the Mountain of the LORD," and other OT shrines originated in altars erected by Abraham.

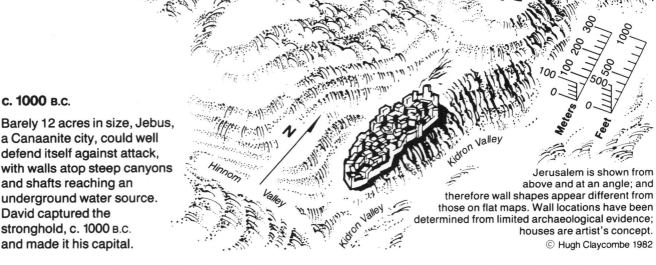

c. 1000 B.C.

Barely 12 acres in size, Jebus, a Canaanite city, could well defend itself against attack, with walls atop steep canyons and shafts reaching an underground water source. David captured the stronghold, c. 1000 B.C. and made it his capital.

Jerusalem is shown from above and at an angle; and therefore wall shapes appear different from those on flat maps. Wall locations have been determined from limited archaeological evidence; houses are artist's concept.

© Hugh Claycombe 1982

For further reference to the development of Jerusalem see: page 73, *Solomon's Jerusalem*; page 99, *Jerusalem of the Returning Exiles*; page 139, *Jerusalem During the Time of the Prophets.*

2 Samuel 5:6-10

David Conquers Jerusalem

The king and his men marched to Jerusalem to attack the Jebusites, who lived there. The Jebusites said to David, "You will not get in here; even the blind and the lame can ward you off." They thought, "David cannot get in here." Nevertheless, David captured the fortress of Zion, the City of David.

On that day, David said, "Anyone who conquers the Jebusites will have to use the water shaft to reach those lame and blind who are David's enemies." That is why they say, "The 'blind and lame' will not enter the palace."

David then took up residence in the fortress and called it the City of David. He built up the area around it, from the supporting terraces inward. And he became more and more powerful, because the LORD God Almighty was with him.

1 KINGS

First and Second Kings were originally one book. The account of the kings begins with the death of David, followed by Solomon's succession to the throne, and it ends with God's chosen people in exile in a foreign land. The authorship of 1 and 2 Kings is questionable, but it is certain that they were written by a single author living during the Babylonian exile who used other sources available at that time.

First and Second Kings serve as a retrospective analysis of Israel's history. The author is attempting to explain to a distraught people in exile in a foreign land the reason for their condition.

First Kings begins with Adonijah's attempt to take the throne from his aging father, David. David is informed of this by both Bathsheba and Nathan, the prophet, and David proceeds to make Solomon king over all Israel. Solomon is God's choice — God loves Solomon (see 2 Samuel 12:24-25) and has set him apart to ascend the throne. In David's charge to Solomon in 1 Kings 2, we find . . .

THE PLAN

> So be strong, show yourself a man, and observe what the Lord your God requires: Walk in his ways, and keep his decrees and commands, his laws and requirements, as written in the Law of Moses, so that you may PROSPER in all you do and wherever you go, and that the Lord may keep his PROMISE to me: "If your descendants watch how they live, and if they walk faithfully before me with all their heart and soul, you will never fail to have a man on the throne of Israel" (1 Kings 2:2b-4, emphasis added).

God's original plan for Israel was continued prosperity and the fulfillment of His covenant promise to David. But this was contingent upon obedience. God's covenant with David — to establish his throne forever — was an *unconditional* covenant (eventually fulfilled in Christ). But individual participation in its blessings was contingent upon obedience to the Mosaic covenant.

The precedent is set in 1 Kings 2, and the entire book hinges on this concept: The welfare of Israel and her kings is directly dependent on their continued obedience or disobedience to the covenant stipulations (2:3-4). From the author's vantage point, he makes it clear that exiled Israel is facing the consequences of her stubborn defiance of God's plan.

What did Solomon ask God for in 1 Kings 3:9, and what did God give to him?

_____

_____

_____

From here through chapter 10, we are given a glimpse of Solomon's great **wisdom, wealth,** and **world acclaim.** It is offered almost as "proof" that God is faithful in keeping His promise to Solomon.

THE PROBLEM

> King Solomon, HOWEVER, loved many foreign women besides Pharaoh's daughter — Moabites, Ammonites, Edomites, Sidonians and Hittites. They were from nations about which the Lord had told the Israelites, "You must not intermarry with them, because they will surely turn your hearts after their gods." NEVERTHELESS, Solomon held fast to them in love. He had seven hundred wives of royal birth and three hundred concubines, and his wives led him astray. As Solomon grew old, his wives turned his heart after other gods, and his heart was not fully devoted to the Lord his God, as the heart of David his father had been (1 Kings 11:1-4, emphasis added).

Solomon's problems actually began much earlier. First Kings 3:1 indicates that he made an alliance with the king of Egypt and married his daughter for political security, disregarding God's express prohibition of intermarrying with foreign women. In chapter 4, Solomon set up tax districts (to provide for his needs) that didn't correspond to the twelve tribal districts. This later caused conflict between the Northern Kingdom, Israel, and the Southern Kingdom, Judah, following Solomon's death. At the end of chapter 5, we learn that he conscripted laborers from all over Israel, an act which slowly built resentment toward him.

But Solomon's greatest evil is idolatry. He allows his wives to worship the gods from their native countries and even builds altars for them to do so — and he follows suit.

THE PRICE

> So the Lord said to Solomon, "Since this is your attitude and you have not kept my covenant and my decrees, which I commanded you, I will most certainly tear the kingdom away from you and give it to one of your subordinates" (1 Kings 11:11).

Why was the division of the kingdom the logical consequence of Solomon's idolatry?

_____

_____

_____

_____

_____

_____

The author is careful to point out that the events that follow the division are a direct result of Israel's sin. On at least eleven occasions, prophecies are recorded and said to have been fulfilled later. Constant references are made to God's control over events, making it clear that what happens in Israel's political life is a result of God's judgment, not chance (e.g. 11:14, 23).

God promises through Ahijah, the prophet, to give Jeroboam the Northern Kingdom and to bless him with an enduring dynasty if he remains obedient.

What did Jeroboam do, and what were the consequences of his actions (12:25–14:18)?

_____

_____

_____

_____

Meanwhile, Rehoboam, Solomon's son, becomes king of Judah, but shows an incredible lack of wisdom (chapter 12) by refusing to listen to the complaints of Israel. But 1 Kings 12:15 notes, ". . . this turn of events was from the Lord. . . ." God is in control, completely omniscient and omnipotent. Judah does evil in the eyes of the Lord, and "There was continual warfare between Jeroboam and Rehoboam" (14:30).

The remaining chapters of 1 Kings are accounts of the kings who reign over Israel and Judah. These kings are not measured by political achievements, but by obedience or disobedience to the laws of God. The author is showing through this history that Israel's continued disobedience to God is the cause of her present troubles.

It is noteworthy that NO king in Israel (the ten northern tribes) is described as being obedient — they all do evil in the eyes of the Lord. And so the Northern Kingdom experiences political chaos, instability and violence. _____ rulers from _____ different dynasties reign from the division of the kingdom (930 B.C.) until the fall of Samaria (722-721 B.C.) — a period of only _____ years.

The Southern Kingdom also has _____ rulers, and all but one (Athaliah) are descendants of David. Their rules extend over a period of about _____ years until the fall of Jerusalem in 586 B.C. Unlike Israel, there are some good kings in Judah: Asa, Jehoshaphat, Hezekiah and Josiah.

THE PROMISE

The reader is constantly reminded throughout 1 Kings of God's promises, especially His promise to establish the house of David (2:4, 33; 6:12; 8:24-26; 9:5; 11:13, 36; 15:4). God's faithfulness is seen — in fulfilling His past promises and in renewing His promise to His people. (The word "promise" is used no less than _____ times.) The author is sharing a message of HOPE for the Jews in exile: God will keep His promise. God promised to secure David's house forever (an unconditional covenant), and He will be faithful.

How did God show His might through the ministry of the prophets?

_____

_____

_____

_____

_____

Chapter 8 serves as a focus for the author's key themes and offers special hope to the Jews in exile. In this chapter, the ark is brought to the Temple, and "the glory of the Lord filled his temple" (8:11b). Solomon's address here brings renewed hope and encouragement for the exiled community.

There is reason for hope, because . . .

1. God is faithful to his promises;

2. God is not limited to the temporal;

3. God is merciful and forgiving.

For personal reflection:

1) What does Solomon's sin (and Jeroboam's) teach us about God's attitude toward idolatry? In what ways do people today still commit idolatry?

2) In what ways is our participation in the blessings of the "New Covenant" contingent upon continued obedience to the Lord?

3) Why do you think Jesus said it is difficult for a rich man to enter the kingdom of heaven? Is there anything in your life right now that is keeping you from depending on God and serving Him with a whole heart?

4) In what ways have you had to pay the consequences for bad decisions or disobedience? Do you think God abandons us when we sin, or is there hope for restoration? Why?

For the next lesson . . .

Read all of 2 Kings and 1 & 2 Chronicles, or at least the following:

- ■ 2 Kings 1:1–2:25
- ■ 2 Kings 4:1–6:23
- ■ 2 Kings 9:1–10, 30-37; 10:18-36
- ■ 2 Kings 11:1–12:21
- ■ 2 Kings 17:1–18:16; 22:1-20
- ■ 2 Kings 25:1-30;
  1 Chronicles 22:1-19; 28:1-21
- ■ 2 Chronicles 15:1-19; 36:15-23

Solomon's Temple

960-586 B.C.

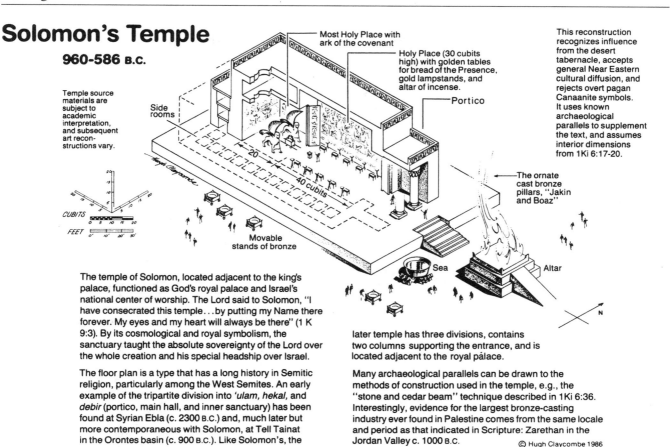

Temple source materials are subject to academic interpretation, and subsequent art reconstructions vary.

Side rooms

20

40 cubits

CUBITS

FEET

Movable stands of bronze

Most Holy Place with ark of the covenant

Holy Place (30 cubits high) with golden tables for bread of the Presence, gold lampstands, and altar of incense.

Portico

The ornate cast bronze pillars, "Jakin and Boaz"

Sea

Altar

N

This reconstruction recognizes influence from the desert tabernacle, accepts general Near Eastern cultural diffusion, and rejects overt pagan Canaanite symbols. It uses known archaeological parallels to supplement the text, and assumes interior dimensions from 1Ki 6:17-20.

The temple of Solomon, located adjacent to the king's palace, functioned as God's royal palace and Israel's national center of worship. The Lord said to Solomon, "I have consecrated this temple...by putting my Name there forever. My eyes and my heart will always be there" (1 K 9:3). By its cosmological and royal symbolism, the sanctuary taught the absolute sovereignty of the Lord over the whole creation and his special headship over Israel.

The floor plan is a type that has a long history in Semitic religion, particularly among the West Semites. An early example of the tripartite division into 'ulam, hekal, and debir (portico, main hall, and inner sanctuary) has been found at Syrian Ebla (c. 2300 B.C.) and, much later but more contemporaneous with Solomon, at Tell Tainat in the Orontes basin (c. 900 B.C.). Like Solomon's, the

later temple has three divisions, contains two columns supporting the entrance, and is located adjacent to the royal palace.

Many archaeological parallels can be drawn to the methods of construction used in the temple, e.g., the "stone and cedar beam" technique described in 1Ki 6:36. Interestingly, evidence for the largest bronze-casting industry ever found in Palestine comes from the same locale and period as that indicated in Scripture: Zarethan in the Jordan Valley c. 1000 B.C.

© Hugh Claycombe 1986

Temple Furnishings

Glimpses of the rich ornamentation of Solomon's temple can be gained through recent discoveries that illumine the text of 1 Ki 6-7.

1 Kings 7:13-51

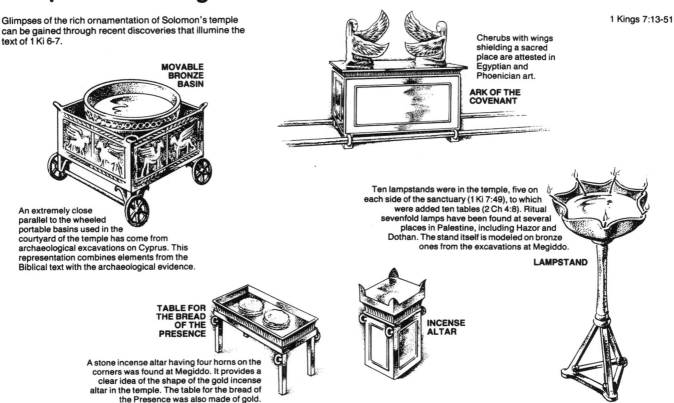

MOVABLE BRONZE BASIN

An extremely close parallel to the wheeled portable basins used in the courtyard of the temple has come from archaeological excavations on Cyprus. This representation combines elements from the Biblical text with the archaeological evidence.

Cherubs with wings shielding a sacred place are attested in Egyptian and Phoenician art.

ARK OF THE COVENANT

Ten lampstands were in the temple, five on each side of the sanctuary (1 Ki 7:49), to which were added ten tables (2 Ch 4:8). Ritual sevenfold lamps have been found at several places in Palestine, including Hazor and Dothan. The stand itself is modeled on bronze ones from the excavations at Megiddo.

LAMPSTAND

TABLE FOR THE BREAD OF THE PRESENCE

INCENSE ALTAR

A stone incense altar having four horns on the corners was found at Megiddo. It provides a clear idea of the shape of the gold incense altar in the temple. The table for the bread of the Presence was also made of gold.

The Divided Kingdom

930-586 B.C.

The division of Solomon's kingdom had geographical and political causes, with roots reaching back to earlier tribal rivalries. Israel was closer to Phoenician cities and major trade routes than Judah, whose heartland was a plateau-like ridge higher than the district around Samaria.

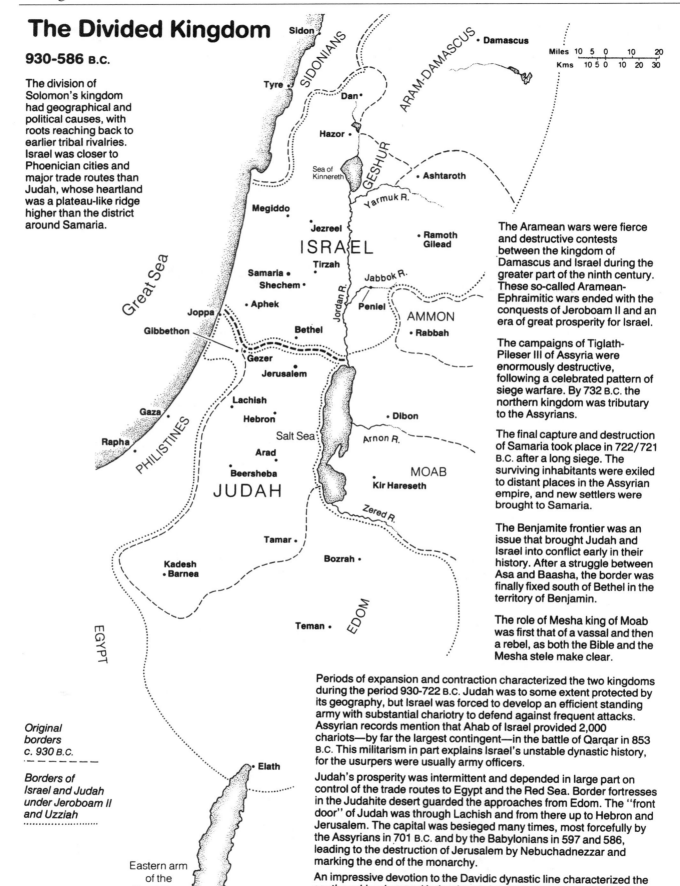

Miles 10 5 0 10 20
Kms 10 5 0 10 20 30

Original borders c. 930 B.C.

Borders of Israel and Judah under Jeroboam II and Uzziah

Eastern arm of the Red Sea

The Aramean wars were fierce and destructive contests between the kingdom of Damascus and Israel during the greater part of the ninth century. These so-called Aramean-Ephraimitic wars ended with the conquests of Jeroboam II and an era of great prosperity for Israel.

The campaigns of Tiglath-Pileser III of Assyria were enormously destructive, following a celebrated pattern of siege warfare. By 732 B.C. the northern kingdom was tributary to the Assyrians.

The final capture and destruction of Samaria took place in 722/721 B.C. after a long siege. The surviving inhabitants were exiled to distant places in the Assyrian empire, and new settlers were brought to Samaria.

The Benjamite frontier was an issue that brought Judah and Israel into conflict early in their history. After a struggle between Asa and Baasha, the border was finally fixed south of Bethel in the territory of Benjamin.

The role of Mesha king of Moab was first that of a vassal and then a rebel, as both the Bible and the Mesha stele make clear.

Periods of expansion and contraction characterized the two kingdoms during the period 930-722 B.C. Judah was to some extent protected by its geography, but Israel was forced to develop an efficient standing army with substantial chariotry to defend against frequent attacks. Assyrian records mention that Ahab of Israel provided 2,000 chariots—by far the largest contingent—in the battle of Qarqar in 853 B.C. This militarism in part explains Israel's unstable dynastic history, for the usurpers were usually army officers.

Judah's prosperity was intermittent and depended in large part on control of the trade routes to Egypt and the Red Sea. Border fortresses in the Judahite desert guarded the approaches from Edom. The "front door" of Judah was through Lachish and from there up to Hebron and Jerusalem. The capital was besieged many times, most forcefully by the Assyrians in 701 B.C. and by the Babylonians in 597 and 586, leading to the destruction of Jerusalem by Nebuchadnezzar and marking the end of the monarchy.

An impressive devotion to the Davidic dynastic line characterized the southern kingdom and helped to maintain stability, in contrast to the more mercurial northern kingdom.

2 KINGS, 1 & 2 CHRONICLES

In 2 Kings, the events of the past six to eight hundred years (from the time of the Exodus) finally come to a head. Throughout her history, Israel continually has disobeyed God and has prostituted herself with idols, even back when Moses was receiving the Ten Commandments. And now is the time of judgment; all the covenant curses — the direct consequences of Israel's disobedience — come to fruition.

God again shows them something He's been trying to teach them all along: There is a . . .

PENALTY FOR SIN

Sin always results in separation from God and physical punishment. In the Garden of Eden, sin resulted in banishment from Eden (the presence of God) and physical death. In Numbers 15:30-31, we read that God wouldn't tolerate deliberate, defiant sin; the offender was to be cut off from his people. And now the nation of Israel experiences the penalty for her sin:

- removal from the Promised Land [". . . he thrust them from his presence" (2 Kings 17:20)].

- physical punishment at the hands of her enemies.

How does this principle of a penalty for sin carry over into the New Testament?

_____

_____

_____

_____

_____

_____

Second Kings is primarily a book of judgment. Chapter 1 records God's judgment on Ahaziah, the wicked king of Israel. Ahaziah sends a captain with a company of fifty men to Elijah (1:9) after Elijah announces that the injured king will not recover. Ahaziah believes, as the pagans do, that Elijah's curse has magical power which only can be nullified by coercing Elijah to retract the curse, or by killing him.

The king is attempting to assert his authority over Elijah, in direct defiance of the covenant nature of Israel's kingship (see 1 Samuel), which stipulated that the king was to be under the authority of God's word spoken through His prophets. Therefore, "Fire fell from heaven and consumed the captain and his men" (2 Kings 1:10b, see also 2 Kings 1:12). Though this punishment seems unusually harsh, the question of who is sovereign in Israel is at stake. Here and throughout the rest of 2 Kings, we find . . .

PROOF OF GOD'S SOVEREIGNTY

List some of the instances in 2 Kings where recorded events were shown to be the direct fulfillment of prophecies (showing God to be ultimately in control of everything that was happening):

_____

_____

_____

_____

_____

Chapter 17 recounts God's repeated warnings to His people and their continual apostasy. "Therefore the Lord rejected all the people of Israel; he afflicted them and gave them into the hands of plunderers, until he thrust them from his presence" (17:20). This penalty is not just a coincidence. God is sovereign — in complete control of historical events. Israel's circumstances are God's direct punishment for their sin. God then brings judgment in chapter 24: "Surely these things happened to Judah according the Lord's command, in order to remove them from his presence because of the sins of Manasseh . . ." (24:3).

We have a tendency to view the "God of the Old Testament" as a God of judgment and wrath, and the "God of the New Testament" as a God of grace and mercy. Nothing could be further from the truth. God is the same God in the Old Testament as He is in the New Testament. All through the history of Israel, God has been faithful, patient and forgiving, despite Israel's continued disobedience.

What evidence do we find in 2 Kings of God's grace in the midst of judgment?

_____

_____

_____

_____

_____

Under Josiah's leadership in chapters 22–23, the Book of the Law is found (either the entire Pentateuch or possibly only Deuteronomy), which leads to a renewal of the covenant and a short-lived revival. Josiah serves the Lord with all his heart, soul and strength (23:25). During his reign there are wonderful reforms, and Israel celebrates the greatest Passover ever.

Why was the Lord still unwilling to forgive (24:4)?

_____

_____

_____

_____

_____

Some very significant events happen during this period that aren't reflected in the account of 2 Kings. When the kingdom divides and the kings of Israel and Judah begin to do evil in the eyes of the Lord, God begins to raise up prophets to proclaim His word. The prophets not only condemn idolatry and immorality and warn of coming judgment, but they also bring focus to God's promise of salvation through a coming Messiah from the house of David. This is God's . . .

PROMISE OF SALVATION

First and Second Kings are written during the Exile, as the Jews look back and ask "Why?" But **1 AND 2 CHRONICLES** are written after the people of Judah are permitted to return to Jerusalem and to their land. Jewish tradition ascribes the work (originally one book) to Ezra. The author writes from the standpoint of a restored community (but no longer an autonomous nation — they have no king) and asks these questions: "What now?" "Is God still interested in us?" "Are His promises still valid?"

First and Second Chronicles serve as a message of hope for the restored community — hope in God's promise of salvation for the remnant of Israel through the coming Messiah, hope of God's continued concern for His people.

The events of 1 and 2 Chronicles parallel those recorded in 2 Samuel and 1 and 2 Kings, but with some striking differences which verify that God's promises are still in effect. In 1 and 2 Chronicles:

A. The Temple receives greater emphasis.

B. The law and **the prophets,** like the Temple, are more crucial to Israel's continued relationship with God than the presence or absence of a king.

C. The author sustains Israel's hope for the promised **Messiah.**

D. "All Israel" is a major concern.

E. The genealogy at the beginning of 1 Chronicles is significant. The author traces Israel's family line back to Adam, showing that God's love for them did not begin with David's reign or the conquest of Canaan, but with creation.

Historically, the books of 2 Kings and 1 and 2 Chronicles are a devastating account of the penalty of sin — they end in exile in Babylon. But at the same time, they are rich with proof of God's sovereignty and His promise of salvation. God is not through with His people — or His redemptive plan.

For personal reflection:

1) Is it hard for you to imagine a God who punishes so severely? What does His punishment teach you about the awfulness of sin?

2) Do you think God is still in control of events today? Explain.

3) Why was God unwilling to forgive Judah (2 Kings 24:4)? Do you think there are ever times when He is unwilling to forgive people today?

4) How can the perspective of 1 and 2 Chronicles be an encouragement to us if we sin or are suffering the penalty for the sins of our nation?

For the next lesson . . .

Read all of Ezra and Nehemiah, or at least the following:
- Ezra 1:1-8; 3:1-13
- Ezra 4:1-24; 6:1-22
- Ezra 7:1-10; 8:15-36
- Ezra 9:1–10:17
- Nehemiah 1:1–2:10; 4:1–5:19
- Nehemiah 6:15–7:3; 8:1–9:38
- Nehemiah 13:1-31

EZRA & NEHEMIAH

The books of Ezra and Nehemiah were originally two separate compositions. However, the earliest Hebrew manuscripts and the oldest manuscripts of the Septuagint (the Greek translation of the Hebrew Old Testament, translated during the intertestamental period) treat Ezra and Nehemiah as one book. These two books of the Bible also have been called "1 and 2 Ezra." Though they contain the memories of both Ezra and Nehemiah, they were written or compiled by a single author, who most scholars believe also was the author of 1 and 2 Chronicles.

In 586 B.C., Jerusalem was destroyed and the Southern Kingdom of Judah was exiled to Babylon. It was the culmination of hundreds of years of apostasy and stubborn defiance of God's laws. But God is not finished with His people yet, as the prophet Jeremiah reminds them: "For men are not cast off by the Lord forever. Though he brings grief, he will show compassion, so great is his unfailing love" (Lamentations 3:31-32).

Jeremiah prophesies that Judah's captivity will last only seventy years (see Jeremiah 25:11), and in fulfillment of that promise, we see in the books of Ezra and Nehemiah that God restores His people. Cyrus, the king of Persia, issues a decree in 538 B.C. allowing all the exiles to return to their homelands and to worship their gods. The Jews also benefit from this change in policy. The books of Ezra and Nehemiah describe the three-stage return:

* Under Zerubbabel in 538 or 537 B.C.

* Under Ezra in 458 B.C. (eighty years later!)

* Under Nehemiah in 445 B.C. (thirteen years after Ezra)

God is restoring Israel to His favor and is continuing His promise of redemption through them. His punishment may have seemed severe, but it was absolutely necessary to rid Israel of idolatry once and for all and to pave the way for the coming Messiah.

Only about fifty thousand Jews return with Zerubbabel. No doubt, the rest have become satisfied with life in Babylon; some never have seen the Promised Land. But God calls a remnant of the faithful to return (Ezra 2).

Ezra 3 begins in the seventh month of the year. What is significant about this month, especially in light of the restoration of the Jews to the Promised Land?

_____

_____

_____

Chapters 3 through 6 describe the building of the Temple under Zerubbabel and the opposition the Jews face from their enemies, who "set out to discourage them and to frustrate their plans" (4:4). They are compelled by King Xerxes to stop construction, but resume building fifteen years later, in the second year of Darius. In chapter 6, the Temple finally is completed and is dedicated in 516 B.C., seventy years after its destruction in 586 B.C.

Almost sixty years pass between chapters 6 and 7, when Ezra comes to Jerusalem along with about fifteen hundred men, plus women and children. Whereas Zerubbabel's mission was THE BUILDING OF THE TEMPLE, Ezra's mission is THE BUILDING OF THE PEOPLE. Ezra is a man devoted to the Word of God and committed to teaching Israel to know and obey God's law (7:6, 10, 25-26).

Tradition tells us that Ezra instituted the synagogue worship and was instrumental in forming the Old Testament canon. His mission was the building of the people by the power of the Word.

Upon his return to Jerusalem, in what condition did Ezra find the people, and what was his response (9:1–10:17)?

_____

_____

_____

_____

_____

_____

Ezra teaches that restoration to God's grace will require . . .

1. **Confession of sin;**

2. **Submission to God's will;**

3. **Separation from pagan influences.**

The book of **NEHEMIAH** continues the description of the restoration of the remnant of "all Israel" to the Promised Land. The book begins in 445 B.C., about thirteen years after the close of the book of Ezra.

REBUILDING THE WALLS (Nehemiah 1–7)

While in exile, Nehemiah has been the "cupbearer to the king," a position of high honor. He has remained in Susa in the Persian Empire, but, upon hearing of the condition of the wall around Jerusalem, he sets forth to rebuild it.

Whereas Ezra was characterized primarily as a man of the WORD, Nehemiah is described as a man of PRAYER (1:4-11; 2:4; 4:4-5, 9; 5:19; 6:9, 14; 13:14, 22, 29, 31). These two men do more to reform and revitalize the nation of Israel than any other has done, most likely because of their dedication to the Word of God and to prayer.

What opposition did Nehemiah encounter once restoration of the wall began (chapters 4, 6)?

_____

_____

_____

_____

_____

Because Nehemiah is a man of prayer, he is able to stand strong in the face of opposition, to keep the Israelites encouraged, and to complete the restoration of the wall in just fifty-two days (6:15).

RENEWING THE COVENANT (Nehemiah 8–10)

Again, we read about the seventh month (significant in the Jewish calendar), when "the people assembled as one man. . . . They told Ezra the scribe to bring out the Book of the Law of Moses" (8:1).

What was the response by the people to the reading and explaining of God's Word?

_____

_____

_____

_____

_____

REFORMING THE NATION (Nehemiah 11–13)

A. REPOPULATING THE CITIES (chapter 11)

B. REDEDICATING THE WALL (chapter 12)

C. REVIVING THE PEOPLE (chapter 13)

Ezra and Nehemiah had an unparalleled impact on the restored community:

> Without the teaching of the law, without the invincible faith and fearless action of these 2 leaders, it is doubtful if a distinctive Jewish religion and community — with all that means for the world through the birth and death of Christ — could have survived (_Eerdmans' Handbook to the Bible_, p. 312).

These men forever changed the course of Israel's history by ridding her once and for all of idolatry and by giving rise to a people who would be devoted to the Word of God, prayer and piety.

So we end Israel's history in Canaan much as it started — full of promise and obedience. They have just come through a second exodus and have been restored to favor with God. God is still faithful to His people, still gracious, still forgiving, and still committed to fulfilling His promises (see Jeremiah 29:10-14).

For personal reflection:

1) What effect do you think God's Word can have on people today? Do you think truly understanding it could spark a revival in your life? in your country?

2) Does the three-fold formula for restoration still work today? Which is most difficult for you?

3) Do you pray about all your decisions, as Nehemiah did? How could a commitment to prayer help you when you face opposition?

4) Based on the examples of Ezra and Nehemiah, what kinds of changes do you think God wants to make in your life? Are you willing to let Him?

For the next lesson . . .

Read all of Esther, or at least the following:
- Esther 1:1-22
- Esther 2:1-23
- Esther 3:1-15
- Esther 4:1–5:14
- Esther 6:1–7:10
- Esther 8:1-17
- Esther 9:1-17, 20-22; 10:3

Return from Exile

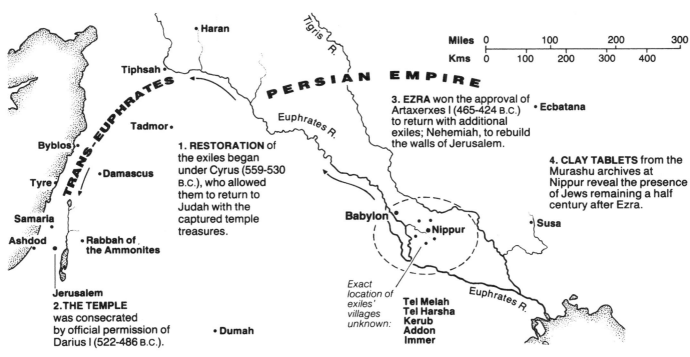

Miles 0   100   200   300
Kms 0   100   200   300   400

• Haran

Tiphsah •

Tigris R.

PERSIAN EMPIRE

Euphrates R.

3. EZRA won the approval of Artaxerxes I (465-424 B.C.) to return with additional exiles; Nehemiah, to rebuild the walls of Jerusalem.

• Ecbatana

TRANS-EUPHRATES

Tadmor •

1. RESTORATION of the exiles began under Cyrus (559-530 B.C.), who allowed them to return to Judah with the captured temple treasures.

4. CLAY TABLETS from the Murashu archives at Nippur reveal the presence of Jews remaining a half century after Ezra.

Byblos •

Tyre •

• Damascus

Babylon •   • Nippur

• Susa

Samaria •

Ashdod •

• Rabbah of the Ammonites

Exact location of exiles' villages unknown:

Tel Melah
Tel Harsha
Kerub
Addon
Immer

Euphrates R.

Jerusalem
2. THE TEMPLE was consecrated by official permission of Darius I (522-486 B.C.).

• Dumah

Zerubbabel's Temple

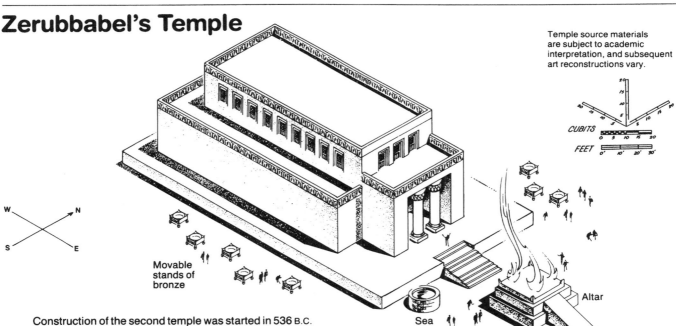

Temple source materials are subject to academic interpretation, and subsequent art reconstructions vary.

CUBITS

FEET

W   N
S   E

Movable stands of bronze

Sea

Altar

Construction of the second temple was started in 536 B.C. on the Solomonic foundations leveled a half-century earlier by the Babylonians. People who remembered the earlier temple wept at the comparison (Ezr 3:12). Not until 516 B.C., the 6th year of the Persian emperor Darius I (522-486), was the temple finally completed at the urging of Haggai and Zechariah (Ezr 6:13-15).

Archaeological evidence confirms that the Persian period in Palestine was a comparatively impoverished one in terms of material culture. Later Aramaic documents from Elephantine in Upper Egypt illustrate the official process of gaining permission to construct a Jewish place of worship, and the opposition engendered by the presence of various foes during this period.

Of the temple and its construction, little is known. Among the few contemporary buildings, the Persian palace at Lachish and the Tobiad monument at Iraq el-Amir may be compared in terms of technique.

Unlike the more famous structures razed in 586 B.C. and A.D. 70, the temple begun by Zerubbabel suffered no major hostile destruction, but was gradually repaired and reconstructed over a long period. Eventually it was replaced entirely by Herod's magnificent edifice.

ESTHER

After seventy years of captivity, Cyrus, king of Persia, issued a decree allowing the Jews to return to Jerusalem to rebuild the temple under the leadership of Zerubbabel. Sixty years elapsed between Ezra 6 and 7, after which Ezra traveled to Jerusalem to teach God's Word. Thirteen years later, Nehemiah rebuilt the wall around Jerusalem.

It was during this sixty-year intermediate period that the events of the book of Esther took place. God's Temple had been rebuilt, but that wasn't the end of Satan's assault on God's chosen people — neither did it end God's gracious deliverance of them.

THE PROVIDENTIAL POSITIONING OF ESTHER

The events of the book of Esther take place in Persia (Babylonia), more specifically in Susa, the winter residence of the Persian kings. The time is approximately 483 B.C., in the third year of the reign of Xerxes (1:3).

What were the events that took place in the first two chapters that providentially brought Esther to the throne in Persia?

_____

_____

_____

The details of the story make it readily apparent that Esther is providentially positioned in the palace. God takes a lowly Jewish orphan and makes her a queen to fulfill His purposes. Similar positionings are recounted throughout Scripture. It is always the least likely person who is placed in a position to do God's will (e.g. Joseph, Gideon, the nation of Israel, the disciples, and Saul of Tarsus).

THE PLOT OF HAMAN

Haman holds the highest position of honor in the court (Esther 3:1-2). Because Mordecai refuses to bow to him, Haman is filled with hatred for Mordecai and his people, the Jews.

How did Haman plan to destroy the Jewish people (3:6-14)?

_____

_____

_____

_____

Mordecai urges Esther to beg the king for mercy, to plead with him for her people. This would not be as easy as it sounded. Approaching the king without being summoned would mean certain death — unless, by chance, he would grant favor and extend the gold scepter to her, sparing her life. Esther, no doubt, is afraid.

How did Mordecai's response put everything in perspective (4:13-14)?

_____

_____

_____

_____

_____

Two fasts are noted in chapter 4 (both by Mordecai, the second also including Esther and her maids), which stand in sharp contrast to the feasting that is prominent throughout the book, and which accentuate the gravity of the situation facing Esther and the Jews. After the three-day fast, Esther determines to go to the king: "I will go to the king, even though it is against the law. And if I perish, I perish" (4:16b).

How is Esther an example for us?

1. **Her life is characterized by obedience.**

2. **She recognizes God's greater purpose in the events of her life.**

3. **She is willing to pay the price of obeying God.**

In chapter 5, Esther goes to the king and is received with favor; he holds out the gold scepter to her and offers to give her up to half the kingdom. She wisely requests only that Xerxes and Haman attend a banquet she has prepared. While at this banquet, Esther requests that they attend a second banquet the next day. By doing this, she wins the favor of the king, heightens anticipation, and allows the other events to take place which affect the outcome.

How does Haman personify evil in the book of Esther?

_____

_____

_____

_____

_____

There always has been a "Haman" in Israel's history, plotting time and again to destroy God's chosen people. Here, Haman builds a gallows with the intention of asking Xerxes to have Mordecai hanged the next morning.

The turning point is marked by the events of chapter 6: A sleepless night brings King Xerxes to learn of Mordecai's part in exposing the earlier conspiracy to assassinate Xerxes (2:19-23). When the king also learns that no reward has been given to Mordecai, he asks Haman what should be done for the man whom the king delights to honor. Since Xerxes doesn't reveal the man's name, Haman naturally assumes that the honor is for himself and finds himself heaping on his enemy honors he thought were intended for him (6:10-11).

At Esther's second banquet, she finally makes her request to the king — she pleads for her own life and the lives of her people, exposing Haman's plot. In a strange twist of events, Haman is hanged on the very gallows he built for Mordecai.

How did the king circumvent the irrevocable law to kill all the Jews, and what was the result (chapters 8 and 9)?

_____

_____

_____

_____

THE PROVIDENCE OF GOD

The most striking literary characteristic of the book of Esther is what is *not* said: there is not one mention of God, prayer (which always accompanied fasting), sacrifice, Israel, or any other religous symbol.

How does the author make use of what is not said to point us to the providence of God in this story?

_____

_____

_____

_____

List some of the similarities between the story of Esther and the story of Joseph in Genesis 37 through 45:

_____

_____

_____

_____

To the Jews, who would be familiar with the Pentateuch, these parallels would be readily perceived. Think of the impact on the Jews still in exile or even in the restored community — just as God, in His providence, had provided for their deliverance in the time of Jacob through Joseph, even now God still is ensuring the deliverance of His people.

THE PLAN OF REDEMPTION

Why is it important that Haman was called an Agagite (a descendant of Agag, king of the Amalekites), and how does that connection give this story greater significance (see Exodus 17; Numbers 24:20; and 1 Samuel 14 and 15)?

_____

_____

_____

_____

_____

THE PURPOSE OF THE STORY

A. For a people in exile or in the restored community:

_____

_____

B. For us:

_____

_____

For personal reflection:

1) Has God placed you in a position where He may want to use you to accomplish His purposes?

2) Are you willing to pay any price to be a disciple, or are there still some things that hold you back?

3) Do you think God is in control of every event in your life? What evidence do you see that He is? Explain.

4) What other personal applications can you draw from the book of Esther?

For the next lesson . . .

Read all of Job, or at least the following:
- Job 1:1–2:13
- Job 3:1-26; 4:6-9; 5:6-7, 17-18
- Job 6:24–7:21; 10:1-9; 11:1-9
- Job 12:9-13; 13:1-5, 15; 16:12-21
- Job 19:23-27; 23:10-12; 28:1-28
- Job 34:10-15; 36:4-17, 26; 38:1-41
- Job 40:1-14; 42:1-17

JOB

The events of Job take place in the days of the patriarchs, probably between 2000 and 1000 B.C. One of Job's friends is identified as Eliphaz the Temanite (Teman being a town in Edom), and may have been one of Esau's sons (Esau was the father of the Edomites) listed in Genesis 36:10.

It is unlikely that Job is the author, since material is recorded of which he would have had no direct knowledge. The bulk of Job comprises the words of Job and his friends, which must have been available to the author in either written or oral form.

The story of Job is simple: A righteous man suffers, receives miserable comfort from so-called friends, and eventually finds vindication and restoration. But, at the same time, it is very complex. The book of Job is possibly the oldest recorded book in the Bible, and it fittingly deals with the oldest question of man: "Why do the innocent suffer?"

It was the logical assumption in ancient Israel that suffering was an indication of sin and wickedness on the part of the one afflicted. But the first two chapters of Job give insight into another element of the problem.

SATAN: ACCUSATION AND RUIN

In Job 1:6-7, the angels come to present themselves before the Lord, and Satan, whose name means "accuser," also comes before Him. This does not appear to have been an uncommon occurrence. In Zechariah 3:1-2, Satan stands before the Lord to accuse Joshua (or Jeshua), and Revelation 12:10 describes Satan as "the accuser of our brothers who accuses them before our God day and night." We learn from chapter 1 of the book of Job that it is Satan, not God, who afflicts the inhabitants of the earth, including Job.

What power has been given to Satan (1:6-12)?

_____

_____

_____

What are the four sources of suffering in our world?

1. _____

2. _____

3. _____

4. _____

We must keep in mind that God is ultimately in control. Notice that it is God who allows Satan to test His righteous servant, and it is God who brings ultimate vindication, putting Satan's accusations to rest. God also sets limits on Satan's power; Satan isn't given unlimited reign. In the first part of this story, Satan is not permitted to lay a finger on Job himself (1:12), then is permitted to do so, but is forbidden to take Job's life (2:6). God is at the same time just and good and all-powerful — nothing and no one is outside His sovereign control.

JOB'S FRIENDS: FRUSTRATION AND REBUKE

Chapters 3 through 27 contain three cycles of dialogue-dispute. Job opens with a lament in chapter 3, and then his friends, each in turn, attempt to explain to Job the reason for his suffering. After each rebuke, Job gives a reply, and the cycle begins again.

Remember that neither Job nor his friends were aware of the events of chapters 1 and 2, so his friends' "words of comfort" reflect the attitudes toward suffering prevalent in Job's day:

    A. ELIPHAZ bases his argument in his three speeches on <u>experience</u> (4:8; 5:6-7).

    B. BILDAD bases his argument on <u>tradition</u>, on the theological tenets of the day (8:8-10, 13, 20; 18:21).

    C. ZOPHAR bases his argument on <u>assumption</u> (11:6; 20:4).

Chapters 29 through 42 contain three monologues: by Job, Elihu, and God. Elihu, being younger than Job's other friends, has remained silent out of deference for his elders. But he finally speaks up and gives very good counsel (chapters 32–37), much of which is repeated by God (chapters 38–42).

Elihu agrees with the others that God is just and right. He points out, however, that suffering isn't always indicative of God's judgment, but often of His discipline and chastening; God always has a higher purpose (33:17-18, 29-30). Elihu also points out that the ways of God are above our understanding (36:26; 37:5, 19).

JOB: DESPERATION AND REMORSE

1. He desires to know what he has done wrong (6:24; 7:20; 10:2; 27:5-6).

2. He assumes that it is God who is afflicting him (10:16; 12:9; 16:9; 31:35).

3. He is honest before God (7:7; 10:1, 3).

4. Even in desperation, Job maintains faith in God and in His ultimate redemption (13:15; 16:19-21; 19:25-27; 23:10).

GOD: RESTORATION AND REWARD

God's "monologue" (chapters 38–42) consists of a series of questions. He never offers an explanation to Job, but demonstrates His supreme power, goodness, wisdom and justice that surpass human understanding. Forms of the word "understand" are used twenty-five times, and of the word "knowledge," thirteen times, emphasizing that it is our lack of understanding that causes the dilemma when the innocent suffer. The entire book hinges on that theme. Even the literary structure supports it:

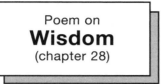

Poem on
Wisdom
(chapter 28)

Three Cycles of
Dialogue-Dispute
(chapters 3–27)

Three
Monologues
(chapters 29–42)

Prologue
(chapters 1–2)

Epilogue
(chapter 42)

The structure of the book points us to its central theme. The poem on wisdom in chapter 28, possibly written (and inserted) by the narrator, is the focal point of the book. It describes how precious stones and metals are found in the deepest mines, while wisdom can neither be found in mines nor be bought with the finest gold or silver (28:15). The writer concludes that wisdom is found only in God and the fear of Him (28:20-28). God alone is the answer to the mystery of why the innocent suffer; He alone understands. The key to our understanding is to fear the Lord and to shun evil.

Happily, in this case, Job is vindicated: God rebukes Job's friends and commends Job, and, after Job forgives and prays for his friends (42:8), God again prospers Job (42:10), giving him twice as much as he had before. "The Lord blessed the latter part of Job's life more than the first" (42:12a). The theme throughout the Bible is redemption, or restoration, and here God restores Job, redeeming him from the hands of Satan.

For personal reflection:

1) Have you ever been afflicted and found yourself blaming God or asking why?

2) Why is it so hard to accept the fact that innocent people suffer? Is it fair for God to allow that to happen?

3) What does this story teach us about listening to the advice of close friends?

4) How does the book of Job help you to understand what "patience" really is? How can you use the lessons from this story to help others who may be hurting?

For the next lesson . . .

Read all of Psalms, or at least the following:

- Psalms 93–100
- Psalms 108–110
- Psalms 113–118
- Psalms 120–134
- Psalms 146–150
- Psalms 32, 51, 119
- Psalms 1, 22, 23, 90, 91, 137, 139

PSALMS

THE HEART OF THE PSALMS

The book of Psalms is not a doctrinal collection to be studied, but a doxological collection to be experienced in worship. The heart of the psalms is the full spectrum of human emotion they convey:

A. _____ (8:3-4; 139)

B. _____ (22:1-2, 6; 6:6; 38:11)

C. _____ (51:1-4)

D. _____ [Note the "imprecatory" Psalms, in which the author calls upon God to bring misfortune to an enemy: Pss. 5; 11; 17; 35; 55; 59; 69; 109; 137; and 140.]

Other emotions that are conveyed include these: trust (27:1; 56:11; 73:25-26); the hope of being with God (23:6; 27:4); praise and adoration (63:3-4; 145:3); worship (95:6-7); and yearning (42:1-2; 84:2).

THE POETRY OF THE PSALMS

Psalms contains some of the finest examples of poetry anywhere in ancient (or even recent) literature. What types of poetry can be found in the psalms?

_____

_____

_____

_____

_____

_____

The most striking feature of Hebrew poetry is parallelism, the "rhyming" of thought. All the poetry of the psalms can be divided into three types of parallelism:

A. SYNONYMOUS — The second segment repeats the first in different words.

B. ANTITHETIC — The second segment contrasts the first.

C. SYNTHETIC — The idea is reinforced or expanded by the second segment.

Why is it significant that Hebrew poetry rhymes thoughts instead of sounds?

_____

_____

_____

_____

_____

_____

THE THEOLOGY OF THE PSALMS

Each psalm must be understood in light of the collection as a whole. Five major themes are woven through the psalms:

A. MAJESTY — The most striking characteristic of the book of Psalms is the absolute centrality of the God of Israel. Psalms describes the majesty of God and his rule over creation and history (93:1-2; 95:3; 96:4-6).

B. JUSTICE — With God as the great, sovereign King, His kingdom will come, and all opposition and rebellion finally will be purged. Though the wicked appear to flourish now, in the end their evil will come back on them (37:13, 37-38; 9:8).

C. KINGDOM — As King over all the earth, God chose Israel to be His servant people. He delivered them and gave them a land of their own, and He united them with himself through the covenant. (A synopsis of Israelite history is interspersed throughout the Psalms.) Israel was redeemed as the initial embodiment of God's kingdom (48:1-3). There are numerous references throughout the psalms to the covenant, Israel, Zion, God as King, His throne, and His rule over the earth. "The Lord reigns" is a phrase that is repeated several times.

D. COMPASSION — God's splendor and majesty and His sovereignty and justice do not nullify His compassion. He is swift to bring forgiveness, strength and provision to those who fear Him. God is seen in the psalms as a God of love, mercy and compassion (34:18; 55:22; 91:14-16).

E. WORSHIP — Each psalm is a revelation of man's response to God — a response of praise, adoration, trust . . . worship (100:1-2, 4; 113:1-3). The collection of psalms is one grand expression of praise to God.

THE HISTORY OF THE PSALMS

The traditional Hebrew title meant "Praises," but the LXX (Septuagint) gave it the title "Psalmoi" — songs to the accompaniment of a stringed instrument. Psalms became the prayer and praise book of the nation of Israel in their Temple worship, and Jews still use the psalms today, in the synagogue. The Christians of the New Testament sang them (see Colossians 3:16 and James 5:13), and all denominations of Christians use the psalms today.

Who wrote the psalms, and when were they written?

_____

_____

_____

_____

_____

_____

Clusters of psalms were collected for a long time, adapted to the language of the users, and used in public worship. List some of these compilations:

_____

_____

_____

_____

_____

It was the post-exilic Temple personnel of the third century B.C. who compiled Psalms into its final form. Let's take a closer look at that form.

THE STRUCTURE OF THE PSALMS

Psalms is divided into five "books," which it has been since the time of Ezra. There is much evidence of conscious arrangement of the psalms in this structure (though they are not in any chronological or thematic order). There is a definite introduction in Psalms 1 and 2, and a conclusion in Psalms 146 through 150. Each book ends with a doxology and consists of material predominantly attributed to a single author.

Many authors and theologians have attempted to account for the details of the Psalter's final form. One theory that is particularly intriguing comes from the *Midrash* (the Jewish commentary): "Moses gave to the Israelites the five Books of the Law, and as a counterpart to these, David gave the Psalms which consists of five books."

Psalms "is the fivefold Book of the Congregation to Jehovah, as the Pentateuch is the fivefold Book of Jehovah to the congregation." It very well could be that each of these "books" was meant to correspond loosely with the first five books of the Bible (see chart on next page).

THE CHRIST OF THE PSALMS

The psalms never were considered to be prophecy, but the Jews always recognized their future fulfillment. Even David, when he was writing his own words, said: "The Spirit of the Lord spoke through me; his word was on my tongue" (2 Samuel 23:2). Jesus applied the psalms to himself, as did His disciples: "Everything must be fulfilled that is written about me in the Law of Moses, the Prophets and the Psalms" (Luke 24:44b).

The psalms are replete with allusions to Christ. The following are some of the principal "messianic" Psalms: 2, 8, 16, 20–24, 31, 35, 40–41, 45, 50, 55, 61, 68–69, 72, 89, 96–98, 102, 109–110, 118 and 132. Psalms is a book about Christ, continuing the theme of redemption that runs throughout the Bible. The law is perfectly fulfilled in Christ. History is perfectly fulfilled in Christ. And we see that poetry — the expression of the human heart — also is perfectly fulfilled in Christ.

For personal reflection:

1) What psalms have been particularly meaningful to you over the years?

2) What have you learned about God through the book of Psalms that you didn't know from reading the rest of the Bible?

3) What have you learned through the psalms about the emotions of mankind? How can the psalms be used in expressing your emotions to God?

4) How can reading the psalms help us to give God more of the praise and worship He deserves? How can Psalms be used as your personal prayer book?

For the next lesson . . .

Read all of Proverbs, Ecclesiastes and Song of Songs, or at least the following:

- Proverbs 1:1–3:35
- Proverbs 4:1-27; 8:1–9:18
- Proverbs 20:1–22:1; 31:10-31
- Ecclesiastes 1:1–3:14
- Ecclesiastes 5:8-20; 9:1-12; 12:1-14
- Song of Songs 1:1–4:16
- Song of Songs 5:1–8:14

	Book 1 Psalms 1–41	Book 2 Psalms 42–72	Book 3 Psalms 73–89	Book 4 Psalms 90–106	Book 5 Psalms 107–150
Doxology	41:13	72:18-19	89:52	106:48	150:6
Authors	Mostly David	Mostly David and Korah	Mostly Asaph	Mostly Anonymous	Mostly David
Similarity to the Pentateuch	**Genesis** Sin and judgment, but with vindication in the midst (Psalm 19)	**Exodus** References in book 2 to the things that made Israel unique as a nation; the nation of Israel began in Exodus.	**Leviticus** Salvation through sanctuary; every chapter in book 3 refers to the Temple, courts of the Lord, etc.	**Numbers** Wilderness wanderings (Psalm 90 written during wanderings?); grumbling and unfaithfulness of Israel	**Deuteronomy** Covenant of love and our response to God (praise)

PROVERBS, ECCLESIASTES & SONG OF SONGS

PROVERBS: THE ACTIONS OF THE GODLY

Who wrote the book of Proverbs, and when were these proverbs compiled?

_____

_____

_____

_____

Proverbs is a textbook of wisdom, formulated to teach young men wisdom, righteousness, and the path to true success. "Wisdom" is used forty-one times in the book. In the pages of Proverbs, every area of life is touched: relationships, home, work, justice, decisions, attitudes, reactions — in a word, everything man does, says, and even thinks. And all this wisdom is based on one ideal: the fear of the Lord.

What is "the fear of the Lord," and why is it important (1:7; 10:27; 14:26-27; 15:16, 33; 19:23; 22:4; 23:17; 24:21; 28:14; and 31:30)?

_____

_____

_____

_____

_____

There are several themes in Proverbs:

1. Wisdom and folly

2. The righteous and the wicked

3. Words and the tongue

4. Family

5. Laziness and hard work

There are several secondary themes in Proverbs: poverty and wealth, plans and decisions, the proud and the humble, friends and neighbors, masters and servants, kings and rulers, hopes and fears, joy and sorrow, sexual temptation and lust, and anger. Every area of life is to be touched by wisdom, which comes from the fear of the Lord. God wants to affect our every action, attitude, word and thought.

At first glance, the literary structure appears to be an entirely random collection of wisdom, but it is actually very well structured. Chapters 1 through 9 contain a series of discourses that contrast wisdom and folly. A key feature in these first nine chapters is the personification of both wisdom and folly, portrayed as women, each seeking to persuade young men to follow her ways.

The book concludes with an acrostic poem in Proverbs 31:10-31, honoring the wife of noble character — the ideal woman who epitomizes the wisdom described throughout the book. The poem serves as a return to the theme of chapters 1 through 9; in a subtle way it advises young men to marry Lady Wisdom. This woman, Wisdom, is aptly described: "Wisdom has built her house; she has hewn out its seven pillars. She has prepared her meat and mixed her wine; she has also set her table" (9:1-2). This is similar to some of the descriptions of the noble woman in chapter 31. So, Proverbs is not only an instruction book on wisdom, but it is also one grand appeal for young men to follow the way of wisdom.

ECCLESIASTES: THE ATTITUDES OF THE GODLY

"Ecclesiastes" comes from the Greek word for "preacher" or "teacher" and is derived from the word for "assembly." The Hebrew title means "one who convenes and speaks at an assembly." The book of Ecclesiastes, then, may have been a sermon intended to be delivered to a congregation. The book contains the philosophical and theological reflections of a man who has come to the end of his life and has realized the meaninglessness of life apart from God — because he foolishly has sought satisfaction and fulfillment apart from God. (Solomon certainly fits such a description.)

A. LIFE IS MEANINGLESS APART FROM GOD.

There are two keys to understanding Ecclesiastes. First, "meaningless" (or "vanity" in KJV, which may mean "breath" or "vapor" in the Hebrew language, thus meaning empty or without substance) is used thirty-five times, and only once elsewhere (see Job 27:12). Second, the meaning of "under the sun," a phrase used twenty-nine times, must be properly defined. It indicates the world seen simply from a human standpoint, a world based on human thought and speculation apart from God. Right from the outset, the message of the author of Ecclesiastes is that life as man lives it, without God, is futile, meaningless, purposeless and empty.

What are some things which the author finds to be meaningless?

_____

_____

_____

_____

B. THERE IS NO SATISFACTION APART FROM GOD.

Solomon tried everything to gain fulfillment in this world. God gave him great wisdom, but that didn't satisfy. He applied himself to wisdom and folly, but it was "chasing after the wind" (1:17). So he tried embracing folly (cheering himself with wine) and amassing great wealth and fame (chapter 2).

The book of Ecclesiastes is not about cynicism and despair. It was never God's intention for man to leave Him out of the picture. God does bring joy into our lives, but our ultimate satisfaction must be in Him, not in the pleasures of life — and certainly not in the "pleasures" of sin!

C. TRUE FULFILLMENT IS FOUND IN GOD ALONE.

God alone brings joy to the "meaninglessness" of life. The only Hebrew word the author uses for God in Ecclesiastes is "Elohim" (thirty times), which emphasizes God's absolute sovereignty. God is ABLE to completely satisfy, and we can trust in His complete sovereignty and justice (2:24-26; 3:11-14; 5:19-20).

The author praises the enjoyment of life (8:15; 9:7, 9; 11:8) and brings the book to its conclusion: "Now all has been heard; here is the conclusion in the matter: Fear God and keep his commandments, for this is the whole duty of man" (12:13).

The conclusion of the book refers back to all the wisdom of Proverbs — fearing the Lord. In Proverbs, the fear of the Lord affects the actions of man. In Ecclesiastes, it affects man's attitude toward life. Fulfillment is found not in the pleasures of life itself, but in the God who gives us life. Obedience to God's commands, not the endless pursuit of happiness itself, results in true happiness (see John 10:10 and 15:10-11).

SONG OF SONGS: AFFECTIONS AND ALLEGIANCES OF THE GODLY

The Hebrew title of this book means "the greatest of songs." Probably written by Solomon, it is a beautiful book showing marital love as a gift from God and showing the absolute devotion required for this level of intimacy. It characterizes marital love as the strongest, most unyielding and invincible force in human experience.

Jews have regarded Song of Songs as an allegory depicting God's love for Israel. How is this book an illustration of Christ's love for the church and of our relationship with Him?

_____

_____

_____

_____

_____

_____

How did the Jews liken the three books discussed in this lesson to the Temple which Solomon built for God?

_____

_____

_____

_____

_____

_____

For personal reflection:

1) Choose one area of your life where you need more wisdom (marriage, job, raising children, use of the tongue, etc.) and find all the proverbs that address that concern. Try to memorize two or three.

2) Why do we sometimes misunderstand the "fear of the Lord"? Do you think people today have the same "fear" as folk in Bible times had? How do you think this affects the "wisdom" of the times?

3) Do you agree that happiness is a by-product of obedience? Do you see any correlations between your own level of obedience to the commands of God and your level of fulfillment or happiness?

For the next lesson . . .

Read all of Isaiah, or at least the following:

- Isaiah 1:10-20; 2:1-22; 4:2-6
- Isaiah 6:1-13; 9:1-7; 10:20–12:6
- Isaiah 14:1-27; 24:1–26:21
- Isaiah 35:1-10; 36:1–38:7
- Isaiah 40:1–42:9; 49:1-26
- Isaiah 51:1-16; 52:7–53:12; 55:1-13
- Isaiah 60:1–62:12; 65:17-25; 66:15-24

ISAIAH

The poetical books were born out of the "Golden Age" of Israel — times of peace and prosperity and obedience to God (during the reigns of David and Solomon). But the prophetical books are the product of the "Dark Ages" of the nation — times of apostasy and ruin.

The PRE-EXILIC prophets were (in order of writing): Obadiah, Joel, Jonah, Amos, Hosea, Isaiah, Micah, Nahum, Habakkuk, Zephaniah and Jeremiah. The EXILIC prophets, writing during the period of exile, were Ezekiel and Daniel; Jeremiah also extended into this period for a short time. The POST-EXILIC prophets were Haggai, Zechariah and Malachi.

What was the role of the prophet?

_____

_____

_____

The prophets had the unique ability to see into the affairs of men and into the mind of God. They always spoke to the issues at hand but also were looking into the future for a more perfect fulfillment of their messages.

As a whole, the prophets focused on:

1. **The Lord as ruler over all history**

2. **The primary need to be right with God**

3. **The moral foundation of religion and society**

4. **A blend of judgment and hope**

5. **The messianic kingdom**

Of the books written by the four major prophets, Isaiah is probably the most often quoted and the best loved. The book is noticeably divided into two sections, which has given rise to the theory that the second half of Isaiah was written by someone else at a much later time. Hence, this second half of the book is often dubbed, "Deutero-Isaiah." What evidence is there that Isaiah truly is (and always was) one book?

_____

_____

_____

_____

Isaiah 1:1 provides the historical setting for the book: "The vision concerning Judah and Jerusalem that Isaiah son of Amoz saw during the reigns of Uzziah, Jotham, Ahaz and Hezekiah, kings of Judah."

One commentator outlines the first thirty-nine chapters of the book according to the king under which Isaiah prophesied:

— Chapters 1 through 6 were written under Uzziah and his son, Jotham. Uzziah (also known as Azariah) began his reign in the Southern Kingdom around 767 B.C. His story is recorded in 2 Kings 15.

— Chapters 7 through 14 were written under Ahaz, who paid tribute to the Assyrians and was king when the Northern Kingdom fell to Assyria.

— Chapters 15 through 39 were written under Hezekiah, the first king of Judah after the fall of Israel (715 B.C.). Assyria was a strong threat to Judah, and Sennacherib, ruler of Assyria, tried to overtake Jerusalem. Hezekiah was a righteous king, and God extended his life by fifteen years, recorded in the historical interlude of chapters 36 through 39 (which acts as a bridge between the two sections), as well as in 2 Kings 18:13 through 20:19.

PART 1: THE BOOK OF JUDGMENT — GOD'S GOVERNMENT (chapters 1–39)

Isaiah 1 serves as an introduction to the entire book:

* Israel has rebelled against God (1:2) and has forsaken the Lord and turned her back on Him (1:4). This is an accurate description of the apostasy of Judah and Israel at this point in history.

* God reveals in Isaiah 1:10-17 that the religion of sacrifices and festivals in Judah and Israel is detestable because of their insincerity and their flagrant lack of justice.

* God declares judgment (1:25).

* But even in the midst of judgment, there is the promise of redemption (1:18, cf. Gen. 3:15).

* But a precedent is set: obedience is required (Isa. 1:19-20, 27-28). The rebellious will perish, but the obedient will prosper. This is developed even further in Isaiah 65:8-16. So, both the beginning and ending of Isaiah repeat the same themes echoed throughout the Old Testament: Where there is sin, there is always judgment; and salvation is contingent upon obedience.

The first thirty-five chapters speak almost entirely of judgment — upon Israel as well as her enemies. But on almost every page, intertwined with God's judgment, are promises of God's grace — just as in the book of Genesis when God gave the promise of ultimate redemption (see Genesis 3:15) in the midst of His judgment on sin.

What are some of the promises of God's grace found in Isaiah?

_____

_____

_____

_____

_____

Israel has broken the covenant and God's arm is raised to execute judgment on her sin, and yet He still is planning to be gracious and to restore them to His favor.

PART 2: THE BOOK OF COMFORT — GOD'S GRACE (chapters 40–66)

Isaiah 1 through 39 closely parallel the Old Testament as a whole. Likewise, the second section of Isaiah closely parallels the New Testament (chapters 40–66).

In chapters 1 through 35, Isaiah prophesied against the backdrop of the Assyrian threat against Judah and Jerusalem. He recorded Assyria's failure and warned about the future rise of Babylon in the historical interlude of chapters 36 through 39. Chapters 40 through 66 were written as if the Babylonian exile of Judah was almost over, even though it hadn't yet begun.

In these final chapters, grace and comfort are predominant, and Isaiah gives us some of the greatest prophecies of the coming Messiah found anywhere in Scripture. Isaiah 42:1-4; 49:1-6; 50:4-9; and 52:13–53:12 are known as the four "Servant Songs," depicting the Messiah as a servant, and describing His suffering. He also is viewed as a high priest who would atone for the sins of the world.

Deliverance from Babylonian captivity is foretold, but more importantly, these twenty-seven chapters foretell Israel's eventual deliverance from the prison of sin.

A. GOD IS ABLE TO DELIVER (chapter 40)

B. GOD IS WILLING TO DELIVER (41:9-10)

C. GOD IS FAITHFUL TO DELIVER (43:19; 44:23)

Why is Isaiah 53 such a significant chapter?

_____

_____

_____

_____

_____

_____

How is the book of Isaiah a "miniature replica" of the Bible as a whole?

_____

_____

_____

_____

_____

Isaiah mirrors in every way the message of the entire Bible. The whole life of Christ can be found within the pages of Isaiah — from Christ's birth, to His death and resurrection, to His second coming in great glory. It is little wonder that the book of Isaiah has been called the "fifth Gospel," and Isaiah the "fifth evangelist." God's plan is beautifully and deliberately unfolded in Isaiah's "microcosm" of the sixty-six books of the Bible!

For personal reflection:

1) If God knew that He planned to restore His people and send a Deliverer, why did He still bring such judgment upon them?

2) What does God's mercy toward Israel teach you about His mercy toward you?

3) How did Isaiah's vision of God recorded in chapter 6 affect his ministry? In what ways does your view of God affect your life and ministry?

4) What do you think it would have been like to be a prophet during the decadent period of the kings? Are there any ways in which Christians are "prophets" today?

For the next lesson . . .

Read all of Jeremiah and Lamentations, or at least the following:

■ Jeremiah 1:4–3:18; 7:1-29

■ Jeremiah 9:13-26; 11:1-17; 14:1–15:6; 16:1–17:14

■ Jeremiah 23:1-8; 25:1-14; 29:1-23

■ Jeremiah 31:31-40; 32:36–33:26

■ Jeremiah 37:1–39:18

■ Jeremiah 44:1-30; 50:4-20; 52:1-34

■ Lamentations 1:1–5:22

Times of the Prophets

Books of Major Prophets

Isaiah | Jeremiah | Lamentations | Ezekiel | Daniel

The Books of Minor Prophets

Hosea | Joel | Amos | Obadiah | Jonah | Micah | Nahum | Habakkuk | Zephaniah | Haggai | Zechariah | Malachi

Israel's prophets are a built-in "reformation" aspect of Old Testament faith. The word "prophet" means "to speak out"—to *forth-tell* God's word as much as to foretell the future. They spoke out against hypocrisy, injustice, immorality and idolatry, warning God's people that He would punish them for such continued disobedience. The prophets also foretold the time when God would save a remnant of His people through whom all nations would be blessed.

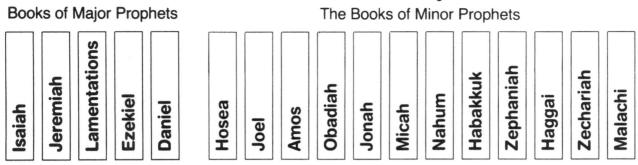

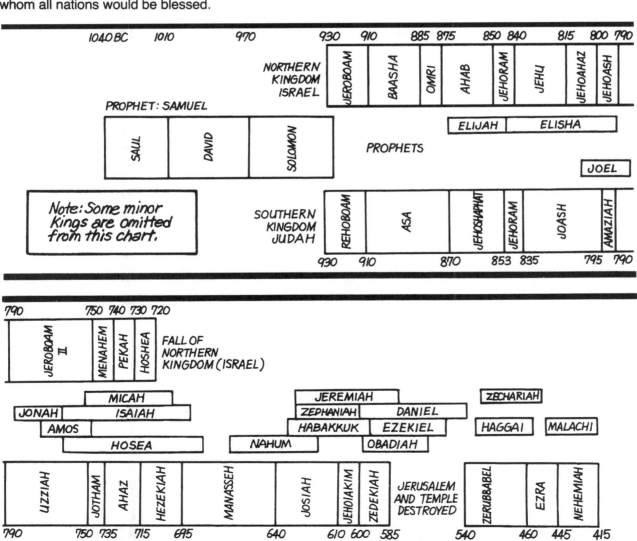

JEREMIAH & LAMENTATIONS

Jeremiah covers the most devastating events in the life of Israel: the destruction of Jerusalem and the Babylonian captivity. Isaiah foretold this exile, but Jeremiah actually lived it. His ministry began approximately sixty years after the death of Isaiah, in about 626 B.C. Jeremiah was immediately preceded by Zephaniah; Habakkuk, Ezekiel and Daniel were contemporaries.

Jeremiah prophesied during a stormy and chaotic time of political transition. Egypt, Assyria and Babylon were all vying for supremacy in western Asia, and Judah was torn between alliance with Egypt or Babylon.

— 612 B.C.: Ninevah, the capital of Assyria, fell to the Babylonians and Medes.

— 607 B.C.: The Assyrian Empire crumbled.

— 605 B.C.: The Egyptians were crushed at Carchemish by Nebuchadnezzar (recorded in Jeremiah 46:2), making Babylon the dominant world power in western Asia.

— 605 B.C.: Nebuchadnezzar also besieged Jerusalem and took his first captives into exile, including Daniel and his three friends.

— 597 B.C.: All the skilled craftsmen, artisans and officials (including Jehoiachin, king of Judah) were carried into exile from Jerusalem to Babylon (24:1; and chapter 29, a letter to these exiles).

— 586 B.C.: The coup d'etat occurred; after an eighteen-month siege, Jerusalem was captured, and every important building, including the Temple of the Lord, was burned. The walls surrounding Jerusalem were broken down, and the remaining people (except a few of the poor) were taken into exile. This is recorded in chapters 39 and 52, and also in 2 Kings 24 and 25.

From a historical standpoint, there is nothing new happening here, but within Jeremiah's prophecies, something significant is revealed concerning God's redemptive plan for His people.

THE PASSING OF THE OLD COVENANT

Jeremiah is keenly conscious of the COVENANT in his writings, using the term at least twenty-three times and referring to it many more. He also mentions circumcision — the sign of the covenant — at least six times, always admonishing his hearers to be circumcised in their hearts, not just in the flesh.

In the first eleven chapters especially, Jeremiah is careful to show that it is Judah, and not God, who has broken the covenant; the penalties they are about to pay are their own fault (2:17, 19, 35; 5:12, 31; 7:9-10, 22-26, 28).

Every chapter through the entire book of Jeremiah carries an indictment against the nation of Israel — for her idolatry, wickedness, rebellion and stubbornness. It is summed up in chapter 11, when God finally accuses His people of breaking His covenant:

> From the time I brought your forefathers up from Egypt until today, I warned them again and again, saying "Obey me." But they did not listen or pay attention; instead, they followed the stubbornness of their evil hearts. So I brought on them all the curses of the covenant I had commanded them to follow but that they did not keep. Both the house of Israel and the house of Judah have BROKEN THE COVENANT (Jer. 11:7-8, 10, emphasis added).

In chapter 3, the covenant relationship is likened to marriage, the most intimate of all human covenants. Israel and Judah are accused of adultery: "I gave faithless Israel her CERTIFICATE OF DIVORCE and sent her away because of all her adulteries. . . . In spite of all this, her unfaithful sister Judah did not return to me with all her heart, but only in pretense . . ." (3:8, 10, emphasis added, cf. 3:1; 12:7).

What were the results of Israel's breaking of the covenant?

_____

_____

_____

In the destruction of Jerusalem and the Lord's Temple, and in the exile of His people, we find the termination and completion of the covenant — with God's chosen people thrust from His presence. But if this were the end of the story, there would be no hope of a Redeemer as promised in Genesis 3:15.

So, in the midst of ultimate judgment on the nation of Israel, almost every page refers to the "remnant" (120 times), to the hope of restoration, or to the fact that the captivity would last only seventy years — that once again "they would be His people and He would be their God" (indicative of a covenant relationship). The old covenant has been broken and fulfilled. But what would be the nature of this new relationship?

THE PROMISE OF THE NEW COVENANT

Jeremiah 30 through 33, often called the prophet's "Book of Consolation," comprise the longest passage in Jeremiah that is concerned exclusively with the future restoration of God's chosen people. What are some of the promises in this section?

_____

_____

_____

_____

Jeremiah uses the term "NEW COVENANT" (31:31), a term found nowhere else in the Old Testament.

> "The time is coming," declares the Lord, "when I will make a NEW COVENANT with the house of Israel and with the house of Judah. It will not be like the covenant I made with their forefathers when I took them by the hand to lead them out of Egypt, because they broke my covenant, though I was a husband to them," declares the Lord. "This is the covenant I will make with the house of Israel after that time,"declares the Lord. "I will put my law in their minds and write it on their hearts. I will be their God, and they will be my people. No longer will a man teach his neighbor, or a man his brother, saying, 'Know the Lord,' because they will all know me from the least of them to the greatest," declares the Lord. "For I will forgive their wickedness and will remember their sins no more" (Jer. 31:31-34, emphasis added).

Why was a new covenant necessary, and how would it be different from the old one?

_____

_____

_____

_____

_____

How is this "new covenant" unfolded in the New Testament?

_____

_____

_____

_____

_____

LAMENTATIONS is a series of five poems, traditionally ascribed to Jeremiah. They convey the overwhelming sense of loss that accompanies the destruction of Jerusalem and the Temple, and the exile of the Jews. Some characteristics of Lamentations include the following:

— Each chapter, except the central chapter (3), has 22 verses. Chapter 3 has 3 x 22, or 66, verses.

— Chapters 1 through 4 are all acrostic poems, with each verse (or series of three verses in chapter 3) beginning with successive letters of the Hebrew alphabet.

— Chapter 3 also stands as the apex of the theology of Lamentations, highlighting the faithfulness and compassion of God.

In the midst of wholesale devastation and slaughter, what evidence was there of God's continued concern for His people?

_____

_____

_____

_____

_____

_____

It is fitting that Lamentations ends in repentance: "Restore us to yourself, O Lord, that we may return; renew our days as of old" (5:21).

In Deuteronomy, God had promised Israel that, if they repented during their captivity, He would hear them and restore them. The hope of the fulfillment of that promise remains — not because of man's inherent goodness, but because of God's compassion and faithfulness to the truly repentant. God is not finished with His people yet. The old covenant has been broken, but God has promised a new covenant to supersede it.

For personal reflection:

1) How does the persecution that Christians face today compare with what Jeremiah went through? How can his perseverance give us strength when we're under attack for our beliefs?

2) Are we still in a covenant relationship with God today? Are there consequences for breaking the covenant? Explain.

3) Have you ever gone through a time of extreme trial when you thought God had abandoned you? What hope is there in Jeremiah and Lamentations that God still cares?

For the next lesson . . .

Read all of Ezekiel, or at least the following:
- Ezekiel 1:1–3:27
- Ezekiel 7:1-27; 10:1-22; 11:16-25
- Ezekiel 15:1-8; 18:14-32; 20:30-44
- Ezekiel 23:1-49; 33:1–34:31
- Ezekiel 36:22–37:28
- Ezekiel 39:17–40:4; 40:48–41:26
- Ezekiel 43:1-12; 47:1-12; 48:30-35

EZEKIEL

In 597 B.C., King Jehoiachin and ten thousand craftsmen, artisans and officials were exiled to Babylon. Among these was a young man studying for the priesthood, Ezekiel, who became God's messenger among the exiles. Ezekiel's designation, "in the thirtieth year" (1:1), is probably a reference to his age.

Why did Ezekiel tell us his age, and why was it significant?

_____

_____

_____

_____

_____

Chapter 1 finds Ezekiel among the exiles by the Kebar River — a canal of the Euphrates just south of Babylon and possibly a place of prayer for the exiles (see Psalm 137:1). It is in this foreign land, in this significant year, that Ezekiel experiences a revelation of God and His call to be a prophet.

REVELATION: A VISION OF GOD (chapters 1–3)

In chapter 1 of the book, Ezekiel sees what appears to be an approaching storm. Instead he finds that it is four living creatures, cherubim, standing wing-tip to wing-tip. They each have four faces: the face of a man, a lion, an ox, and an eagle. Beside each creature is a wheel intersected by another wheel and covered with eyes. Above this astounding sight is a throne of sapphire with "a figure like that of a man" high above it and surrounded by the brilliant radiance of a rainbow.

Verse 28 explains, "This was the appearance of the likeness of the glory of the Lord." What did this vision reveal about the glory and sovereignty of God?

_____

_____

_____

_____

_____

What Ezekiel saw is not as significant as the fact *that* he saw. For centuries, God's glory had been associated uniquely with the Temple in Jerusalem. But now God has left His Temple and appears to His exiled people in Babylon. This has a profound implication from a theological perspective: God is not inextricably tied to the Temple.

Chapters 2 and 3 relate Ezekiel's commissioning by God to be His messenger. The year that should have marked the beginning of his ministry as a priest instead becomes the year of his commissioning as a prophet. God reveals to Ezekiel that his words will fall on deaf ears, but still God appoints him as a "watchman."

In ancient Israel, watchmen were stationed on the highest parts of the city wall to inform the city's inhabitants of the progress of battle or of approaching messengers. The prophets were spiritual watchmen sent to warn God's people of coming judgment and to teach them that God held each one responsible for his own behavior. This commission is repeated in Ezekiel 33:7-9 and is spelled out in chapter 18.

How did God/Ezekiel use symbols to prophesy the coming siege of Jerusalem?

_____

_____

_____

_____

Chapter 6 shows that the purpose of God's coming judgment is to turn their eyes heavenward to finally see that God is the sovereign Lord (6:7, 10, 13-15). The entire book reinforces this concept, sixty-five to seventy times! But so that God isn't accused of being capricious just to assert His sovereignty, chapter 7 makes it clear that God's judgment is the direct result of Israel's sinfulness (7:3-4, 8-9, 27).

RETRIBUTION: A VISION OF JUDGMENT
(chapters 8–11)

Chapters 8 through 11 record Ezekiel's vision in 592 B.C. of the Temple in Jerusalem. In the vision, he is transported to Jerusalem (by a hand carrying him by the hair), to the entrance of the Temple. He again sees the "glory of the God of Israel, as in the vision I had seen in the plain" (8:4). The defilement of the Temple stands in sharp contrast to the glory of God, providing ample justification for God's stern judgments on Judah.

List some examples of the people's sinfulness at this point and throughout the rest of the book of Ezekiel:

_____

_____

_____

_____

What happened to the glory of God because of the sinfulness of God's people?

_____

_____

_____

_____

_____

The indictments against God's people build with every chapter until the climax in chapter 24 — in 588 B.C., when Nebuchadnezzar lays siege on Jerusalem. Jerusalem is likened to a rusty cooking pot, set on the fire to burn. It is at this point, on the verge of the destruction of the Temple, that God pronounces judgment on the surrounding nations (chapters 25–32).

RESTORATION: A VISION OF NEW LIFE (37:1-14)

Ezekiel uses several symbols/metaphors to convey the restoration that is to come. What are these symbols, and what is their New Testament significance?

A. GOOD SHEPHERD

_____

_____

_____

B. COVENANT OF PEACE

_____

_____

_____

C. NEW HEART

_____

_____

_____

D. NEW LIFE

_____

_____

_____

REDEMPTION: A VISION OF A NEW TEMPLE
(chapters 40–48)

Ezekiel has a final vision in 573 B.C. — a vision of a new Temple. It is described in great detail, along with the reinstated Temple worship, reminiscent of the final chapters of Exodus. Following Israel's deliverance from Egypt, God had given instructions to Israel for building the Tabernacle to worship Him. Here in the book of Ezekiel, following the anticipated restoration, the prophet is given instructions for a new Temple and continued worship. What are some possible interpretations of this vision?

- hope in exile

_____

_____

- the New Testament church

_____

_____

- the new Jerusalem

_____

_____

A diagram of the book of Ezekiel helps us to understand the prophet's theme:

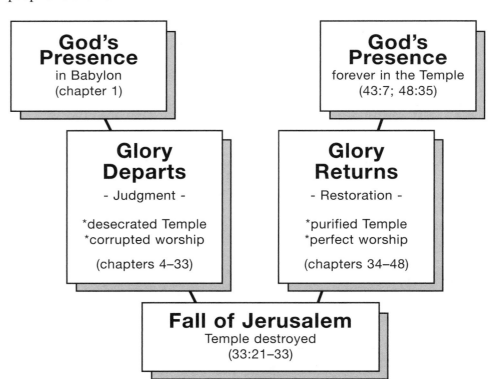

The prophet Ezekiel has been preparing for the priesthood, so it is no wonder that he expresses his messages in terms of the Temple — from its desecration to its destruction to its restoration. He's also uniquely concerned with the presence of God. After all, it is God's presence that has given Israel her identity. The book of Ezekiel shows God's presence in a foreign land, departing from the Temple, and returning to the Temple to dwell among men forever. The closing verse in Ezekiel describes the name of the city where the Temple will be as, "The Lord is There."

The theme running from the beginning of judgment to the climax of redemption and restoration is, "Then they will know that I am the Lord." This is Ezekiel's message to a people in exile. It gives them hope for the present and the future.

What is the application for the church today?

_____

_____

_____

_____

From beginning to end in the book of Ezekiel, we see God — the sovereign Lord — in control of every event in history, moving toward the fulfillment of His purposes: to give new life, a new heart, a new covenant, and a new Shepherd. Then all the world will know that He is the Lord!

For personal reflection:

1) In what ways do you think God has appointed us as "watchmen" for Him? Are we responsible for the blood of those we fail to warn? Explain.

2) What is the purpose of God's judgment? Why is it necessary that a holy and loving God also be just?

3) In view of your study in Ezekiel, what do you think are the consequences of sin being tolerated in the church or in your nation?

4) What do you think is the significance of the new Temple in Ezekiel's vision? What relevance does it have to your life today?

For the next lesson . . .

Read all of Daniel, or at least the following:
- Daniel 1:1-21
- Daniel 2:1-49
- Daniel 3:1-30
- Daniel 4:28–5:30
- Daniel 6:1–7:28
- Daniel 8:1–9:27
- Daniel 11:29-35; 12:1-13

DANIEL

When Cyrus issued the decree in 539 B.C. allowing all the exiles to return to their homelands, no doubt the returning Jews greatly anticipated a restored monarchy and the immediate fulfillment of the prophecies concerning the messianic kingdom. And yet we know from history that there is a gap of about four hundred years between the Old and New Testaments. The Messiah would come, but not for four centuries! Just as the Jews had spent four hundred years in Egypt awaiting deliverance and return to Canaan, so they would have to wait four hundred years for their Messiah.

But so far in our studies, none of the prophets has foretold any intermediate events — that is, until we get to the book of Daniel. This book was meant for encouragement, as well as for warning. Contrary to the Jews' hopes and anticipations, their restoration to the Promised Land would not inaugurate the messianic kingdom. Perilous times awaited them, but God's eternal kingdom *would* come. Without the book of Daniel, the Jews would have lost hope quickly in the midst of their coming tribulations and may have abandoned their hope of the fulfillment of God's promises.

THE SETTING

In chapter 1, we learn that Daniel and his three friends — Hananiah, Mishael and Azariah — are among the first exiles taken to Babylon in 605 B.C. This chapter explains how these faithful exiles are placed into positions of honor in the king's court where they are taught the language and literature of Babylon and are to be trained for three years before entering the king's service.

Why did they refuse to eat the King's food, and what was the result?

_____

_____

_____

_____

_____

_____

"And Daniel remained there until the first year of King Cyrus" (1:21). It is in the first year of Cyrus that the decree would be issued allowing the exiles to return to their homeland. So Daniel becomes God's messenger in the king's court, in a foreign land, throughout the entire period of exile. This is the setting for the rest of the book.

GOD'S SOVEREIGNTY IN THE PRESENT (chapters 2–6)

Chapter 2 begins in Nebuchadnezzar's second year (c. 604 B.C.), while Daniel and his friends are still in training. The king has a troubling dream, which his court magicians, enchanters, sorcerers and astrologers are unable to interpret. Nebuchadnezzar orders all the wise men to be put to death, which would include Daniel and his three friends, whose names were changed to Shadrach, Meshach and Abednego. But God reveals the dream and its message to Daniel, who informs the king the next day and is rewarded (2:48-49).

Chapter 3 recounts the well-known story of the fiery furnace. Shadrach, Meshach and Abednego refuse to bow to the ninety-foot-high golden image of the king. Their response to the king's threats show that they recognize that God is able to deliver them, though they aren't sure if He is *willing* (3:17-18). What was the outcome of this event?

_____

_____

_____

_____

_____

_____

Chapter 5 introduces Belshazzar, the last king of Babylon. Verses 2, 11, 13 and 18 refer to Nebuchadnezzar as Belshazzar's "father," but the implication in the original Hebrew text is that Nebuchadnezzar was Belshazzar's forefather or grandfather (see Jeremiah 27:7). In Daniel 5, Belshazzar, a thousand of his nobles, and his wives and concubines are drinking wine from the gold goblets that were taken from the Lord's Temple in Jerusalem. "As they drank the wine, they praised the gods of gold and silver, of bronze, iron, wood and stone" (5:4).

How did God reveal His displeasure, and what were the consequences which Babylon was forced to pay?

_____

_____

_____

_____

_____

_____

Throughout these first five chapters, Daniel has been prospering and advancing in position in the kingdom. In chapter 6, a familiar story, Daniel is thrown into the lion's den as the result of a conspiracy by the administrators and satraps. After a night in the lion's den, he is removed, and "no wound was found on him, because he trusted in God" (6:23).

The first six chapters of Daniel, comprising mostly historical information, reveal three important concepts:

A. THE PRESERVATION OF A REMNANT

_____

_____

_____

B. THE FAITHFULNESS OF GOD

_____

_____

_____

C. THE RESULT: GOD IS EXALTED

_____

_____

_____

Troubling times await the restored community. Chapters 7 through 12 reveal some of the events Israel would encounter. But these chapters, like the first six, show that God is faithful; He is in complete control of every event in history — He is sovereign. And ultimately, His kingdom will be established and will endure for all time. He will be exalted.

GOD'S SOVEREIGNTY IN THE FUTURE
(chapters 7–12)

In a series of visions, God unfolds for Daniel the history of the Near East until the coming of Christ (chapters 7–12). An angel interprets these visions for Daniel as being representative of four kingdoms. List these kingdoms, along with some historical information about each one:

1. The first kingdom (2:38)

_____

_____

_____

2. The second kingdom (5:28; 8:20)

_____

_____

_____

3. The third kingdom (8:21)

_____

_____

_____

4. The fourth kingdom (chapter 2; 7:20, 24)

_____

_____

_____

The history foretold here doesn't end with Antiochus IV Epiphanes or with the Roman Empire that follows (read 2:44 and 7:13-14, 27). There would be a FIFTH KINGDOM, an eternal kingdom initiated by Christ. This was Jesus' primary teaching — that the Kingdom _had come_. It was now within His believers, but would be realized fully when His heavenly kingdom would be established on earth.

In chapter 9, following Daniel's beautiful prayer of repentance, he realizes that the seventy-year exile is near completion when the angel Gabriel reveals to him that seventy "sevens" have been decreed for Israel (9:24).

Many regard the letter of Artaxerxes I (see Ezra 7:11) as the beginning point of the first sixty-nine of these sevens (483 years). Others regard the commission of Nehemiah by the same king to begin rebuilding Jerusalem as the starting point. By using either a solar calendar with the former date (458 B.C.) or a lunar calendar with the latter (445 B.C.), we arrive remarkably close to the date of the beginning of Jesus' public ministry.

What are some of the possible interpretations of Daniel 9:26-27?

_____

_____

_____

_____

_____

_____

For the Jews living during the troubling times of rising and falling empires and the martyrdom under Antiochus IV Epiphanes and the early Roman Empire, the book of Daniel was a vital source of encouragement. It revealed that God was still in control of history — every event was specifically foretold — and that, even though the kingdoms of the world seemed to prevail over His people, He was bringing an everlasting kingdom, one that would never fail and would endure forever.

What is the significance of the book of Daniel for us today?

_____

_____

_____

_____

_____

_____

_____

For personal reflection:

1) What are some of the various interpretations of the book of Daniel with which you are familiar?

2) How can the story of the fiery furnace help us in times of trial? Do you think there are times God wants us to be "thrown into the fire"? Explain.

3) Daniel and his friends refused to compromise in some very difficult circumstances. In what areas are you sometimes tempted to compromise?

4) What is the result (in our lives as well as in our nation) when we remain faithful to God?

5) In what way(s) does the book of Daniel provide encouragement and hope that God's kingdom will ultimately triumph over evil in our world? Are you ever tempted to think that God is *not* in control, that evil has the upper hand?

For the next lesson . . .

Read all of Hosea, Joel, Amos, Obadiah, Jonah and Micah, or at least the following:

- Hosea 1:1–3:5; 11:1-11
- Hosea 13:4–14:9
- Joel 2:12-14; 28-32; 3:1-21
- Amos 4:1–5:6; 5:18–6:7; 9:11-15
- Obadiah 1-21
- Jonah 1:1–4:11
- Micah 4:1-8; 5:2–6:8; 7:14-20

Identification of the Four Kingdoms

Chronology of Major Empires in Daniel

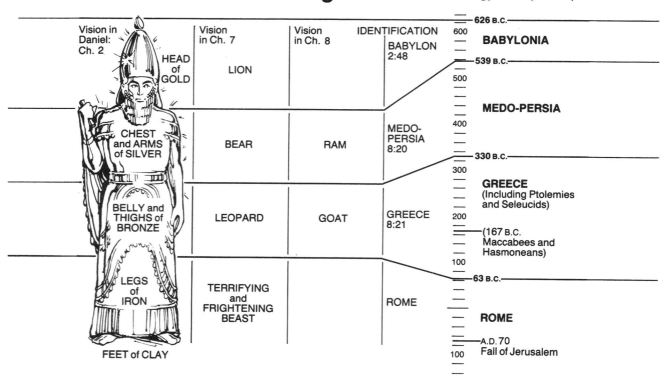

Vision in Daniel: Ch. 2	Vision in Ch. 7	Vision in Ch. 8	IDENTIFICATION
HEAD of GOLD	LION		BABYLON 2:48
CHEST and ARMS of SILVER	BEAR	RAM	MEDO-PERSIA 8:20
BELLY and THIGHS of BRONZE	LEOPARD	GOAT	GREECE 8:21
LEGS of IRON	TERRIFYING and FRIGHTENING BEAST		ROME
FEET of CLAY			

626 B.C. — **BABYLONIA**
600
539 B.C.
500
MEDO-PERSIA
400
330 B.C.
300
GREECE (Including Ptolemies and Seleucids)
200
(167 B.C. Maccabees and Hasmoneans)
100
63 B.C.
ROME
A.D. 70 Fall of Jerusalem
100

The Neo-Babylonian Empire

626-539 B.C.

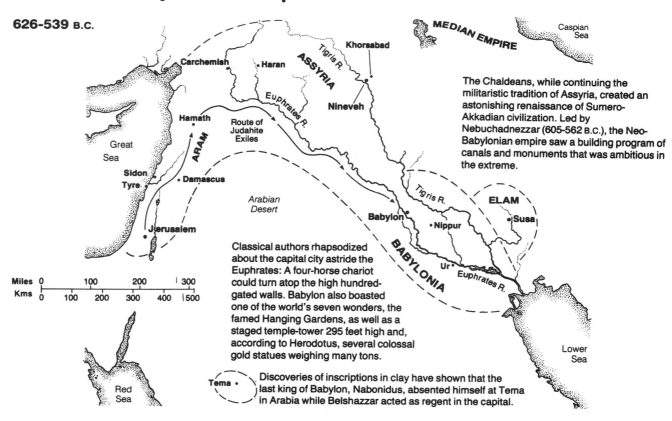

The Chaldeans, while continuing the militaristic tradition of Assyria, created an astonishing renaissance of Sumero-Akkadian civilization. Led by Nebuchadnezzar (605-562 B.C.), the Neo-Babylonian empire saw a building program of canals and monuments that was ambitious in the extreme.

Classical authors rhapsodized about the capital city astride the Euphrates: A four-horse chariot could turn atop the high hundred-gated walls. Babylon also boasted one of the world's seven wonders, the famed Hanging Gardens, as well as a staged temple-tower 295 feet high and, according to Herodotus, several colossal gold statues weighing many tons.

Discoveries of inscriptions in clay have shown that the last king of Babylon, Nabonidus, absented himself at Tema in Arabia while Belshazzar acted as regent in the capital.

MINOR PROPHETS (PART 1)

The entire Old Testament so far has been a record of the triumphs and failures of God's chosen nation — the Israelites. Throughout the history of Israel, God slowly has been revealing His plans, purposes, and expectations for His people. An outline of His revelation is discernible:

I. THE PENALTY FOR SIN

_____

_____

_____

II. THE ACCEPTANCE OF A SUBSTITUTE

_____

_____

_____

III. THE NECESSITY OF OBEDIENCE

_____

_____

_____

IV. THE PROMISE OF DELIVERANCE

_____

_____

_____

All of Israel's history has borne out these principles. God slowly has been teaching His people, revealing His plan so that, in the fullness of time, they would understand the message and significance of Christ's life, death and resurrection. Even during Israel's darkest hours, God still has tried to help them understand His purposes — through His prophets.

The first six books of the minor prophets — Hosea, Joel, Amos, Obadiah, Jonah and Micah — were all written during the period of Assyrian power.

What were some of the characteristics of this period of history as it related to Israel?

_____

_____

_____

During these turbulent years, God sent the prophets, His messengers, to warn Israel of their impending doom and to urge them to repent:

— Amos and Hosea preached to Israel.

— Joel and Micah preached primarily to Judah.

— Jonah and Obadiah preached to the Gentile nations of Assyria and Edom, respectively.

Let's look at these prophets in the order they're presented, looking for the distinctive theme of each.

HOSEA: GOD'S COMPASSION FOR ISRAEL

Many times in the Old Testament, especially in Jeremiah, Israel's relationship to God is described in terms of the marriage relationship, the most intimate of all human relationships. Here, God uses Hosea as a living illustration of His tremendous love for Israel.

How was Hosea's relationship with his wife an illustration of God's relationship with Israel?

_____

_____

_____

_____

_____

_____

Hosea loves his wife so much that he is willing to buy her back, to pay the ransom price, even though she is rightfully his. This is an illustration of God's love for Israel. It is not just symbolic of Israel's restoration after exile, but of the continuation of God's plan of redemption; this is the same provision God would make for Israel through the coming Messiah (see 1 Corinthians 6:20 and 7:23).

But even though Hosea buys his wife back, there is still a condition on their relationship (a covenant): "Then I told her, 'You are to live with me many days; you must not be a prostitute or be intimate with any man, and I will live with you'" (Hos. 3:3). In order for Gomer to receive Hosea's love, she has to change her lifestyle and be faithful to their marriage.

This also applies to Israel: "Afterward the Israelites will return and seek the Lord their God and David their king" (3:5). In order for Israel to receive God's love again, it will require returning and seeking the Lord — and "David," referring to the Messiah. God will provide for the ransom price to be paid, through Christ, but He requires faithfulness: "You shall acknowledge no God but me, no Savior except me" (13:4b).

The overwhelming plea in the book of Hosea is for Israel to return to God. No matter what the sin of her past, God is waiting with open arms for her to return. God affirms His undying love for her throughout Hosea (7:13; 10:12; 11:1, 4, 8; 14:4). This book is reminiscent of the story of the prodigal son in Luke 15 — both reveal a hint of the extent of God's great compassion, of His unfailing love for His people.

JOEL: GOD'S CALL FOR REPENTANCE

In Joel, the dominant theme is "the day of the Lord" (1:15; 2:1, 11, 31; 3:14), a time of God's divine judgment. His purpose in revealing the calamity about to overtake Israel is to drive them to repentance.

Write out Joel 2:12-14.

_____

_____

_____

_____

_____

_____

AMOS: GOD'S CONTEMPT FOR COMPLACENCY

When Amos was written, Assyria had not yet become a conquering world power. At this time, Israel is spiritually smug. God takes Amos, a shepherd from Tekoa in Judah, and sends him to the Northern Kingdom to stir Israel from her complacency. Israel needs to be reminded of her covenant obligations and that judgment is not reserved just for her enemies. God shows His utter contempt for her complacency.

What were some of the sins of Israel that Amos denounced?

_____

_____

_____

_____

_____

God had been trying all along to rouse Israel from her complacency through various natural disasters (famines, locusts, plagues and fire), but what was her response?

_____

_____

_____

_____

_____

Though God declares judgment on Israel in these chapters, still His overwhelming desire is their repentance. God's message is that He requires more than just empty performance of rituals — He demands righteousness and piety. His people have become complacent because they know they are God's chosen people, but they have forgotten that there are responsibilities to go along with their privileges. They are not immune to judgment.

OBADIAH: GOD'S CONDEMNATION OF THE ENEMY

In Obadiah, the shortest book in the Old Testament, God promises judgment on Edom. The Edomites were the descendants of Esau, Jacob's brother. They, too, were sons of Abraham and should have been Israel's closest ally. But Edom was hostile toward Israel throughout her history. The Edomites never failed to help any army who attacked Israel.

The capital of Edom was Sela, or Petra (one of the seven wonders of the world), a seemingly impregnable fortress carved in rock. There was only one entrance, a mile-long cleft in a rock with seven-hundred-foot-high cliffs on either side. The Edomites were proud of their own security, thinking themselves invincible. They gloated over Israel's devastation at the hand of the Babylonians.

What judgment was pronounced on Edom?

_____

_____

_____

How does Obadiah give us an indication of the final outcome of history?

_____

_____

_____

_____

_____

JONAH: GOD'S CONCERN FOR GENTILES

Jonah was written during a period of great national pride in Israel. The Israelites were proud of their prosperity, military strength and favored position with God. Jeroboam II had restored their traditional boundaries, but Assyria still posed a real threat from the north at this time.

God called Jonah to preach to the people of Nineveh, the capital of Assyria. Why was Jonah reluctant to go? What changed his mind?

_____

_____

_____

_____

_____

_____

God sets an important precedent in this book: His compassion is not limited to Israel. His concern is for people. God says, "But Nineveh has more than a hundred and twenty thousand people who cannot tell their right hand from their left, and many cattle as well. Should I not be concerned about that great city?" Ezekiel 33:11 sums it up: ". . . I take no pleasure in the death of the wicked, but rather that they turn from their ways and live. . . ." God's concern always has been for the whole of creation, not just the Israelites. They were chosen by Him, not to be sole heirs of His mercy and salvation, but to be the vehicle through which Christ would come, making salvation available to all.

God's promise to Abraham was not that his nation would be blessed, but that through them the whole world would be blessed. God has been hinting at this all along, but here it is unmistakable. The book of Jonah shows God's concern for all, including the Gentiles.

MICAH: GOD'S CULMINATION OF THE PROMISE AND CONTINUATION OF A REMNANT

The book of Micah alternates between oracles of judgment and oracles of hope. God's deliverance and ultimate fulfillment of His promises are central in Micah. A glorious future is foretold and the coming of the Messiah is prophesied in chapters 4 and 5.

There is an important concept repeated time and again in Micah (and throughout the books of the prophets) that is important to our understanding of the fulfillment of God's promises: the continuation of a REMNANT (2:12; 4:7; 5:7-8; 7:18).

The remnant always has been the embodiment of the true Israel. God has been faithful continually to the nation of Israel, but individual participation in the blessings of the covenant always has been contingent upon obedience to that covenant. This is a vital concept if we are to properly understand the role of Israel and God's plan of salvation. The fulfillment of the promise in Micah is for the remnant — those who are faithful to the covenant.

What impact does this have on our understanding of the New Testament?

_____

_____

_____

_____

_____

_____

To a people arrogant in their prosperity and complacent in their favored position as "the chosen of the Lord," these prophets offer quite a warning. They reaffirm God's love for His people, but it is not an exclusive love. God's compassion knows no boundaries. Evil will be defeated, just as Edom was. But Israel is not immune to judgment — it is only the repentant and the faithful who are truly "Israel" and who will experience the blessings of the coming Kingdom.

God is preparing them for Christ's message; He slowly is unraveling His plan of redemption.

For personal reflection:

1) Do you have trouble accepting the fact that God required Hosea to marry a prostitute? How was this situation unique?

2) Are there any ways in which God's people are sinfully complacent today (as they were in Amos' day)?

3) Does God ever show compassion on the sinful people of today? In what ways? Are there times when His mercy on others makes you feel threatened?

4) How does the idea of a remnant influence your understanding of salvation in Christ? What are some of the responsibilities of being part of God's remnant?

For the next lesson . . .

Read all of Nahum, Habakkuk, Zephaniah, Haggai, Zechariah and Malachi, or at least the following:

- Nahum 1:1–3:19
- Habakkuk 1:1–3:19
- Zephaniah 1:14–2:3; 3:1-20
- Haggai 1:1–2:23
- Zechariah 4:1-14; 6:9–8:23
- Zechariah 9:9–10:9; 11:4-17; 13:1–14:21
- Malachi 2:17–4:6

MINOR PROPHETS (PART 2)

The last six books of the minor prophets reveal God's final messages to Israel before the New Testament begins. Nahum, Habakkuk and Zephaniah prophesied during the reign of Josiah, the last good king of Judah (reigning from 640 to 609 B.C., after the Assyrian exile), during the collapse of Assyrian power. Haggai, Zechariah and Malachi prophesied to the restored community of Israel following the Babylonian captivity.

NAHUM: GOD'S RETRIBUTION / CONTINUED OBEDIENCE

One hundred fifty years earlier, Jonah preached to Nineveh, and they were spared from destruction because they repented and turned to God. But God's graciousness on this occasion did not ensure His unqualified grace in the future. The people of Ninevah soon reverted to their extreme wickedness, brutality and excessive pride (Nahum 3). In the book of Nahum, God declares the destruction of Nineveh because of her atrocities. When and how were these prophecies fulfilled?

_____

_____

_____

_____

_____

_____

Nahum reveals the certainty of God's punishment of the wicked and also the necessity of continued obedience and repentance. God would not spare present-day Nineveh, Nahum tells Judah, even though He spared the city 150 years earlier. This is a comfort to Israel: Her enemies ultimately will be destroyed. But it is also a warning: God's grace cannot be presumed upon. God requires continued obedience.

HABAKKUK: GOD'S RELIABILITY / COVENANT FAITHFULNESS

Habakkuk prophesied at the end of Josiah's reign and probably lived to see the attack on Jerusalem by Babylon in 597 B.C. The book of Habakkuk is a dialogue between the prophet and God, but it represents the voice of all the godly in Judah who are struggling to understand the ways of God. His questions to God are an attempt to understand why God is silent at a time when the wicked prevail and justice is perverted.

God tells Habakkuk that His justice is pure and that Babylon, too, will be punished. God will be faithful to His covenant promises. All He asks is that the faithful in Israel trust Him and wait for His justice to prevail.

What was God's ultimate answer to Habakkuk's questions?

_____

_____

_____

_____

_____

What does it mean to walk in faith?

_____

_____

_____

_____

_____

ZEPHANIAH: GOD'S REMNANT / CONTINUED PROMISES

Zephaniah, a fourth-generation descendant of King Hezekiah, echoes the message of the other prophets: warning of coming exile and the destruction of those who follow false gods and have turned from the Lord (chapter 1); urging to seek the Lord (2:3); judgment against enemy nations (2:4-15); and the future of Jerusalem (chapter 3). The prophet also shows the love, mercy and faithfulness of God (3:5, 17).

According to Zephaniah, who would be restored?

_____

_____

_____

_____

_____

The books of **HAGGAI, ZECHARIAH** and **MALACHI** are all post-exilic, written during the period of Ezra-Nehemiah, when the restored community was struggling in Jerusalem. When Cyrus issued the decree in 538 B.C. allowing the exiles to return to their homeland, only about fifty thousand returned with Zerubbabel to the Promised Land. The vast majority of God's chosen people remained scattered throughout Babylon and Assyria.

The returning exiles faced opposition and hardship, famine and drought, apathy and discouragement. Haggai and Zechariah were God's messengers of encouragement to this newly restored community. They had begun rebuilding the Temple immediately, but had given up the work because of opposition. So now, in 520 B.C., these two prophets come to rebuke God's people and encourage them to complete His Temple.

HAGGAI: GOD'S RETURN / CONDITIONAL BLESSINGS

Haggai shows Israel in chapter 1 that her present hardships are a result of mixed-up priorities. What were the people supposed to be doing?

_____

_____

_____

_____

_____

_____

_____

Everything is futile as long as their priorities are wrong. So, at Haggai's urging, the "whole remnant" (1:12, 14) begins to work on the house of the Lord.

What was the reaction of the older priests and Levites when they saw the foundation of the Temple? What was God's reaction?

_____

_____

_____

_____

_____

_____

_____

God reveals to all Israel that it is not a Temple that brings glory to God, but it is God who brings glory to the Temple. In Ezekiel 10, God's glory had departed from Solomon's Temple prior to its destruction. But now God reveals that His glory will return (Hag. 1:7, 9). How was this fulfilled?

_____

_____

_____

_____

_____

_____

In Haggai 2:10-19, God reveals that even though His people are back in the "Holy Land," being in contact with holy objects will not make them pure; they must continue to obey the Lord (which includes rebuilding the Temple) and remember the penalty they are paying for neglecting the Lord's house. God promises to bless them from this day on — blessings will be theirs when He becomes their first priority.

ZECHARIAH: GOD'S REMEMBRANCE / COMING MESSIAH

Haggai prophesied for only four months, but Zechariah, for about two years. There are more prophecies concerning the coming of Christ in Zechariah than in any other Old Testament book except Isaiah.

Zechariah is a book of encouragement for the restored community — God has not forgotten them. Even Zechariah's name points to this — it means, "the Lord remembers." God remembers His covenant with His people and will send His promised Messiah (3:8-9; 6:12-13; 9:9; 10:4-12; 12:10; 13:7; 14:9).

The entire book is built around this encouraging theme: God still loves His people and has a glorious future in store for them. He will enable them to complete the Temple (4:6-9; 8:9) and will live among them. In Zechariah 1:7 through 6:8, the prophet records eight "night visions," all of which point to this central theme, offering encouragement for the present task and promising future blessing.

In chapter 10, the chosen remnant is restored and gathered in; they will remember God. But in chapter 11 (the parable of the two shepherds), the fate of the remainder of those who call themselves "Israel" is revealed — they will reject the Messiah and will be thoroughly abandoned.

Chapters 12 through 14 offer encouragement for Israel that God will make Jerusalem an immovable rock for all nations (12:3); a fountain will be opened to the house of David and the inhabitants of Jerusalem to cleanse them from sin and impurity (13:1); they will be refined by fire (13:9); living water will flow from Jerusalem (14:8); and a time will come when the Lord will be king over the whole earth (14:9).

What are some possible interpretations of these passages?

_____

_____

_____

_____

_____

_____

MALACHI: GOD'S REQUIREMENT / COMPLETE OBEDIENCE

Malachi is the final voice of God to His people prior to the New Testament. The Jews completed the Temple in 516 B.C. In 445 B.C., Nehemiah returned to Jerusalem from Babylon to rebuild the walls around the city, which took fifty-two days.

In 433 B.C., Nehemiah returned to the service of the Persian king, but during His absence the Jews fell into sin. When Nehemiah returned, he found that they had been neglecting the tithe, breaking the Sabbath, and intermarrying with their pagan neighbors. Even priests had become corrupt. Malachi probably prophesied during Nehemiah's absence.

What caused the Israelites to fall away in such a short time?

_____

_____

_____

_____

_____

What was Malachi's message to the Jews?

_____

_____

_____

_____

_____

God demands obedience not only to the ritual of worship, but also to the spirit of worship — complete conformity to the righteous life He requires.

These last six books of the minor prophets show that past grace and salvation from judgment are not a guarantee of God's unqualified blessing — for Nineveh or for Israel. God requires complete and ongoing obedience, not just to an outward form of religion, but in every aspect of life. God is not pleased with mechanical, routine worship. He is to be Israel's highest priority. His people are to wait patiently for His coming, to live by faith in His promises.

All these themes recur in the New Testament as they pertain to God's righteous followers of the new covenant. Everything written by the prophets in the Old Testament was designed as preparation for the New Testament, which would fulfill prophecy completely.

For personal reflection:

1) Have there been times when you presumed on the grace of God, thinking that He wouldn't punish you because He had been gracious in the past? Explain.

2) What have you learned about the justice and holiness of God through your study of the prophets?

3) Like Habakkuk, do you ever question God? Do you think it's okay to ask God such honest questions? Explain.

4) In your own words, what does it mean to walk by faith?

5) How do people today neglect the Lord's house? Are you faithful in giving to the Lord His tithes and your offerings?

OLD TESTAMENT STUDY QUESTIONS

1. What is the primary theme in each of the first five books of the Bible, and how do they complement one another in revealing the character of God?

2. How are the exodus from Egypt (described in Exodus) and the acquisition of Canaan (described in Joshua) illustrations of the Christian life?

3. What is the dominant theme of the book of Judges, and how does the literary structure contribute to our understanding of it?

4. What is the significance of the book of Ruth?

5. Compare and contrast the lives and reigns of Saul and David, Israel's first two monarchs, as described in 1 and 2 Samuel.

6. What was the consequence of Solomon's sin, and how did it affect the nation of Israel, both spiritually and historically?

7. When were the books of 1 and 2 Chronicles written, and how did that affect the perspective of the material presented there?

8. What significant events are recorded in Ezra and Nehemiah, and what was the impact of them on the Jews?

9. What is the peculiarity in the book of Esther, and how does it focus our attention on the sovereignty of God expressed in the book?

10. How does the book of Job contribute to our understanding of the nature of suffering, and what comfort does it offer for the suffering Christian?

11. How does the collection of the Psalms mirror the five books of the Law?

12. How can the writings of Solomon (Proverbs, Ecclesiastes and Song of Songs), who built the Temple, be compared to the Temple? What is the theme of each book?

13. What is the primary message of the book of Isaiah, and how does it mirror the Bible as a whole?

14. Why is Jeremiah referred to as the "weeping prophet," and what major contribution do his writings (Jeremiah and Lamentations) make to our understanding of God's plan of redemption?

15. How did Ezekiel's age and anticipated vocation influence his prophecies, and how was this a comfort to the people in exile?

16. What political events are prophesied in the book of Daniel, and why was it important for the restored community of Israel to understand these prophecies?

17. What do the books of Jonah and Nahum have in common? How do they differ? What are the primary theological implications of the prophecies in these two books?

18. How did God use Hosea as an illustration of His love for Israel and His plan of redemption?

19. When and why were the books of Haggai, Zechariah and Malachi written?

NEW TESTAMENT INTRODUCTION

To understand the social, political and religious climate during the period covered by the New Testament, we must look at the intertestamental period — the four hundred "silent years" ("silent" because of the lack of any biblical record or of any prophets) between the end of Nehemiah's governorship (c. 407 B.C.) and the birth of Christ (6–4 B.C.). These years are called "silent," but they were anything but silent. They had a major impact on the world of the New Testament and on the spread of Christianity.

POLITICAL DEVELOPMENTS

A. PERSIAN RULE

This period began in 538 B.C. and lasted until 333 B.C. During the time of Persian rule, the rival worship of the Samaritans became established.

What was the cause of the tension between the Jews and Samaritans?

_____

_____

_____

_____

_____

_____

_____

B. GREEK RULE

At the age of twenty, Alexander the Great swept through the known world and conquered all of it in the name of Greece. After Alexander's untimely death, his kingdom was divided among his four generals. Two of these founded dynasties: the Ptolemies, who ruled over Egypt; and the Seleucids, who reigned over Syria and Mesopotamia. These two kingdoms were in constant conflict for over a century.

1. The ruler of the **Ptolemies** was tolerant and even considerate of the Jewish religion. During the rule of the Ptolemies, the Septuagint (the Greek translation of the Old Testament) was produced.

2. The **Seleucids** gained control over Palestine in 198 B.C. This ushered in a period of great tragedy, but also a period of great heroism in Jewish history. When Antiochus IV Epiphanes came to power, he began a campaign of radical Hellenization and sought to eradicate the Jewish religion.

3. Opposition to Antiochus by the **Maccabeans** was led by Mattathias, an elderly priest, and his five sons. The Maccabean Revolt (166-142 B.C.) resulted in the independence of Judah.

C. ROMAN RULE

Palestine was conquered by Rome in 63 B.C., putting an abrupt end to Jewish independence. The bitter struggle with Rome, along with the heavy taxation which soon was imposed, sparked great resentment among Jews of the Roman Empire, a resentment readily apparent in the gospel accounts.

All this political turmoil, persecution and oppression influenced the messianic expectations of the Jews. They saw their greatest need as political liberation, and so primary focus centered on prophecies concerning the One who would rule on David's throne and would overthrow Israel's enemies. These prophecies were particularly comforting to the Jews at this time. By the time Jesus was born, the Messiah was understood almost exclusively as bringing political liberation and conquest.

RELIGIOUS DEVELOPMENTS

Not only were there sweeping political changes in the Near East during the intertestamental period, but there were also some very significant religious developments.

A. LITERARY WORKS

1. Septuagint

_____

_____

_____

_____

_____

2. Talmud

_____

_____

_____

_____

_____

3. Apocrypha

_____

_____

_____

_____

4. Dead Sea Scrolls

_____

_____

_____

_____

B. INSTITUTIONS

1. The synagogue appears to have developed during the period of exile when the Jews' Temple had been destroyed. Dispersed throughout the world by exile, the Jews struggled to find a meaningful way to worship God without breaking His command that sacrifices could be offered only at the Temple in Jerusalem. The synagogue was not a place of sacrifice, but of preaching and expounding on the Law. When the Jews returned from exile, this form of worship returned with them.

How did the development of the synagogue pave the way for Christianity?

_____

_____

_____

_____

_____

_____

2. The Sanhedrin, the highest tribunal of the Jews, was given authority over civil and religious matters. It consisted of 71 members: the high priest, 24 chief priests, 24 elders and 22 scribes. Tradition attributes its origin to the 70 elders appointed to assist Moses (see Numbers 11), a council which probably was reorganized under Ezra and which became a recognized ruling body during the intertestamental period.

SOCIAL DEVELOPMENTS

The Judaism of Jesus' day was influenced greatly by the events taking place between the testaments. Not only were there new writings and institutions, but also various religious groups within Judaism:

1. Pharisees

_____

_____

_____

_____

2. Sadducees

_____

_____

_____

_____

3. Scribes

_____

_____

_____

_____

4. Essenes

_____

_____

_____

_____

5. Zealots

_____

_____

_____

_____

_____

OTHER DEVELOPMENTS

How did each of the following influence the later spread of Christianity?

A. THE DIASPORA:

_____

_____

_____

_____

_____

B. THE PAX ROMANA:

_____

_____

_____

_____

_____

C. THE ROMAN ROAD SYSTEM:

_____

_____

_____

_____

_____

It's easy to see that the introduction of Christianity came at the perfect point in history. There was one common language, and the Old

Testament had been translated into that language. There was freedom of movement throughout the world, made possible by the Roman peace. The increased trade that resulted, along with the Roman road system, provided for a rapid spread of the gospel that would have been impossible prior to the establishment of the Roman Empire. The dispersion of the Jews throughout the known world gave the Christian church "little footholds" throughout the empire with which to share the gospel. None of this happened by accident. It was all part of God's divine plan to make known His plan of redemption through Jesus Christ to the entire world.

NEW TESTAMENT OVERVIEW

In all the books of the New Testament, the predominant theme is FULFILLMENT. These books show unequivocally that Jesus Christ is the fulfillment of the Old Testament. The concepts of animal sacrifice, the covenant, the monarchy, a remnant and a Messiah, all prevalent in the Old Testament, were pointing to something yet to come.

The Old Testament covered thousands of years of history; the New Testament spans only one hundred years. The Old Testament told the history of a nation; the New Testament, the history of a Person. The Old Testament pointed to one who was coming; the New Testament focuses on One who has come and will come again. The Old Testament focused on the law and introduced the curse; the New Testament centers on grace and introduces the cure.

The Bible is one complete revelation of God's plan of redemption. The Old Testament is but a shadow of the New Testament. God's plan of redemption continues to be unfolded.

For personal reflection:

1) How did God perfectly prepare the world for Christ's coming?

2) While all these events were taking place, do you think the Jews understood that God was carefully putting everything in place to fulfill His promises? Explain.

3) How can what you learned from this lesson help you during the "silent years" in your life?

4) Pray this week that God would help you to see His working in history (even now) as He continues to work out His plan of redemption.

For the next lesson . . .

Read all of Matthew, or at least the following:

- Matthew 1:18–2:12; 3:1–4:11
- Matthew 5:1–7:28
- Matthew 9:35–10:42;11:1-29
- Matthew 13:1-52; 16:13–17:13; 18:1-35
- Matthew 20:1-16; 21:28–22:14
- Matthew 23:1–25:46
- Matthew 26:47-56; 27:32–28:20

Between the Testaments

Malachi c. 430 B.C.

From Malachi to Christ

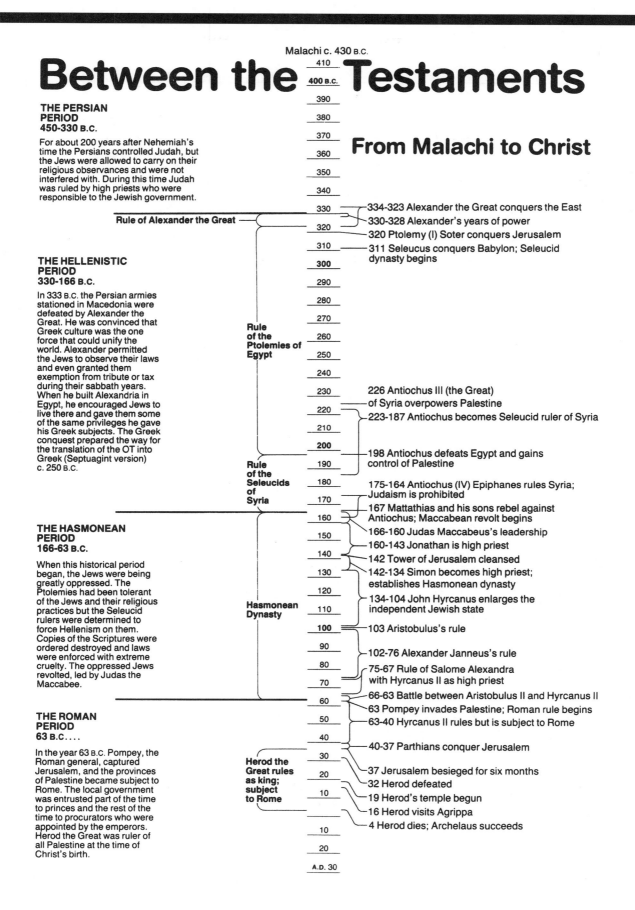

THE PERSIAN PERIOD 450-330 B.C.

For about 200 years after Nehemiah's time the Persians controlled Judah, but the Jews were allowed to carry on their religious observances and were not interfered with. During this time Judah was ruled by high priests who were responsible to the Jewish government.

Rule of Alexander the Great

THE HELLENISTIC PERIOD 330-166 B.C.

In 333 B.C. the Persian armies stationed in Macedonia were defeated by Alexander the Great. He was convinced that Greek culture was the one force that could unify the world. Alexander permitted the Jews to observe their laws and even granted them exemption from tribute or tax during their sabbath years. When he built Alexandria in Egypt, he encouraged Jews to live there and gave them some of the same privileges he gave his Greek subjects. The Greek conquest prepared the way for the translation of the OT into Greek (Septuagint version) c. 250 B.C.

Rule of the Ptolemies of Egypt

Rule of the Seleucids of Syria

THE HASMONEAN PERIOD 166-63 B.C.

When this historical period began, the Jews were being greatly oppressed. The Ptolemies had been tolerant of the Jews and their religious practices but the Seleucid rulers were determined to force Hellenism on them. Copies of the Scriptures were ordered destroyed and laws were enforced with extreme cruelty. The oppressed Jews revolted, led by Judas the Maccabee.

Hasmonean Dynasty

THE ROMAN PERIOD 63 B.C....

In the year 63 B.C. Pompey, the Roman general, captured Jerusalem, and the provinces of Palestine became subject to Rome. The local government was entrusted part of the time to princes and the rest of the time to procurators who were appointed by the emperors. Herod the Great was ruler of all Palestine at the time of Christ's birth.

Herod the Great rules as king; subject to Rome

410
400 B.C.
390
380
370
360
350
340
330
320
310
300
290
280
270
260
250
240
230
220
210
200
190
180
170
160
150
140
130
120
110
100
90
80
70
60
50
40
30
20
10
10
20
A.D. 30

334-323 Alexander the Great conquers the East
330-328 Alexander's years of power
320 Ptolemy (I) Soter conquers Jerusalem
311 Seleucus conquers Babylon; Seleucid dynasty begins

226 Antiochus III (the Great) of Syria overpowers Palestine
223-187 Antiochus becomes Seleucid ruler of Syria

198 Antiochus defeats Egypt and gains control of Palestine

175-164 Antiochus (IV) Epiphanes rules Syria; Judaism is prohibited
167 Mattathias and his sons rebel against Antiochus; Maccabean revolt begins
166-160 Judas Maccabeus's leadership
160-143 Jonathan is high priest
142 Tower of Jerusalem cleansed
142-134 Simon becomes high priest; establishes Hasmonean dynasty
134-104 John Hyrcanus enlarges the independent Jewish state
103 Aristobulus's rule
102-76 Alexander Janneus's rule
75-67 Rule of Salome Alexandra with Hyrcanus II as high priest
66-63 Battle between Aristobulus II and Hyrcanus II
63 Pompey invades Palestine; Roman rule begins
63-40 Hyrcanus II rules but is subject to Rome
40-37 Parthians conquer Jerusalem
37 Jerusalem besieged for six months
32 Herod defeated
19 Herod's temple begun
16 Herod visits Agrippa
4 Herod dies; Archelaus succeeds

Matthew	Mark	Luke	John
King Lion: symbol of strength and kingship	**Servant** Ox: symbol of lowly service	**Ideal Man** Man: highest intelligence of all God's creation	**Son of God** Eagle: symbol of heavenliness and divinity
Jews Matthew shows how Jesus fulfilled Old Testament messianic prophecies—has the most Old Testament quotes and allusions.	**Romans** Luke is more interested in deeds than words—has only 4 parables, but 20 miracles.	**Greeks** (Lovers of culture and poetry.) Luke records "songs"; uses "all" to show that Christ is Lord of the Gentiles, too.	**Whole World** John shows Jesus as the eternal, incarnate Son of God; Goes back to eternity and looks ahead to eternity.
Son of Abraham (Jesus is the father of the Jews.) Matthew shows Jesus' royal position as the Son of David.	**None** No one is interested in the genealogy of a servant.	**Son of Adam** (Jesus is the ideal man) Jesus is not just the son of the Jews but of all mankind.	**In the beginning . . .** John reveals Jesus' eternal nature; Jesus is shown as God.
"All authority in heaven and on earth has been given to me" (Matthew 28:18b). The King commissions His disciples. Resurrection: the crowning proof of Jesus' messiahship.	Ascension: the Lowly One is exalted to a place of honor and glory. "And the Lord worked with them and confirmed his word by the signs that accompanied it" (Mark 16:20b). Jesus was still serving with His disciples.	Ascension: the Perfect Man ascends to the Father. The promise of the Holy Spirit, who gives men power to fulfill the Great Commission.	"Until I return" points to Jesus' second coming—His eternity. "Jesus did many other things. . . . If every one of them were written down . . . even the whole world would not have room for the books that would be written" (John 21:25). The Son of God is not confined to the present world.
Proves that Jesus is the Messiah	Spurs Christians on during times of persecution	Provides an orderly account of Jesus' life, so that we might "know the certainty" of what we've been taught (Luke 1:1-4).	That all might believe that Christ is the Son of God and might "have life in His name" (John 20:30-31).

MATTHEW

Matthew was written expressly for the Jews in order to reveal to them that Jesus was the complete fulfillment of all the Old Testament prophecies concerning the promised Messiah. More than any other Gospel, the book of Matthew provides the link between the Old and the New Testaments, which is probably why it was placed first among the Gospels from earliest times.

List some of the unique features of the book of Matthew which support the assertion that it was written to the Jews:

_____

_____

_____

_____

_____

_____

As we study the book of Matthew, we will focus on the Jews' expectations for the coming Messiah and will compare these with who Jesus really was. Matthew wanted his fellow Jews to understand that Jesus was the perfect fulfillment of the Old Testament Scriptures, and that it was the Jewish expectations which were amiss.

THEY WERE EXPECTING A KING.

The Jews long had been awaiting a king, but instead God sent a baby, a frail and helpless child born not in a palace, but in the humblest of circumstances. But this wasn't just a child . . .

He was conceived by the Holy Spirit (1:18, 20);

He was born of a virgin (1:25);

He was the long-awaited Savior (1:21);

He was God incarnate (1:23);

He was the King (2:2, 6).

THEY WERE EXPECTING A CONQUEROR.

In chapter 3, Jesus begins His public ministry at the age of about thirty (the customary age for beginning service in the Temple). His baptism serves to announce the arrival of the Messiah and to show that Jesus completely identifies himself with man's sin and failure, though He himself has no need of repentance or cleansing from sin.

Here, His reign as Messiah begins, but not with the political conquest anticipated. Instead, in chapter 4, we read of His temptation in the wilderness. Satan's final temptation is an offer to give Jesus all the kingdoms of the world in exchange for His homage to Satan. But physical, political conquest is not important to Jesus; the conquering of temptation is. Jesus has come to conquer sin and temptation, not nations.

What does the Sermon on the Mount reveal about the Kingdom and the Conqueror (chapters 5–7)?

_____

_____

_____

_____

_____

THEY WERE EXPECTING A LIBERATOR.

The Jews were expecting the Messiah to liberate them from Roman rule and oppression, to vindicate them before their enemies. But their greatest enemy was sin, and their greatest bondage was to the power and effects of sin. When sin entered the world, so did sickness and disease — the marks of a fallen world. And so, in chapters 8 and 9, Jesus liberates — both physically and spiritually — those who come to Him from the bondage of sin.

THEY WERE EXPECTING A KINGDOM.

For what kind of kingdom were the first-century Jews waiting?

_____

_____

_____

_____

_____

How was Jesus' concept of a kingdom different?

_____

_____

_____

_____

_____

What additional insights concerning the Kingdom do the "Kingdom parables" offer (13:1-52; 18:21-35; 20:1-16; 22:1-14; 25:1-30)?

_____

_____

_____

_____

_____

This wasn't at all the type of kingdom the Jews were expecting. It is no wonder that few of the religious leaders understood Jesus' parables. This was an eternal kingdom that would begin in the hearts of men and would spread throughout the world. It was both a present reality and a future hope. Its worth was far greater than any earthly kingdom that would be limited in both scope and endurance.

THEY WERE EXPECTING A VICTOR.

The Jews were looking for a conquering hero who would restore the thrill of victory to Israel. In chapter 21, they laud Jesus with shouts of "Hosanna!" as He enters Jerusalem. They spread their cloaks on the road in front of Him, an act of royal homage. They anticipate victory. And yet the same week, the crowd who cried, "Hosanna!" now shouts, "Crucify Him!" Little do they understand that it will be through His death and subsequent resurrection that true victory will be won.

What significant events happened at the moment of Christ's death, and how did these events show Jesus to be a victor (27:45-54)?

_____

_____

_____

_____

_____

Chapter 28 records Jesus' glorious resurrection and victory over death. Though the people think they have destroyed Him, Jesus Christ becomes the greatest victor ever and is given all the kingdoms of the earth as His footstool. He is able to say, "All authority in heaven and earth have been given to me" (28:18b).

The Jews were looking for a political victor. But after three days in the grave, Christ arises *the* victor, making possible the same victory over the power of sin and death for all who believe. He makes that victory available to us! Here in Matthew's gospel, as in the books of the prophets, it is made clear that the Jews are not exclusive heirs to the Kingdom.

List some of the steps in the progression of thought in Matthew (i.e. the Magi; John the Baptist; Jesus' healing ministry; the faith of the Roman centurion; the commissioning of the disciples; the Canaanite woman; Peter's confession; the parables of the tenants and the wedding banquet; and Jesus' final rejection by the Jews):

_____

_____

_____

_____

The Jews were expecting a king, a conqueror, a liberator, a kingdom and a victor. Jesus was all of these, but the Jews rejected Him because He wasn't exactly what they wanted. People still do the same to Jesus today.

What do you think was the purpose of the literary arrangement of this Gospel?

_____

_____

_____

For personal reflection:

1) With all that the Jews had read concerning the Messiah in the the books of the prophets, why do you think they failed to recognize Jesus?

2) How do people today sometimes have erroneous expectations of who Jesus should be and what He should do?

3) What goes through your mind when you read that we're supposed to be "perfect" (Matt. 5:48)? Are the standards of the Kingdom as expressed in the Sermon on the Mount applicable to Christians today? Explain.

4) What are the implications of Christ's death and resurrection for the Christian? Does it make any difference in our everyday lives? What was accomplished?

For the next lesson . . .

Read all of Mark, or at least the following:
- Mark 1:1-28; 2:1-12
- Mark 3:1-6, 20-30; 4:1-32
- Mark 5:1-20; 6:1-5
- Mark 6:6-29; 7:31-37; 8:27-38
- Mark 9:33-50; 10:17-45
- Mark 11:27-33; 12:28-44; 14:1-11
- Mark 14:66-72; 15:1-15; 15:33–16:20

MARK

The Gospel of Mark is altogether different from that of Matthew. Matthew quoted at least forty-seven Old Testament passages; Mark quotes only two. Matthew abounded with the teachings and parables of Jesus; Mark records only four parables. Ninety-one percent of Mark's gospel is found in the Gospel of Matthew. Matthew showed Jesus as the King, but Mark paints a portrait of Jesus as a servant, actively ministering and working among the people He has come to redeem (Mark 10:45). Earliest traditions point to John Mark as the author of this Gospel (John being the Jewish name, and Mark, the Latin).

What do we know about John Mark?

_____

_____

_____

_____

The Gospel of Mark was recorded for the immediate use of those in Rome. The fact that the recipients were not Jews is indicated by Mark's explanation of Jewish customs (7:3-4 — ceremonial washings; 15:42 — Preparation Day) and translation of Aramaic words. Mark doesn't seek to prove to His Roman readers who Jesus is by quoting the Old Testament, with which they would be unfamiliar, but by giving the testimony of witnesses and also confirmation through miracles. Mark isn't as concerned with what Jesus *said* as with what He *did*. Jesus' miracles confirmed His message and offered undeniable proof of His authority. Mark records twenty miracles, not a token two or three that easily could be dismissed. He gives enough evidence to convince any unbelieving Roman that Jesus is indeed the Son of God.

This Gospel probably was written in the mid-to-late 60s. In A.D. 64, Nero set fire to Rome, blaming it on the Christians, which provoked widespread persecution of the church. If indeed Mark wrote during this time, his purpose may have been to encourage the young Christians in their faith by reminding them of the life and works of Jesus Christ, and to offer to the Roman world an indisputable argument for the claims of Christ. Mark is offering to Christians a look at the nature of discipleship, or servanthood.

THE CALL TO DISCIPLESHIP

Right away in chapter 1, we see Jesus calling disciples. The call to discipleship is at the heart of the Gospel of Mark. One of the most striking characteristics of this Gospel is that, throughout the book, Mark records for us the responses of the people who encountered Jesus.

What were some of the reactions of the people to Jesus?

_____

_____

_____

_____

We see here in Mark that Jesus' miracles influenced not only what people felt, but also what they *did*. List some of the responses to Jesus' miracles:

_____

_____

_____

_____

_____

Mark records only four parables, each of which highlights the reactions or responses of people to Jesus:

1. The parable of the sower (4:1-20)

_____

_____

_____

2. The parable of the growing seed (4:26-29)

_____

_____

_____

3. The parable of the mustard seed (4:30-32)

_____

_____

_____

4. The parable of the tenants (12:1-11)

_____

_____

_____

We almost get the sense that Mark is standing among the throngs of people, watching their every reaction to Jesus! A new section begins in Mark 8:31, when Jesus predicted His death. Here, we also see a geographical shift from Galilee, where most of Jesus' public ministry recorded by Mark took place, to Jerusalem and the closing days of Jesus' life.

How did the reactions to Jesus' ministry change at this point?

_____

_____

_____

_____

_____

Everything Jesus did was a confirmation of who He was. And being confronted with that confirmation demanded a response. The people either would follow Him or would crucify Him. His presence among them constituted a CALL TO DISCIPLESHIP.

THE COST OF DISCIPLESHIP

Remember, Mark wrote not only for the unsaved Romans, but also for Christians undergoing intense persecution. His gospel served as a reminder of the tremendous cost of discipleship.

What lessons does Mark's gospel teach about the cost of following Christ?

_____

_____

_____

_____

_____

THE CRITERION FOR DISCIPLESHIP

Our criterion for discipleship — the standard on which we base our understanding of discipleship — is Jesus Christ himself. He is our model, our example, our standard.

A. He had a mission to serve and to save.

_____

_____

B. He had a determination to follow the will of God.

_____

_____

THE COMMISSION OF DISCIPLESHIP

Jesus never intended for His disciples to follow Him and learn from Him *just* for their own spiritual edification. Their three short years with Jesus were not just a time of learning, but of training (3:13-15; 6:7; 9:14-29). This was the very purpose for which He called them. It is no wonder then that His final words to them as recorded in Mark constituted the commission to "Go into all the world and preach the good news to all creation" (16:15). Discipleship not only affects what we are, but it influences what we *do*.

"Then the disciples went out and preached everywhere, and the Lord worked with them and confirmed his word by the signs that accompanied it" (16:20). Here we see the disciples carrying on the ministry of Jesus. Just as Jesus performed miracles as a confirmation of His message, so now His disciples carried His message, and it was confirmed by signs. In both of these cases, the preaching of the gospel necessitated a response by those who heard it.

For the unbeliever, then, the Gospel of Mark shows Jesus for what He did. Jesus couldn't have been anyone other than the Son of God himself. And one cannot be confronted with these claims of Christ without making a conscious decision to accept or reject Him. This is the CALL TO DISCIPLESHIP.

For the believer in Rome during a time of persecution, this Gospel was a tremendous source of encouragement. Mark shows that there is a COST OF DISCIPLESHIP to Christ, but he encourages believers to continue serving as Jesus — who is the CRITERION FOR DISCIPLESHIP — served, by giving our lives for the ransom of many. This COMMISSION OF DISCIPLESHIP applies even in the face of persecution. For comfort comes in knowing that, even though Jesus is not present physically, He still is working to confirm His message. The believer is not alone in the work of spreading the gospel.

For personal reflection:

1) What are some ways in which people respond to Jesus today?

2) Based on our study, what do you think it means to be a disciple of Jesus Christ? Is it possible to be a Christian without being a disciple? Explain.

3) What is your response to the message of Mark?

For the next lesson . . .

Read all of Luke, or at least the following:
- Luke 1:1–3:23
- Luke 4:1-13; 6:1-49; 7:18-50
- Luke 9:1–10:37; 11:1-54
- Luke 12:1–15:32
- Luke 16:19-31; 18:1-30; 19:1-27
- Luke 22:7-53; 23:26-56
- Luke 24:1-53

LUKE

How do we account for the differences in the Gospel accounts?

1. Divine inspiration

2. Language barrier

3. Multiple teachings

4. Different perspectives

Although he never identifies himself, the author of the Gospel of Luke has been identified from earliest times as Luke. He also penned the book of Acts, and from his use of "we" in chapters 16, 20, 21 and 27 of Acts, we deduce that he was at times a traveling companion of Paul. Paul tells us in Colossians 4:14 that Luke was a doctor, and Paul also refers to him in Philemon 24. Luke was a learned man and the only Gentile writer in the New Testament. With the book of Acts, he wrote more of the New Testament than any other new Testament author, including Paul, in sheer number of words.

Both Luke's gospel and the book of Acts were written to Theophilus, who some believe was a Roman official, or at least a man of high position and wealth. Others believe he was an influential layman in Greece. In any case, he was a patron of Luke who was responsible for circulating copies of Luke's writings.

What was Luke's purpose in writing his gospel, and how did his purpose influence the facts he included?

_____

_____

_____

_____

_____

Throughout the Gospel of Luke, we see not just a history of events, but, in a sense, a history of God's plan of salvation. God broke into history, fulfilling His promise of redemption through Jesus Christ. The key verse and focal point of the entire book is Luke 19:10: "For the Son of Man came to seek and to save what was lost." Luke shows that Christ's life, death and resurrection were the fulfillment of God's plan of salvation. Christ's purpose to seek and to save the lost could be accomplished only by completing God's plan of redemption.

THE INAUGURATION OF GOD'S PLAN OF SALVATION (chapters 1–3)

Throughout the history of Israel, God has been promising salvation for His people. The prophets foretold that one would come to "prepare the way of the Lord" — that "Elijah" would come as forerunner of the Messiah. The Gospel of Luke begins by showing us the events surrounding the birth of John the Baptist, who specifically fulfills the prophecy of Malachi (Luke 1:16-17, cf. Mal. 4:5-6). Four hundred years of silence have been broken. God remembers His people Israel.

What unique information does Luke provide concerning the birth of Jesus Christ?

_____

_____

_____

_____

_____

It becomes clear through some of these events that this marks the inauguration of God's plan of salvation (2:11, 29-32, 38; 3:6). With the baptism of Jesus and God's declaration that Jesus is His son, Jesus' public ministry begins. And so does another phase of God's plan.

THE IMPLEMENTATION OF GOD'S PLAN OF SALVATION

Luke records Jesus' ministry according to His movement from place to place: from Galilee (4:14–9:9) to Judea and Perea (9:51–19:27); and finally to Jerusalem (19:28–24:53).

But for Luke, the people *to whom* Jesus ministers are more important than the place *where* He ministers. Luke shows us Christ's compassion for the poor, the helpless, the social outcasts, the sinners, the women and the Gentiles. We see in this Gospel a Jesus who is full of love and compassion, not just for the religious and the righteous, but for all mankind, especially the outcasts. "For the Son of Man came to seek and to save what was lost" (19:10).

THE EXPLANATION OF GOD'S PLAN OF SALVATION

Many of the teachings recorded by Luke are especially important for understanding the way of salvation. What insights do these passages give us concerning God's plan?

1. The parable of the good Samaritan (10:25-37):

_____

_____

2. The parable of the rich fool (12:13-21):

_____

_____

3. The narrow door (13:22-30):

_____

_____

4. The cost of being a disciple (14:25-35):

_____

_____

5. The parables of the lost sheep, lost coin and lost son (14:4-7, 8-10, 11-32):

_____

_____

6. The rich man and Lazarus (16:19-31):

_____

_____

7. The Pharisee and the tax collector (18:9-14):

_____

_____

THE CULMINATION OF GOD'S PLAN OF SALVATION

The culmination of God's plan of salvation is seen in Christ's substitutionary death on the cross and His victory over death through the Resurrection. The focus of this Gospel has been the Cross. Jesus is thoroughly consumed with His purpose and mission, and He speaks often about its fulfillment in the Cross. It is only through Jesus' death on the cross that we can receive salvation from our sins.

Why is it important to our understanding of salvation that Christ was fully human and fully divine? In what way did Jesus fulfill the meaning of the Passover?

_____

_____

_____

_____

We mustn't forget that the Cross is meaningless without the Resurrection. If Christ merely had died in our place and had remained dead, there would be no hope of life for us. But in chapter 24, we read that He conquers death by rising from the grave victorious, and that He appears to two disciples on the road to Emmaus and also to the eleven disciples. Jesus shows them that He is the final fulfillment of God's plan of redemption — the culmination of God's plan of salvation (24:44).

THE PERPETUATION OF GOD'S PLAN OF SALVATION

But the story doesn't end with the Resurrection. Luke records in his "Volume 2" — the book of Acts — that the ministry of Christ continues in and through His church. How do we see this foreshadowed in Luke?

_____

_____

_____

_____

_____

_____

For personal reflection:

1) Why do you think it's important to maintain belief in the authority, inspiration and integrity of Scripture, despite critics' objections?

2) In Jesus' teachings on the nature and way of salvation, which teaching do you think is most misunderstood by Christians today? Did you learn anything new? Jot it down.

3) What role do you think the Holy Spirit plays in the life of the believer today? How is the Spirit-filled life different from that of the person?

4) Reread the passages in Luke that talk about prayer unregenerate or unsanctified (e.g. 11:1-13; 18:1-14). What new insights do you find? What is the result of a life characterized by prayer?

For the next lesson . . .

Read all of John, or at least the following:
- John 1:1-18, 29-34; 2:1–3:21
- John 4:1-42; 5:16-47; 6:25-59
- John 7:1–8:59; 9:35-41
- John 10:1–11:57; 12:20-50
- John 13:1-17; 14:1–16:33
- John 17:1–18:11; 19:28-42
- John 20:19–21:25

JOHN

The Gospel of John is strikingly different from the other three Gospels. Matthew, Mark and Luke are commonly called the "synoptic Gospels" because they have a "similar view." But John, possibly writing in the last decade of the first century, assumes that his readers already know the basic facts about Jesus' life. John's account serves as a supplement, offering information not shared by the others.

During the years of the early church, heresies regarding Christ arose. Some denied Jesus' humanity, while others denied His deity. John's purpose in writing his gospel is made clear in John 20:30-31: "Jesus did many other miraculous signs in the presence of his disciples, which are not recorded in this book. But these are written that you may [or "may continue to," in some manuscripts] believe that Jesus is the Christ, the Son of God, and that by believing you may have life in His name."

THE PROOF OF HIS SONSHIP

Each of the other Gospels record some twenty miracles each, but John records only seven in addition to the Resurrection. They were carefully chosen as proof of Jesus' sonship. SEVEN was considered the number of perfection or completeness, so John offers a complete testimony of who Jesus was and is.

A. SEVEN SIGNS

These are presented in John to prove that Jesus is the Christ, the Son of God. What do these "signs" reveal about who He is?

1. The turning of water into wine (2:1-11):

_____

_____

2. The healing of the official's son (4:43-54):

_____

_____

3. The healing of the invalid at the pool of Bethesda (5:1-15):

_____

_____

4. The feeding of the five thousand (6:1-15):

_____

_____

5. Jesus' walking on water (6:16-24):

_____

_____

6. The healing of the man born blind (9:1-12):

_____

_____

7. The raising of Lazarus from the dead (11:38-44):

_____

_____

These seven miracles are ample proof of who Jesus is. They are signs pointing to something beyond themselves. Jesus isn't just a miracle-worker. He is the Master over the whole realm of creation. Nothing is outside His control. These signs show His complete transcendence and sovereignty over humanity. The miracles are proof that He is the Son of God (10:25, 38; 14:11).

B. TESTIMONY OF SEVEN WITNESSES

Who were the seven witnesses in the Gospel of John, and what did they proclaim concerning Christ?

_____

_____

_____

_____

_____

_____

_____

For those in the latter half of the first century who proposed that Jesus was just a prophet or a good man or teacher, John offers undeniable proof of Jesus' sonship. Not only is He the Son of Man, He also is the one and only Messiah, the Son of God. But our belief is not without foundation. We have the evidence of miracles and eyewitness testimony. "These are written that you may believe" (20:31a).

THE PROPERTIES OF HIS SONSHIP

John doesn't stop with just proving that Jesus is the Christ, the Son of God; John goes on to define that sonship and to tell us what properties are inherent in the title "Son of God." He does this by recording the seven "I am" statements of Jesus.

What do these statements reveal about the Son of God?

1. "I am the bread of life" (6:35):

_____

_____

_____

2. "I am the light of the world" (8:12; 9:5):

_____

_____

_____

3. "I am the gate" (10:7, 9):

_____

_____

_____

4. "I am the good shepherd" (10:11, 14):

_____

_____

_____

5. "I am the resurrection and the life" (11:25):

_____

_____

_____

6. "I am the way and the truth and the life" (14:6):

_____

_____

_____

7. "I am the vine" (15:5, cf. 15:1 — "true vine"):

_____

_____

_____

It is difficult for us to comprehend fully the impact of these statements upon the Jews. The Jews understood what Jesus was really saying; He was claiming equality with God the Father (8:58-59; 10:30-31; 18:6). What do we learn about the properties of Jesus' sonship in John 1?

_____

_____

_____

_____

_____

Partnership (and participation) in the Godhead is the ultimate property of Jesus' sonship. This is entirely different from anything the Jews would have expected concerning the coming Messiah. They never imagined that God himself would become man in order to deliver them from the bondage of sin.

THE PURPOSE OF HIS SONSHIP

John 20:30-31 tells us that there is a purpose behind the sonship of Jesus — "that by believing you may have life in his name" (20:31b). John emphasizes time and again that belief in Jesus is a mandatory prerequisite for eternal life. The purpose of God becoming man was to complete His plan of redemption, in order to offer that redemption to the world, that they might have life.

How do we see this evidenced in Jesus' encounters with people?

_____

_____

_____

_____

_____

Throughout the Old Testament, it was only through the Temple and the Temple sacrifices that people had access to God, fellowship with God, and atonement before God. Everything in the Temple pointed to God's plan of redemption. In John 2:19, Jesus refers to His body as "this temple." It is through Him that we have access to God, fellowship with God, and atonement before God.

How does John take us through the Temple in his gospel, showing Christ to be the fulfillment of it?

1. The bronze altar:

_____

_____

_____

2. The basin for cleansing:

_____

_____

_____

3. The table for the bread of the presence:

_____

_____

_____

4. The golden lampstand:

_____

_____

_____

5. The altar of incense:

_____

_____

_____

6. & 7. The ark of the covenant and the atonement cover:

_____

_____

_____

The purpose of the Temple was to point mankind to God's plan of salvation. And this was the purpose of Christ — to be the fulfillment of that plan and to point all men toward it, that they might have life in Him: "But these are written that you may believe that Jesus is the Christ, the Son of God, and that by believing you may have life in his name" (20:31).

For personal reflection:

1) How does it make a difference to you that Jesus is God? Do you think John gives ample proof? Explain.

2) How could you use what you learned in this lesson to share Christ with an unbelieving friend?

3) Have you ever made a life-changing commitment to Jesus Christ? If not, what is keeping you from doing so?

4) If you were a Jew during Jesus' time, do you think you would have been convinced that Jesus is the Son of God? Do you think it is harder or easier to believe today? Explain.

For the next lesson . . .

Read all of Acts, or at least the following:

- Acts 1:1–3:26
- Acts. 4:1-35; 5:1-42
- Acts 6:8-15; 7:51–8:3
- Acts 9:1-31; 10:9-48; 12:1-19
- Acts 15:1-21; 16:6-34; 18:1-6
- Acts 19:23-31; 20:13-38; 21:10-36
- Acts 24:1-27; 27:27–28:31

ACTS

The Gospel of Luke recorded all that Jesus **began** to do and to teach. Acts records what Jesus **continues** to do and to teach through His apostles, who are empowered by the Holy Spirit. So, here we have the continuation of God's plan of salvation through His church.

At the time of the writing of Acts (A.D. 70-75), Christians had begun to realize that Christ was not returning immediately to set up His kingdom. Acts served as an encouragement and a reminder of what God was accomplishing through His church. The book provided a model for the churches to follow and an explanation for why the Lord tarried.

Acts records the first thirty years of the Christian church — how the Holy Spirit filled and guided His church, and how the gospel was spread throughout the then-known world. In the midst of all this history, we begin to see what the characteristics of the early church were and why the gospel spread so quickly and with such power. This church was . . .

A PRAYING CHURCH

From the beginning, this infant church was a church of prayer (1:14, 24; 2:42; 4:24). Forms of the word "pray" occur some thirty times in Acts. This was one of Luke's major themes in his gospel: that even though Jesus no longer was present physically to lead them, they would have access to the power and will of God through prayer. In Acts, we find the church devoted to prayer. They are not developing their own missions strategy, but are relying on the direction of God.

A POWERFUL CHURCH

Jesus had chosen twelve men to be His disciples. One betrayed Him, one denied Him, they all scattered when He was arrested, and they often lacked in faith and were slow to understand. And yet these same unlearned, undisciplined men were to be the foundation on which God's kingdom would be built.

If Christianity were to survive, the church would have to be empowered for the task. Throughout His ministry, Jesus had told the disciples that He would send the Holy Spirit to comfort them and to guide them into all truth. His last words to them were that they would receive power when the Holy Spirit came on them. And that is exactly what we find happening in Acts 2.

What was significant about the timing of the outpouring of the Holy Spirit?

_____

_____

_____

In what ways were the apostles and believers empowered by the Holy Spirit?

_____

_____

_____

_____

_____

_____

_____

This is not a weak and timid church. It is bold and effective because it possesses supernatural power. What a reminder to Luke's readers facing times of persecution and testing — that the church's effectiveness and power, which began at Pentecost, is available to every believer and is continuing to empower and guide the church of Christ.

A PURE CHURCH

One of the factors contributing to the power of the early church is its unity (2:44-45; 4:32). The church is one in heart, mind, spirit and purpose, and it shares generously with those in need. There is a special unity, the unity that Jesus prayed for in John 17. And this unity is a witness to the world of the truth of what the church preaches.

The unity of the church indicates a *wholeness* in the church — they are untarnished by division, strife and selfishness. Anbanias and Sapphira show a lack of regard for unity and purity (Acts 5) by acting in accordance with their own selfish desires, neglecting the best interests of the body as a whole.

What was the sin committed by Ananias and Sapphira, and how were they punished?

_____

_____

_____

_____

_____

_____

This act of judgment fills the early church with fear, but it sets the precedent. God desires a pure church. He does not tolerate hypocrisy and deceit in His church. The Spirit cannot be deceived. This is a harsh lesson, but a necessary one. As a result, the church becomes a pure one.

A PERSECUTED CHURCH

In Acts 5:17, we find the beginnings of the persecution of the church. Luke shows us two sides of the coin: sometimes God allows them to escape persecution; yet, at other times He allows them to be put to death. Luke records for us the responses of the believers (5:41; 7:60). The persecution that is intended to discourage and crush the church has just the opposite effect! Nevertheless, "On that day a great persecution broke out against the church at Jerusalem, and all except the apostles were scattered throughout Judea and Samaria" (8:1).

A PENETRATING CHURCH

Up until this time, the believers have ministered exclusively in Jerusalem, often congregating at the Temple. How did persecution actually serve to spread the gospel and to bring about the fulfillment of Jesus' commission in Acts 1:8?

_____

_____

_____

_____

_____

_____

In chapter 9, we learn a great lesson. Not only does the gospel have the power to cross geographical and national boundaries, but it also has the power to pervade the most calloused heart. Saul, who had given approval to the death of Stephen (8:1) and had begun to "destroy the church" by dragging men and women off to prison, now has a miraculous encounter with God on the road to Damascus and becomes God's "chosen instrument" in spreading the gospel he previously sought to squelch.

Because the Jews in Damascus try to kill Saul, he is sent by his followers to Jerusalem, then to Caesarea, and off to Tarsus, pushing the gospel still farther into Roman territory.

How did Peter's vision in chapter 10, and the events stemming from it, mark a transition point in the spread of the gospel?

_____

_____

_____

_____

_____

Beginning at chapter 13 and continuing through chapter 20, Luke traces three missionary journeys taken by Paul. Peter is no longer the central character; the focus is now on Paul. It has been Paul's custom to preach first in the synagogues to the Jews, since the synagogue provides a ready-made preaching situation and offers the opportunity to speak to large numbers of Jews at once. Only after opposition from the Jews would Paul and his companions go to the Gentiles with their message.

A PERSEVERING CHURCH

Summarize the important points of Paul's three missionary journeys.

_____

_____

_____

_____

_____

_____

_____

Right from the outset of his missionary ventures, Paul is met with opposition. The Jews incite leaders in Psidian Antioch, who then expel Paul and Barnabas from their region. In Iconium, the Jews and Gentiles plot to mistreat and stone the two missionaries. In Lystra, a mob stones Paul and drags him outside the city, thinking he is dead.

On the second journey, Paul and Silas are thrown into prison, into the inner cell reserved for torture. In Thessalonica, the Jews form a mob and start a riot in the city, dragging off some of the Christians. When Paul and Silas move on to Berea, the Jews from Thessalonica follow them there and agitate the crowds against the two missionaries. In Corinth, the Jews attack Paul again and take him to court.

On his third journey, Paul is opposed greatly in Ephesus. Chapters 21 through 28 refer to Paul's trip to Jerusalem, where he knows that persecution awaits. His ministry, as recorded in the book of Acts, ends in imprisonment.

Through all of this persecution, what was Paul's attitude, and how was his ministry affected?

_____

_____

_____

_____

_____

A PREVAILING CHURCH

With Paul's arrival in Rome, Luke's purpose ends. He has provided for us a history of the fulfillment of Acts 1:8: "But you will receive power when the Holy Spirit comes on you; and you will be my witnesses in Jerusalem, and in all Judea and Samaria, and to the ends of the earth."

Throughout the book of Acts, we see the church of God prevailing. No matter what the opposition, the believers continue to preach the Word of God boldly. Every imprisonment provides opportunity to witness — to jailers, Judean governors and angry mobs. Anyone who will listen is told the glorious news of the gospel. Acts is a book about a prevailing church.

Acts covers the first thirty years of the history of the church, and was meant to be an encouragement and an example to the church of the first century. Its message still applies to us today.

The church should be a PRAYING church, a POWERFUL church, and a PURE church. It may well be a PERSECUTED church, and it *must* be a PERSEVERING and PREVAILING church. God still is working out His plan of redemption through His church. We are His witnesses in Jerusalem, all Judea, and Samaria — to the ends of the earth. Like the early church, we must be a PENETRATING church!

For personal reflection:

1) In what ways are the church today and the early church different? How are they similar?

2) In Acts, all kinds of miraculous phenomena accompanied the outpouring of the Spirit (tongues of fire, miracles, etc.). Why do we see relatively little of that today?

3) What was the believers' secret to persevering under persecution? How could they keep such a joyful attitude? How can these principles help you when you are facing distressing times?

4) The church isn't a building or an organization. It is the *people* of God. Thinking of yourself as "the church," how do you measure up to the standard of the early church?

For the next lesson . . .

Read all of Romans, or at least the following:
- Romans 1:18–2:29
- Romans 3:1–4:25
- Romans 6:1-23; 7:7–8:17
- Romans 8:28-39; 9:1-9; 9:30–10:21
- Romans 11:1-24; 12:1-21
- Romans 14:1-8, 19-23
- Romans 15:23–16:27

The Spread of the Gospel

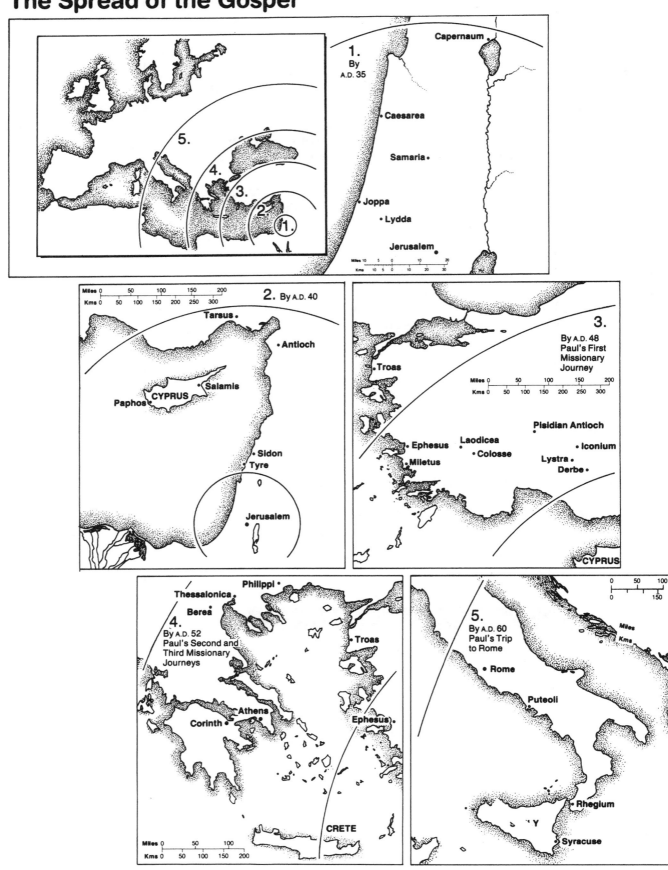

1. By A.D. 35

Capernaum
Caesarea
Samaria
Joppa
Lydda
Jerusalem

2. By A.D. 40

Tarsus
Antioch
CYPRUS
Salamis
Paphos
Sidon
Tyre
Jerusalem

3. By A.D. 48 Paul's First Missionary Journey

Troas
Pisidian Antioch
Ephesus
Laodicea
Colosse
Iconium
Miletus
Lystra
Derbe
CYPRUS

4. By A.D. 52 Paul's Second and Third Missionary Journeys

Philippi
Thessalonica
Berea
Troas
Athens
Corinth
Ephesus
CRETE

5. By A.D. 60 Paul's Trip to Rome

Rome
Puteoli
Rheglum
Syracuse

Paul's First Missionary Journey

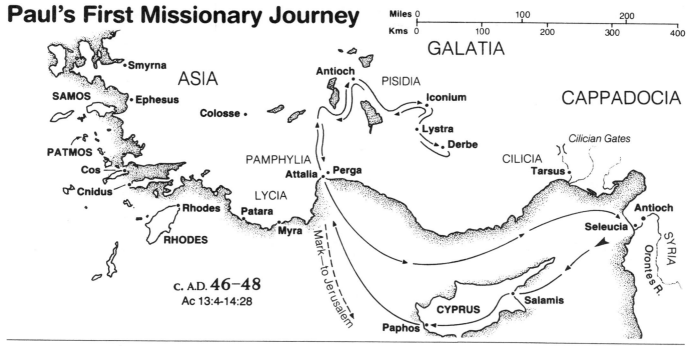

Miles 0 — 100 — 200
Kms 0 — 100 — 200 — 300 — 400

GALATIA

ASIA

Smyrna

SAMOS

Ephesus

Colosse

PATMOS

Cos

Cnidus

Rhodes

RHODES

Patara

Myra

LYCIA

PAMPHYLIA

Attalia · Perga

Mark—to Jerusalem

c. A.D. **46–48**
Ac 13:4-14:28

Antioch

PISIDIA

Iconium

Lystra

Derbe

CAPPADOCIA

CILICIA

Cilician Gates

Tarsus

Antioch

Seleucia

SYRIA

Orontes R.

Salamis

CYPRUS

Paphos

Paul's Second Missionary Journey

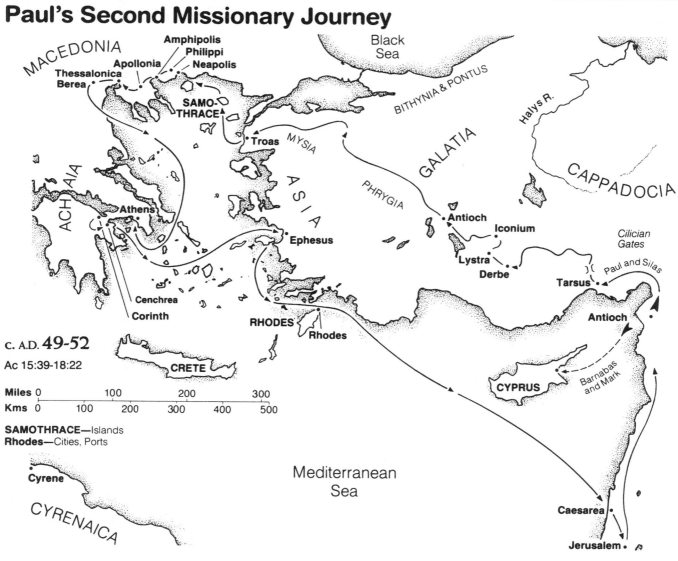

MACEDONIA

Amphipolis
Philippi
Apollonia
Neapolis
Thessalonica
Berea

SAMO-
THRACE

Black
Sea

ACHAIA

Athens

Troas

MYSIA

ASIA

BITHYNIA & PONTUS

Halys R.

GALATIA

CAPPADOCIA

PHRYGIA

Antioch
Iconium

Lystra
Derbe

Cilician
Gates

Tarsus

Paul and Silas

Cenchrea

Corinth

RHODES

Rhodes

Ephesus

Antioch

c. A.D. **49-52**

Ac 15:39-18:22

CRETE

CYPRUS

Barnabas
and Mark

Miles 0 — 100 — 200 — 300
Kms 0 — 100 — 200 — 300 — 400 — 500

SAMOTHRACE—Islands
Rhodes—Cities, Ports

Cyrene

CYRENAICA

Mediterranean
Sea

Caesarea

Jerusalem

Paul's Third Missionary Journey

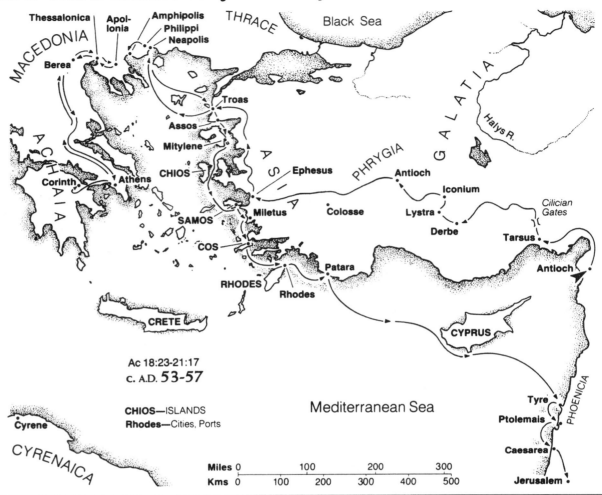

Ac 18:23-21:17
c. A.D. **53-57**

CHIOS—ISLANDS
Rhodes—Cities, Ports

Mediterranean Sea

| Miles 0 | | 100 | | 200 | | 300 | |
| Kms 0 | 100 | 200 | 300 | 400 | 500 | | |

Paul's Journey to Rome

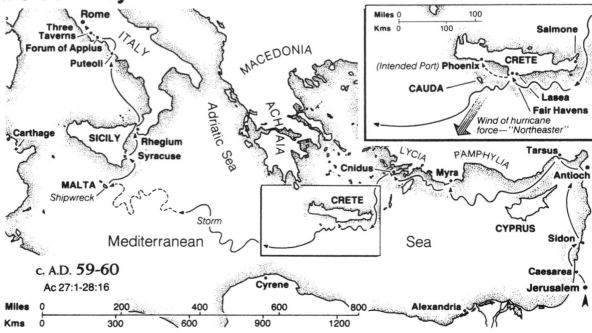

c. A.D. **59-60**
Ac 27:1-28:16

| Miles 0 | | 200 | | 400 | | 600 | | 800 |
| Kms 0 | 300 | | 600 | | 900 | | 1200 | |

ROMANS

Romans was written by Paul (though Romans 16:22 tells us that Tertius was Paul's "secretary" who actually wrote it down) on his third missionary journey, probably from Corinth. At the time of the writing of Romans, Paul was preparing to return to Jerusalem with an offering from the churches in Macedonia and Achaia (15:25-26). Paul always had desired to visit Rome (1:8-13; 15:23-24) and this letter was intended to prepare for his future visit.

Describe the situation in the church in Rome at this time.

_____

_____

_____

_____

THE GRIEVANCE OF GOD

Paul begins by addressing God's rightful complaint against mankind. Paul paints a portrait of the sinfulness of man and God's subsequent judgment (1:18–3:20). What were the criteria given for God's judgment, and how did mankind measure up?

_____

_____

_____

_____

THE GIFT OF GOD

Salvation never could be earned by human effort. But God began working out His plan of redemption the moment sin entered the world (see Genesis 3:15). God would send someone to crush the head of Satan, the author of sin. God would provide our righteousness (Rom. 3:21-26). Now a righteousness, apart from the law, has been given to all who believe and who have faith in Christ.

A. IMPUTED RIGHTEOUSNESS

Chapter 4 gives historical evidence that God has been using this principle all along. It was not new with Christ, but began with Abraham. Paul shows that it was Abraham's *faith* that was "credited to him as righteousness" (4:3, cf. Gen. 15:6), and *not* the work of circumcision.

(God instituted circumcision some fourteen years after His first promise to make Abraham into a great nation.) Circumcision was the seal, the outward sign, of the righteousness which God already had credited to him (Rom. 4:11). Therefore, Paul concludes that Abraham is the father of all who have faith (4:13, 16), and that righteousness also is credited to us who have faith (4:23-24).

What does it mean to be "justified" (to be declared righteous)?

_____

_____

_____

_____

What are the results?

_____

_____

_____

_____

B. IMPARTED RIGHTEOUSNESS

In chapters 6 through 8, Paul describes this aspect of righteousness. We are not to continue in sin, because Christ gives us the ability to live consistently in righteousness.

1. Power over sin (chapter 6)

_____

_____

2. Power over the futility of the law (chapter 7)

_____

_____

He who once was "a prisoner of the law of sin" (7:23) now has been "set free from the law of sin and death" (8:2). Christ has accomplished what the law was powerless to do. He became our sin offering. His death gave us power over the bondage of sin and made it possible for the "righteous requirements of the law [to] be fully met in us" (8:4). The futility is gone.

3. Power of the Holy Spirit (chapter 8)

_____

_____

Paul's conclusion: We are "more than conquerors" through Christ (8:37). From the beginning of time, God determined that those who would believe in Christ would be morally conformed to the likeness of his Son (8:29). Therefore, "If God is for us, who can be against us?" (8:31). Who can condemn us when Christ is at the right hand of God making intercession for us? Who can separate us from God's love? No one!

What a wonderful gift God has given to us! The law and the power of sin and death have been conquered, and we have been justified freely. Not only have we been declared righteous, but we have been given inner power over sin! This is the gift of God.

THE GRACE OF GOD

Chapter 9 begins by recounting how God gave Israel everything to lead them to Him: the covenants, the law, the Temple worship, the promises, the patriarchs and Christ. And yet Paul anguishes over Israel because, though they have pursued a law of righteousness, they have not attained it. As a nation, they have rejected the salvation of Christ. Does this mean that all the promises God made to Israel are void?

_____

_____

In Romans 11:11-24, Paul tells us that the Jews have not stumbled beyond recovery. God still would be gracious to the nation of Israel. If they would turn to Christ, they too would be saved (11:23). Belief in Christ is the criterion — for those yet to be saved, as well as for those already saved (11:22).

In what way did Paul say that "all Israel will be saved" (11:26)?

_____

_____

_____

_____

_____

THE GROUNDS TO LIVE FOR GOD

"Therefore, I urge you brothers, IN VIEW OF GOD'S MERCY . . ." (12:1a, emphasis added). Paul has revealed the tremendous gift of God and the grace of God, in that "While we were still sinners, Christ died for us" (5:8b). In view of all this, we should live for God: ". . . offer your bodies as living sacrifices, holy and pleasing to God — this is your spiritual act of worship" (12:1).

Christ put an end once and for all to the endless offering of sacrifices, but there is still one sacrifice left to be made: not the dead sacrifice of a slaughtered animal, but the living sacrifice of God's consecrated people. This is their worship — not through the law, but through the Spirit, offering themselves to God with their heart, will and mind.

List some of the practical expressions of the Christian life found in chapters 13 through 16:

_____

_____

_____

_____

_____

Romans has been called aptly, "The Gospel according to Paul." Paul takes us all the way back to creation and the sin that entered the world through Adam. Paul shows us the effects of that sin and the subsequent perversity of mankind. "The wages of sin is death, but the gift of God is eternal life in Christ Jesus our Lord" (6:23). Christ paid the penalty for our sin by dying on the cross, thereby satisfying God's justice and reconciling us to God. Through faith in Him, we are credited with righteousness and are given the power to live a righteous life apart from the law.

The key verses in Romans touch every major theme, and we would do well to memorize them. Paul says:

> I am not ashamed of the gospel, because it is the power of God for the salvation of everyone who believes: first for the Jew, then for the Gentile. For in the gospel a righteousness from God is revealed, a righteousness that is by faith from first to last, just as it is written: "The righteous will live by faith" (Rom. 1:16-17, see also 16:25-26).

For personal reflection:

1) Do you think it's possible for someone to live up to the requirements of the law (to be perfect) and, subsequently, to be free from condemnation? If so, how?

2) What do you think would be the result if Christ gave us imputed righteousness without imparted righteousness?

3) What does it mean to be a living sacrifice? Do you feel that you're living that kind of life right now? Explain.

For the next lesson . . .

Read all of 1 Corinthians, or at least the following:
- 1 Corinthians 1:1-17; 3:1–4:21
- 1 Corinthians 1:18–2:16; 5:1-12
- 1 Corinthians 6:12-20; 8:1-13
- 1 Corinthians 9:1–10:13; 10:23-33
- 1 Corinthians 11:1-16; 12:1–13:13
- 1 Corinthians 14:1-40
- 1 Corinthians 15:1-58

1 CORINTHIANS

Acts 18 provides the historical background for 1 Corinthians. Paul founded the church at Corinth on his second missionary journey and, while there, stayed with Priscilla and Aquila, who had come from Rome. After being forced out of the synagogue where he was preaching, Paul moved next door to the home of Justus. Acts 18:11 tells us that Paul spent one and a half years at Corinth, a significant amount of time in one city. He obviously regarded Corinth as an influential city and a vital key to the spread of the gospel.

What were some of the unique characteristics of the city of Corinth, and how did they influence the church there?

_____

_____

_____

_____

The church was supposed to be in Corinth, but Corinth had gotten into the church.

After Paul left Corinth, He went to Ephesus. During his two years and three months there, he received reports of problems in the church which he had founded at Corinth (1 Cor. 1:11; 5:1; 7:1; 16:17). So it is at this point that Paul wrote 1 Corinthians. The book was meant to instruct and correct an immature, unspiritual church.

THE WISDOM OF THE CHURCH

The city of Corinth, only forty miles from Athens, becomes heir to Athen's philosophic wisdom. The Corinthian Christians pride themselves on their superior wisdom and intellect, which Paul tells us is the beginning of their downfall — it is causing divisions in the church. They are following the teachings of individual men, and they divide themselves as a church by whose teaching they follow. Their trust is in words of human wisdom.

What was Paul's attitude toward "human wisdom," and whose wisdom did he encourage the Corinthians to follow (1:18–2:16)?

_____

_____

_____

_____

_____

From a study of this initial problem, it's easy to see how immorality slowly creeps into the church. Human wisdom and logic teach them that fulfilling desires for pleasure is the right of every man, and that freedom from the law is a license to do anything they please.

THE WITNESS OF THE CHURCH

Here in Corinth, we find a church that is a poor witness in their world. They are, in some ways, no better than the general population at Corinth.

What example of immorality is cited in chapter 5, and what was Paul's advice regarding the matter?

_____

_____

_____

_____

_____

Chapter 6 addresses still another problem area in the Corinthian church: lawsuits. Though believers may have legitimate grievances against one another, Paul condemns their practice of taking their cases before the ungodly and, in the process, destroying their witness as believers.

One cannot live like the world and expect to be a part of the kingdom of God, says Paul (6:9-10). But the Corinthian Christians quote this statement in their defense: "Everything is permissible for me" (6:12a), claiming their Christian liberty from the law. Paul counters this by saying, ". . . but not everything is beneficial. . . . I will not be mastered by anything" (6:12). When we sin, we become slaves to sin, and we lose our freedom. We are free in Christ — not free to be immoral, but free to be righteous and obedient to Him.

All of chapter 7 is devoted to answering questions which the Corinthian church must have been asking concerning marriage. It may be that Paul's initial comment (7:1) is simply another quote from Corinthian wisdom: "It is good for a man not to marry."

Summarize Paul's attitudes toward marriage.

_____

_____

_____

_____

Even in this chapter concerning marriage, Paul's primary concern is the witness of the church. Marital fidelity and devotion to God are much needed in a wicked and licentious society.

In chapter 8, Paul turns to the issue of eating food which has been sacrificed to idols. Here again, "freedom" is an issue to the Corinthian Christian. But Paul says that Christians have a responsibility to limit their freedom in order to be a pure witness, not only to those outside the church, but also to the weaker brother or sister inside.

What specific admonitions for propriety in worship does Paul give in chapter 11 (see also chapter 14), and how are they to be understood today?

_____

_____

_____

_____

_____

On every page, we hear the Corinthian church crying, "Freedom! Liberty!" while Paul calls back, "Witness!" We are to be an example, a witness to the world (taking our culture into account). The principle hasn't changed — WATCH YOUR WITNESS!

THE WORSHIP IN THE CHURCH

The early church is in the practice of holding "agape" (love) feasts following their services, during which they share the Lord's Supper. But instead of sharing, some get drunk while others go hungry. Paul reminds "revelers" that there is no room for self-centeredness in worship.

Chapters 12 through 14 explain the use of spiritual gifts in worship. Paul provides some general information about, and principles for using, spiritual gifts:

— The gifts are given by the Spirit, as God determines, for the edification of the church, and not for selfish advantage (12:7; 14:12).

— The church is a body with many parts (12:12-27), and each member is indispensable.

— Not everyone has the same gift (12:28-30).

— Without love, every gift is useless (chapter 13).

Now, concerning the use of tongues in chapter 14, Corinth is the only church to whom Paul writes concerning the gift of tongues (languages), because here it is being abused. When the gift was given originally at Pentecost (see Acts 2), it was a witness to, and a confirmation of, the gospel to a large group representing many different languages. No doubt, people of many languages often would gather in Corinth because of its location on the major trade routes. So, perhaps this gift of languages is necessary here in Corinth. But there are problems.

What general principles does Paul give regarding the use of tongues in worship?

_____

_____

_____

_____

THE WALK OF THE CHURCH

Lifestyle is always based on doctrine. Paul gives some doctrinal instruction in 1 Corinthians 15 concerning the Resurrection. Apparently, there are some in Corinth (maybe former Sadducees?) who are saying that there was no resurrection from the dead. But Christ's resurrection is the proof and guarantee of our resurrection. Without the Resurrection, Paul says, his preaching would be foolishness, and so would faith (15:14, 17) — we would still be in our sins.

How does our doctrine affect how we live?

_____

_____

_____

_____

_____

_____

We normally tend to think of the New Testament church as a church free from problems and immorality. But from its inception, Satan has been trying to destroy the church from the inside as well as from the outside. We would do well today to heed the principles taught by Paul to this struggling first-century church.

For personal reflection:

1) What are the causes of division in the church today?

2) How do you assess the church today? Are we impacting our culture or is our culture impacting us (has "Corinth" gotten into the church)?

3) Is it possible to be a "sinning Christian"? Why or why not?

4) If we are to show propriety in worship, what kinds of practices which are acceptable in our culture today should we be careful of adopting?

For the next lesson . . .

Read all of 2 Corinthians, or at least the following:
- 2 Corinthians 1:3-11; 2:5–3:18
- 2 Corinthians 4:1–5:10
- 2 Corinthians 5:11–7:1
- 2 Corinthians 7:2–9:15
- 2 Corinthians 10:1–11:15
- 2 Corinthians 11:16–12:10
- 2 Corinthians 12:11–13:11

2 CORINTHIANS

How different this letter is from 1 Corinthians! Paul's first letter was full of rebuke and criticism and pain — the pain of a pastor seeing the church he painstakingly founded now filled with corruption and worldliness. How relieved he was when he finally met up with Titus in Macedonia and learned of the response of the Corinthian church — "He told us about your longing for me, your deep sorrow, your ardent concern for me, so that my joy was greater than ever" (2 Cor. 7:7).

While 1 Corinthians was written in distress and heaviness of heart, 2 Corinthians was occasioned by great joy, yet continued concern for a young church in the midst of a decadent society. But the intriguing charm of 2 Corinthians comes not just from what we learn about Corinth, but from what we learn about Paul.

What personal information do we learn about Paul from this letter?

_____

_____

_____

_____

Second Corinthians reveals to us Paul's secret of success in his ministry — the secret of his boldness, his steadfast endurance, his persistence in ministry:

PAUL'S CONFIDENCE

Ten times in this short book, Paul tells us that he is "confident." He sees God's great purpose in everything, in the way that all things are being worked together for the good of those who believe (see Romans 8:28). Because Paul can see past the earthly, temporal hardships to God's greater purpose, he is able to approach everything in life with a great degree of confidence:

A. CONFIDENCE IN GOD'S COMFORT

_____

_____

B. CONFIDENCE IN GOD'S PEOPLE

_____

_____

C. CONFIDENCE IN GOD'S COVENANT

_____

_____

D. CONFIDENCE IN A FUTURE HOPE

_____

_____

E. CONFIDENCE IN THE WORK OF CHRIST

_____

_____

Second Corinthians 6 shows the effects of this great confidence that we possess as Christians: "great endurance . . . purity . . . sincere love . . . truthful speech . . . power of God . . . weapons of righteousness . . . genuine . . . making many rich . . . having nothing and yet possessing everything" (6:3-10). We are not yoked together with unbelievers, but are separate; there is purity. "Since we have these promises . . . let us purify ourselves" (7:1a). Our understanding of who God is and what He has promised prompts us to live a life worthy of our calling.

PAUL'S CONCERN

Paul has a great concern for people and for the ministry of the church. It is this concern that prompts him to write about a subject which most pastors find extremely delicate — MONEY.

In chapters 8 and 9, Paul addresses the collection of funds for the Jerusalem church (cf. Rom. 15; 1 Cor. 16). Evidently, the Corinthians began to do their part in this relief effort a year earlier, but have not completed it. So Paul tells them he is sending Titus back to Corinth to complete the work — first, because of his concern for the oppressed in Jerusalem, and second, because of his concern for the Corinthians themselves, that their faith would be proven genuine by their actions.

Paul also is concerned for the prosperity and witness of the Corinthian church, because He understands how God works. Paul wants the Corinthian Christians to learn to be generous, thereby unleashing God's generosity upon them, which will in turn enable them to give away even more!

What is the result when obedience accompanies profession (2 Cor. 9:13-14)?

_____

_____

_____

_____

_____

PAUL'S COMMENDATION

Not surprisingly, Paul seems to have had much opposition in Corinth. Why was he being criticized (10:1–11:15)?

_____

_____

_____

_____

Paul begins to show the Corinthians in chapter 11 what authenticates him as God's apostle — the proofs of his commendation by the Lord:

* His message is confirmation of his authority — it is not self-serving, but is edifying for the church.

* Paul's adversaries hold that, since Paul refuses to accept payment from the Corinthians for his preaching, his message is worthless. But his concern is more for the welfare of the Corinthians and his witness in that community than for his own financial needs. This is actually a proof of his apostleship.

* These same false teachers have boasted much about themselves, belittling Paul in the process. In 2 Corinthians 11:16 through 12:10, Paul uses their tactics and shows how much more he has to boast about than any of them.

Why did God give Paul a "thorn in the flesh" (12:7-10)?

_____

_____

_____

_____

Paul closes his letter by showing again his great concern for the Corinthians, which is possibly his greatest credential as an apostle. His love for them and his concern about their spiritual welfare are his commendation, his confirmation of authority as God's messenger. Because of his concern, he warns, admonishes, and entreats them to examine themselves (13:5, 7, 9-11). What was Paul's prayer for them?

_____

_____

_____

_____

Second Corinthians gives us an inside, intimate view of a man mightily used of God. Paul was undaunted in his efforts to spread the gospel throughout the world, even though he met with opposition, tribulation, criticism, and sometimes what seemed like futility. The ordinary person, if he or she were to encounter half of what Paul did, would lose heart, become discouraged, and possibly would falter in ministry. But Paul had inner strength, drive and boldness that serve as a powerful incentive for us and make Paul an example for us to follow.

What are some practical applications from Paul's example for us today?

_____

_____

_____

_____

_____

Paul didn't intend this letter to be about himself. He wrote it because his heart overflowed with joy at the repentance of the Corinthians. But his life shines through; his example is evident. God wants each of us to be a "Paul" — to allow God to use us to minister effectively and persistently for Him.

For personal reflection:

1) How can Paul's example help us when we're going through times of great trial and tribulation?

2) How do you feel when pastors talk about "money matters"? Do you agree or disagree that "you can't love without giving" and that our generosity is a reflection of the reality of the gospel?

3) In what ways do you sometimes measure yourself by the world's standards instead of God's? What is the problem with doing that?

4) Do you ever feel inadequate to do what God has called you to do? Why should your inadequacy be a source of comfort rather than condemnation?

For the next lesson . . .

Read all of Galatians and Ephesians, or at least the following:

- Galatians 1:11–2:21
- Galatians 3:1-25
- Galatians 3:26–4:21
- Galatians 5:1–6:18
- Ephesians 1:3–2:10; 2:19-22
- Ephesians 3:7–4:32
- Ephesians 5:1–6:20

GALATIANS & EPHESIANS

Paul founded the Galatian churches — in Antioch, Iconium, Lystra and Derbe — on his first missionary journey (see Acts 13–14) and visited them on at least two other occasions (Acts 16:6; 18:23). Immediately after his first journey, Paul finds that false doctrines have been introduced into the church, so he immediately addresses the problem in a letter to be circulated among those churches.

THE PREREQUISITES OF THE CHURCH

What were the teachings of some "false brothers" to the Galatians?

_____

_____

_____

_____

_____

In the letter to the Galatians, Paul is distraught that these Christians in Galatia so quickly have deserted the gospel to embrace this false "gospel," which, says Paul, is really no gospel at all — it is a perversion of the gospel. Paul calls them "foolish" (3:1), and exclaims, "I am perplexed about you!" (4:20). So Paul is determined to set them straight by telling them that justification is by faith in Jesus Christ *alone*. There are two fundamental benefits that flow from this great truth:

A. FREEDOM FROM THE LAW

_____

_____

_____

B. FRUITFULNESS

_____

_____

_____

In this letter, Paul teaches freedom, but that freedom from the law doesn't mean freedom to practice immorality. On the contrary, it is this freedom that allows us, even compels us, to do what is right.

The letter to the **EPHESIANS** may have been a "circular letter" intended to be circulated among various churches. What evidence of this can you find?

_____

_____

_____

_____

THE PECULIARITY OF THE CHURCH

Paul begins to unfold for us in the book of Ephesians the uniqueness of God's church. It is not an administration or organization. It has many facets, and no one illustration thoroughly describes it. So Paul gives us several:

    A. FAMILY (2:19)

    B. TEMPLE (2:20-22)

    C. BODY (1:22-23; chapter 4)

    D. BRIDE (5:22-32)

This relationship we have with Christ is characterized by . . .

    1. Love — a conscious, self-sacrificing commitment;

    2. Submission — to the Word of God and to the will of God;

    3. Purity — as a perfectly pure virgin bride;

    4. Loyalty — to our relationship with Christ, just as to the marriage relationship, which is not to be taken lightly and should not be broken by adultery or divorce.

THE PURPOSE OF THE CHURCH

The entire book of Ephesians focuses on the purpose of the church. Words like "intent," "purpose," "in order to," or references to God's will are on every page. Paul says that the purpose of the church is . . .

    A. To be holy and blameless and to bring glory to God (1:4, 11-12; 4:24);

    B. To do good works (2:10);

    C. To spread the gospel through the heavens and the earth (3:10).

In every way, the purpose of the church is to glorify God and to reflect His glory throughout the world. We are a beacon for God. As His church, our lives and our works shout out a message to all the world. This is another fulfillment of God's covenant promise to Abraham. God has established the church so that all the world will be blessed through our message and our Christ.

THE PROVISION FOR THE CHURCH (chapter 1)

In and of ourselves, apart from Christ, it would be utterly impossible to accomplish God's purposes in this world. What spiritual blessings are recorded in chapter 1 that enable us to fulfill His will?

_____

_____

_____

_____

_____

_____

What is the result of these provisions?

_____

_____

_____

_____

_____

_____

_____

_____

THE PRACTICE OF THE CHURCH

Chapters 2 through 6 are replete with references to the walk of Christians in the world. Ephesians 2:1-10 describes the salvation of individuals: though once we were following the ways of the world and Satan and were slaves to the sinful nature, through the grace of God we have been saved and raised up to the heavenly realms. Because of this, Paul prays that the Ephesians might become rooted and established in Christ's love, so that they might be filled with all the fullness of God (3:14-21). He urges them: to "live a life worthy of the calling [they] have received" (4:1). Concerning the practice of the church, Paul tells them to be humble, gentle, patient and forbearing; to live in unity; to use spiritual gifts for the edification and perfection of the body; to grow up in Christ; and to live as children of light, not darkness.

List some of the specific practices Paul mentions in which Christians should and should not be engaged (4:25–5:15):

_____

_____

_____

_____

_____

_____

In what ways should our relationships be influenced by our relationship with Christ?

_____

_____

_____

_____

_____

_____

_____

THE POWER OF THE CHURCH

In Ephesians 6:10-18, Paul describes the armor of God. Why is this armor needed by the church?

_____

_____

_____

_____

_____

_____

Truth, righteousness, readiness in the gospel, and faith in Christ are necessary to withstand the attacks of the enemy. Salvation is our helmet. For soldiers, the helmet was for protection, but also was a striking symbol of military victory. Our salvation likewise proclaims our victory in the battle. The only weapons we have are the Word of God (our sword) and prayer (our communication with the Commander-in-Chief). God and His Word are our true sources of power.

How can we take advantage of the power that has been made available to us?

_____

_____

_____

_____

_____

_____

Throughout time, God has had a "church." Even in the Old Testament, He always preserved a remnant. God was preparing the remnant of Israel to be the vehicle through which Christ would come physically into the world. Now God has called us, the church, to proclaim the message of salvation through Christ. We are still the vehicle through which Christ comes to the world. No wonder the church is so complex and distinctive . . . and powerful.

Even now, God's church is moving forward to fulfill God's purpose. In every denomination, every nation, every tongue, there are Christians who are part of the church universal, and each one has his or her part in God's redemptive plan.

For personal reflection:

1) In what ways do you see the tension between freedom and fruitfulness in the church today? How about in your life?

2) Which one of Paul's illustrations of the church is closest to how you view the church? What happens if too much emphasis is placed on just one aspect to the exclusion of the others?

3) Why do you think there is seemingly so little power in the church today? Do you see as much power in your life as you would like? If not, why not?

For the next lesson . . .

Read all of Philippians.
- Philippians 1:1-11
- Philippians 1:12-30
- Philippians 2:1-18
- Philippians 2:19-30
- Philippians 3:1-21
- Philippians 4:1-9
- Philippians 4:10-23

PHILIPPIANS

The city of Philippi was located on the Via Egnatia, part of the 250,000 miles of paved roads built by the Roman Empire beginning in the third century before Christ. In Acts 16:12, Luke tells us that Philippi was "a Roman colony and the leading city of that district of Macedonia." The citizens of Philippi enjoyed special rights and privileges (because it was a Roman colony) of which they were particularly proud.

The Philippians had great cause for civic pride, which is reflected in Paul's letter to the church there. Paul stresses humility and unity. His reference to their citizenship being in heaven (Phil. 3:20) would have special meaning to a people who prided themselves in their earthly citizenship.

The founding of the church at Philippi is recorded in Acts 16, during Paul's second missionary journey. This was the first church established in Europe (northern Greece), and was a response to Paul's vision of the Macedonian man calling, "Come over to Macedonia to help us" (Acts 16:9). What were some of the events that happened there?

_____

_____

_____

_____

_____

_____

The book of Philippians was written by Paul from prison in either Rome or Ephesus. Allusions throughout Philippians make it clear that death is a very real possibility for Paul. He is not in the most favorable of circumstances. Paul is keenly conscious of his situation and makes numerous references to his imprisonment and hope of deliverance. But we learn that Paul is full of joy, despite his circumstances — he uses forms of the word "joy" some sixteen times in four short chapters. And this from a man has in prison who is expecting to be put to death! If ever a man has had reason to be depressed or forlorn, Paul certainly has reason. So how can Paul possibly have joy? As we study this book, we will learn the secret of his joy.

JOY IN THE FRUITFULNESS OF PEOPLE

It is evident throughout Paul's writings that he has an intense love for people. He spends his whole life sharing God's Word with people; he finds great joy in seeing people mature and grow in Christ.

What kind of life did Paul encourage the Philippians to live?

_____

_____

_____

_____

_____

_____

Paul is concerned about the Philippians' joy (1:25-26). Whenever we focus on the welfare of others instead of on our own circumstances, we are filled with joy. Depression is sometimes caused by self-centeredness. Paul finds his joy in seeing the spiritual progress of others and in encouraging them to live up to all that God desires for His holy people.

Paul goes on to teach them how they can have joy and peace (4:6-8). In verse 4, he commands them twice to REJOICE, then proceeds to tell them to pray about everything with thanksgiving and to think about what is pure, right and praiseworthy. This goes a long way in solving our worry or anxiety, the ultimate robbers of joy.

JOY IN THE FURTHERANCE OF THE GOSPEL

Paul has a wonderful ability to see past earthly circumstances to God's eternal purposes. Paul can have joy in the midst of persecution because he can see God's hand at work in the furtherance of the gospel (1:12-14).

What good could Paul find in his imprisonment and in the preaching of those who were trying to cause more trouble for him?

_____

_____

_____

_____

_____

_____

_____

JOY IN THE FULLNESS OF SALVATION

You may be thinking by now that Paul's joy is based on circumstances alone — on the fruitfulness of God's people and the furtherance of the gospel. But what about the times when even God's people begin to wax cold and the gospel seems to be thwarted on every hand? Paul shows us here that, even though circumstances can be the occasion of great joy, our joy is not contingent upon circumstances. True joy comes not from what happens *to* us, but from what happens *in* us.

What was the meaning of life for Paul, and how could it bring him joy, despite his circumstances?

_____

_____

_____

_____

_____

_____

JOY IN THE FUTURE OF BELIEVERS

Paul's writings abound with a confidence in ultimate salvation, when we will live with Christ forever and our bodies will be transformed from perishable to imperishable. A glorious future awaits the Christian. How can we not have joy? We are God's children and heirs to all the riches of heaven.

JOY IN THE FAITHFULNESS OF GOD

We have marveled time and again at Paul's ability to see God and how He works in and through all circumstances. Paul can see God working because he has confidence in God's faithfulness and goodness.

List some of the things Paul knew about God that added to his joy:

_____

_____

_____

_____

These four short chapters stuck into the middle of the New Testament serve as a wonderful example for us. Paul shares with us the secret of joy in the Christian life. But Paul's great concern is that the Philippians find joy:

> And I will continue with all of you for your progress and joy in the faith, so that through my being with you again your joy in Christ Jesus will overflow on account of me (Phil. 1:25b-26).

> So you too should be glad and rejoice with me (Phil. 2:18).

> Rejoice in the Lord (Phil. 3:1, see also 4:4).

Paul wants the Philippians to find the secret of joy. Surely this is a message for us as well! Satan has no tool greater than a discouraged, joyless Christian. Such a person cannot be a witness for Christ! Christians should be the most optimistic and joyful people around, shining like stars in the universe. We have every reason to be glad, because our joy is based not on circumstances, but on a vibrant relationship with Jesus Christ and the hope of His coming.

For personal reflection:

1) What are some positive things you can begin doing in your own life to increase your joy?

2) Always remember that joy comes from the inside; it is the overflow of a relationship with Christ. Have you made a personal commitment to Jesus Christ yet?

3) How can you use what you learned from Philippians to help another Christian suffering from discouragement or depression?

4) Do you agree with the statement that "joy is a by-product of obedience"? Why or why not?

For the next lesson . . .

Read all of Colossians.
- Colossians 1:1-14
- Colossians 1:15-23
- Colossians 1:24–2:5
- Colossians 2:6-23
- Colossians 3:1-17
- Colossians 3:18–4:6
- Colossians 4:7-18

COLOSSIANS

Most commentators agree that the books of Ephesians, Colossians and Philemon all were written at about the same time. The letters to the Ephesians and Colossians both identify Tychicus as the bearer of their letters. The book of Colossians mentions that Onesimus, a runaway slave, was accompanying Tychicus to Colossae, where Philemon was a prominent member. The short letter from Paul to Philemon addresses the problem with Onesimus. The books of Colossians and Philemon also mention Epaphras, John Mark, Aristarchus, Demas and Luke. So, all three of these books are linked together. As we saw in lesson 33, Ephesians may have been a circular letter, the letter referred to in Colossians 4:16 as "the letter from Laodicea," which Paul intended to be read in Colossae also.

Colossae was a second-rate market town surpassed in both power and importance by its neighboring towns of Laodicea and Hierapolis. It was located about one hundred miles east of Ephesus, six miles from Laodicea, and fourteen miles from Hierapolis. Paul probably did not visit the churches at Colossae, Laodicea and Hierapolis (all situated in the Lycus Valley) personally. But, no doubt during Paul's three years at nearby Ephesus, many traveled to hear Paul preach and returned to their hometowns with the good news of Jesus Christ. This was almost certainly the case with Colossae.

Colossians 1:7 tells us that Epaphras (who was himself a Colossian, see 4:12) was a "faithful minister of Christ" and had brought news about the Colossian church to Paul in prison at Rome (A.D. 60). Paul may have written his letter in response to this visit. His opening remarks to this young church are words of thankfulness for their love and faith and for the fruitfulness of the gospel throughout the world — including Colossae.

What was Paul's purpose in writing this letter?

_____

_____

_____

What were the basic beliefs of Gnosticism (of which we see an early form refuted in Colossians)?

_____

_____

_____

_____

_____

Paul sets out to lay the foundation of Jesus Christ and to show the deceitfulness of these heretical philosophies that promised much in the way of salvation, but delivered nothing. It is Christ alone who can reconcile sinful man with a holy God.

THE SUPREMACY OF CHRIST

What does the hymn in Colossians 1:15-20 reveal about the supremacy of Christ?

_____

_____

_____

_____

_____

What did Paul mean when he said Christ was the "firstborn" over all creation?

_____

_____

_____

_____

_____

Understanding the supremacy of Christ is essential for standing firm and for refuting false doctrine. It is the key to recognizing error.

The supremacy of Christ is seen not only in creation, but also in redemption. Only Christ, the fullness of God, could bring about reconciliation with God "by making peace through his blood, shed on the cross" (1:20). "But now he has reconciled you by Christ's PHYSICAL BODY through death . . ." (1:22, emphasis added).

Only a supreme Christ could accomplish this. It is not attainable through secret knowledge, ceremonialism or asceticism, but only "if you continue in your faith, established and firm, not moved from the hope held out in the gospel" (1:23a). Paul tells the Colossians that there is only one way to be holy, without blemish, and free from accusation — only one way to be reconciled to God: through faith in Jesus Christ.

Christianity often has been accused of being exclusive, narrow and intolerant of other religions. Rather, Christianity always has trumpeted the Bible's proclamation of the supremacy of Jesus Christ, who is the fullness of God and who alone is able to redeem the world through faith. This is the very foundation of Christianity, and it cannot be compromised for any reason.

THE SUFFICIENCY OF CHRIST

The heresy threatening the church has alleged that Christ alone is not sufficient, that Christians need some special hidden knowledge and need to follow some of the ceremonial laws of Judaism. According to them, Christ alone is deficient. To those being tempted by the Colossian heresy, Paul says not to look to some mystery religion to somehow be made perfect or complete, because only Christ is sufficient to effect completeness, wholeness and perfection in the lives of His people.

In contrast to what other teachings did Paul show that Christ was sufficient (2:6-23)?

_____

_____

_____

_____

THE SUBJECTIVE RESPONSE OF CHRIST

The Gnostics view the law as entirely objective in the sense that there is no requirement to obey it personally. Licentiousness is permissible for them because the body is sinful anyway. But, knowledge of the supreme Christ always necessitates a personal, subjective response, which is highlighted in chapter 3 by such words as "since/if then," "therefore," and "but now" (3:1, 5, 8).

Paul is admonishing the Colossians to put into practice what they already have in position. He's telling them to appropriate what God has made available, to live like the children they are.

What sorts of things were they to "put off" (3:5-11)?

_____

_____

_____

_____

What were they to "put on" (3:12-17)?

_____

_____

_____

_____

The message of the gospel necessarily changes our lives. We cannot hear it and remain neutral, nor can we accept it and continue in our old pattern of living. It necessitates a subjective, continued response. Paul reminds these Christians that they must CONTINUE in Christ — in correct doctrine and lifestyle — if they are to be presented holy and free from accusation (1:23; 2:6). This is the subjective response to Christ.

What was Paul's primary concern in his final instructions in chapter 4?

_____

_____

_____

_____

Paul's concern for the well-being of the Colossian church is readily apparent. He wants to see them standing firm and mature, not taken captive by vain philosophies. Throughout the Old Testament, God never tolerated idolatry; He never tolerated the slightest variance from His commands. Obedience to God's law was intended to lead His people to a correct understanding of who God was and what He required for salvation; His whole plan of redemption hinged on their proper understanding.

And the God of the Old Testament is the God of the New Testament. There still is no room for variance. The book of Colossians reveals to us that God does not tolerate heresy, or even syncretism. There is one supreme Christ and only one way to be reconciled to God. Christ is both supreme and sufficient. And God expects His people to live in a manner worthy of the name they bear.

The threat to the early church was a mixture of truth and error, the same threat we face today. We must stand firm on the Word of Christ.

For personal reflection:

1) What are some of the heresies confronting the church today? How does Satan still mix in "a little truth" with error?

2) Do you think syncretism is really a threat today, or are we supposed to be tolerant of the beliefs of others?

3) What changes have you seen in your life since you began following Christ? What have you "put off" and "put on"?

4) In what ways do Christians sometimes behave as if Christ is not sufficient?

For the next lesson . . .

Read all of 1 Thessalonians.
- 1 Thessalonians 1:1-10
- 1 Thessalonians 2:1-16
- 1 Thessalonians 2:17–3:5
- 1 Thessalonians 3:6-13
- 1 Thessalonians 4:1-12
- 1 Thessalonians 4:13–5:11
- 1 Thessalonians 5:12-28

1 THESSALONIANS

Paul's letters to the church at Thessalonica are the earliest of all his Epistles, with the possible exception of Galatians. The first letter to the Thessalonians was written c. A.D. 50 or 51, nearly twenty years after Jesus' death and resurrection. The two letters provide a vital element in our understanding of God's process of redemption that began in the book of Genesis.

What is the historical setting of 1 Thessalonians (see Acts 17), and what prompted Paul to write this letter?

_____

_____

_____

_____

One thread that runs throughout 1 Thessalonians is "encouragement" — for both Paul and the Thessalonians. Forms of the word are used eight times (2:12; 3:2, 7; 4:1, 18; 5:11, 14), where they are variously translated as "appeal," "urge," "instructed" and "encourage." The word "encouragement" has the sense of comforting and exhorting at the same time. First Thessalonians is a book of encouragement — of comfort and exhortation — for first-century Christians undergoing persecution, and also for us today.

THE MODEL OF ENCOURAGEMENT

The Thessalonian church is a model of encouragement, for this church brings encouragement to Paul and to the whole world (3:7-9). Paul's comments regarding this church are particularly impressive when we realize how very young this church is and how little time Paul has spent in establishing it.

In chapter 1, he commends them for their "work produced by faith," their "labor prompted by love" and their "endurance inspired by hope" (1:3). In every way, their relationship with Jesus Christ is affecting their actions. In spite of severe suffering, they become imitators of Paul, Timothy and Silas (1:6); they model their teachers. Paul has a ministry of encouragement among them, and they, in turn, model encouragement for others.

What were the three marks of true conversion as modeled by the Thessalonian Christians (1:2-10)?

_____

_____

_____

THE MINISTRY OF ENCOURAGEMENT

What were some of the accusations being made against Paul, and why do you think his opponents tried to discredit him (2:1-16)?

_____

_____

_____

_____

_____

In refuting these false accusations, Paul gives us a vivid description of the tenor of his ministry of encouragement among them (2:1-16; 3:6-9):

A. IT IS BASED ON THE WORD OF GOD.

_____

_____

B. IT IS PROMPTED BY A LOVE FOR PEOPLE.

_____

_____

C. IT IS REINFORCED BY PURITY OF LIFESTYLE.

_____

_____

D. IT IS REWARDED BY EVIDENCE OF FAITH AND GROWTH.

_____

_____

THE MESSAGE OF ENCOURAGEMENT

In chapter 4, Paul gives a distinct message of encouragement to the Thessalonians. He begins and ends with exhortations, with comfort mixed in, throughout chapters 4 and 5.

Paul's message to the Thessalonians is twofold:

A. SANCTIFICATION

Paul knows that they are already living to please God, but he urges them to do so more and more. The Greek word which Paul uses to "urge" them to continue living for God — "we . . . urge you" (4:1) — is the same as that for "encouraged." This is Paul's continued message of encouragement. Part of this message is instruction in godly living, which is God's will for every Christian; Paul tells them that it is God's will that they be "sanctified" (4:3).

What does it mean to be sanctified, and what example does Paul give?

_____

_____

_____

_____

_____

Notice 1 Thessalonians 4:6 and 4:8, which say that those who live like the unregenerate, no matter what they claim their relationship with God to be, will be punished, and their rejection of this teaching constitutes rejection of God! This seems very harsh, but it is a vital element in Paul's message of encouragement.

What is the most notable evidence of the sanctified life?

_____

_____

_____

_____

B. SECOND COMING

Actually, the Second Coming has been Paul's sub-theme all along. Notice that every chapter ends with a reference to Christ's second coming (the Parousia), when His presence will again be with His people (1:10; 2:19; 3:13; 4:17; 5:23).

In 1 Thessalonians 4:13 through chapter 5, the message of the Second Coming is integral to everything else. This is a crucial element in our understanding of God's plan of redemption. Christ came the first time to free man from the bondage of sin, to make salvation available to all (even the Gentiles) through His atoning sacrifice, and to secure life through His resurrection for all who believe. The glorious message which Christ declared was that He would come back to consummate God's full plan of redemption — to destroy death, hell, Satan, and all the forces of evil once and for all (the fulfillment of the promise in Genesis 3:15). This is the message of encouragement (comfort and exhortation) in the face of persecution!

What was the misunderstanding in the Thessalonian church concerning the second coming of Christ, and how did Paul deal with it?

_____

_____

_____

_____

Paul does not intend to offer them a timeline by which to gauge the nearness of the Lord's coming. This is why he reminds them that the day will come like "a thief in the night" (5:1-2) — unexpectedly. But, unexpected as that day may be, it should come as no surprise to the Christian (5:4), because we should live every day as if Christ were coming back immediately.

Paul is concerned in chapter 5 with the lifestyle resulting from their expectancy of the Lord's coming. The fact of the Parousia is an encouragement to live the life that God requires.

How should our expectation of Christ's return affect our lifestyles?

_____

_____

_____

_____

The summary of Paul's message of encouragement — a message of sanctification and the Second Coming — is found in in his closing prayer: "May God himself, the God of peace, SANCTIFY you through and through. May your whole spirit, soul and body be kept BLAMELESS at the COMING of our Lord Jesus Christ. The one who calls you is faithful and he will do it" (5:23-24, emphasis added).

God is able to sanctify us wholly and to keep us pure and blameless until Christ returns (cf. Philippians 1:6). Christ is coming back, but we don't have to wait until then to have victory over sin and to be set apart thoroughly unto God. The Christian life that God requires is a possibility NOW. God is faithful, and He will do it.

For personal reflection:

1) How does this letter help you better understand the role of an encourager?
2) If we have a "family" relationship with other Christians, how should that affect our relationship with them?
3) Do you consider yourself to be living a "sanctified" life? Explain.
4) Is the expectation of the second coming of Christ an encouragement to you? In what ways?

For the next lesson . . .

Read all of 2 Thessalonians, or at least the following:
- 2 Thessalonians 1:1-2
- 2 Thessalonians 1:3-12
- 2 Thessalonians 2:1-12
- 2 Thessalonians 2:13-17
- 2 Thessalonians 3:1-5
- 2 Thessalonians 3:6-15
- 2 Thessalonians 3:16-18

2 THESSALONIANS

First Thessalonians was primarily a book of encouragement — of comfort and exhortation to live a sanctified life, though many other general admonitions were mentioned (esp. 1 Thess. 5:12 ff.). Second Thessalonians is more focused and specific. Paul has a definite purpose in mind, something distinctly different from his purpose in writing 1 Thessalonians.

What words does Paul use frequently in this second letter that give us a clue to its purpose?

_____

_____

_____

It's obvious that, throughout this letter, Paul is very concerned about what the Thessalonians believe, what teachings they follow. He is anxious about their faith and is concerned that they follow the truth and are not deceived in any way.

Remember, Paul spent only about six months (some think as little as three weeks) at Thessalonica before being driven away by fierce opposition. He left a young, inadequately discipled church in the midst of persecution and tribulation. His primary concern is that they are not led astray by false teachings or misunderstandings. Paul is emphatic, because he wants them to know . . .

THE TRUTH ABOUT THEIR PERSECUTION

Paul begins this letter by thanking God for his Thessalonian brothers, and he records a direct answer to his prayer of 1 Thessalonians 3:12-13.

How did God answer Paul's prayer?

_____

_____

_____

The Thessalonians' attitude and response to their trials are evidence that God is working among them — He is providing the strength to endure. In fact, God actually is using these trials to enrich their spiritual and moral character, bringing them to perfection. Paul wants them to know this truth about their persecution. God hasn't abandoned them. He still is in control and is using their trials to make them fit for the kingdom of God, that Christ would be glorified in and through them.

THE TRUTH ABOUT GOD'S RETRIBUTION

How easy it would have been for these young Christians to become discouraged. Serving the Lord has brought them hardship, while the wicked apparently have flourished. That's why Paul is careful to share with them the truth about God's justice and the retribution in store when Christ returns. Paul wants them to understand that God *is* just and that a day of reckoning *is* coming.

When does Paul say these events would take place, and what would be the retribution for the just and the unjust (1:5-10)?

_____

_____

_____

_____

_____

THE TRUTH ABOUT CHRIST'S REVELATION

In 1 Thessalonians, Paul corrected some misunderstandings which the Thessalonian Christians had concerning the Second Coming. He expressed to them in that letter the imminence of Christ's coming. But they confused that with the *immediacy* of Christ's coming. Some among them must have been teaching that Christ already had returned and that the completion of the final days was imminent — and this they attributed to Paul. There was a heightened anticipation and emotionalism in Thessalonica. They were undergoing fierce opposition and persecution, so they naturally assumed that the return of Christ was at hand.

Paul doesn't want them to be deceived (2 Thess. 2:3), and he sets out to correct their misunderstanding and to share the truth about Christ's revelation.

> Concerning the COMING of our Lord Jesus Christ and our being GATHERED to him, we ask you brothers, not to become easily unsettled or alarmed by some prophecy, report or letter supposed to have come from us, saying the DAY OF THE LORD has already come (2 Thess. 2:1, emphasis added).

Paul's message is very simple. To a people who are convinced that since they are experiencing tribulation, the final days have been initiated, Paul says they haven't been.

What two things did Paul say must happen first (2:3-4)?

_____

_____

_____

_____

_____

List some of the speculations as to the identity of the "man of lawlessness" (or the Antichrist) and the "restrainer," "the one who now holds [the secret power of the lawlessness] back" (2:3-7).

_____

_____

_____

_____

_____

All attempts to identify this man of lawlessness and the restraining power, and to correlate them with events which already have taken place, only proves that the mystery of lawlessness is already at work and that many "antichrists" already have come. It is a continuation of the enmity expressed in Genesis 3:15 that will come to a head in the last days.

Paul's primary concern is not to gratify the Thessalonians' curiosity concerning these things. He actually gives very little detail about what this man of lawlessness does. Paul's underlying purpose is to show God's unchallenged sovereignty. God is in complete control of circumstances. The Antichrist will be revealed in his *proper time,* but is now being restrained by some force; he doesn't have ultimate power. Everything will happen according to God's timetable. Most importantly, Paul wants the Thessalonians to know that Christ is the victor; the man of lawlessness will be overthrown by the breath of the Lord's mouth (with great ease) at the splendor of His coming (2:8)!

Where will Christians be during the time in which these events take place?

_____

_____

_____

_____

_____

THE TRUTH ABOUT THEIR PRESERVATION

How disturbing to hear about some of these future events and to learn of the condemnation of those who are deceived by the man of lawlessness (2:10-12)! But the Thessalonians need not be distraught; they have been set apart for God through the Holy Spirit and have believed the truth (2:13). Paul's concern is that they CONTINUE in the truth, standing firm (2:15), that they might "share in the glory of our Lord Jesus Christ" (2:14). Paul is concerned about their spiritual preservation.

Paul encourages them with God's faithfulness, that He is able to keep them strong and to protect them from the tumultuous times that lay ahead (2:16-17; 3:3, 5). God has not left them alone!

THE TRUTH ABOUT HIS EXPECTATION

In Paul's previous letter, he had warned the Thessalonians about idleness. Apparently, the problem has not been resolved, but has worsened. Paul makes no concessions in sharing his expectations — concerning those who are idle and the responsibility of the church. Paul reminds the Thessalonians of his never-ceasing labor among them, and that he expects them to follow his example (3:7-10). In fact, the reason he doesn't ask for their help or eat their food without paying for it is for the express purpose of making himself a model for them to follow (3:9).

Paul's rule among them is that if a man is not willing to work, he shouldn't eat. Paul expects everyone to carry his or her own weight and not to take unfair advantage of the generosity of fellow Christians. He urges them to settle down and earn the bread they eat (3:12).

What was Paul's expectation of the church in regard to those who were sinning by their idleness?

_____

_____

_____

_____

_____

For personal reflection:

1) How has God used affliction in your life to strengthen and perfect your faith?

2) Is it difficult to know what the "truth" is today, since so many varying opinions exist? How can you be sure that what you believe is the truth?

3) Do you find it disturbing to think that God will ultimately punish all the wicked? What would be the result if God changed His mind and left the guilty unpunished?

4) What do you think the Thessalonian Christians' response would have been to those who preach today that Christians will never have to go through the tribulation?

For the next lesson . . .

Read all of 1 Timothy.
- 1 Timothy 1:3-20
- 1 Timothy 2:1-15
- 1 Timothy 3:1-16
- 1 Timothy 4:1-16
- 1 Timothy 5:1-25
- 1 Timothy 6:1-10
- 1 Timothy 6:11-21

1 TIMOTHY

Paul's letters to Timothy and Titus, two of his closest companions, are commonly referred to as the "pastoral Epistles." They were written late in Paul's ministry, with 2 Timothy being Paul's final letter before his execution. The Pauline letters we've studied so far have been addressed to churches, but the pastoral Epistles are personal letters to individual pastors, and they are significantly different from Paul's other letters.

List some of the unusual characteristics of these letters:

_____

_____

_____

_____

In 1 Timothy 1:3, we learn that Paul had urged Timothy to stay in Ephesus, where Paul had pastored previously for two years and three months. Timothy, a native of Lystra, possibly had been converted through Paul's ministry on his first missionary journey. On Paul's second visit to Lystra, others spoke very well of Timothy, and Paul was so impressed that he wanted Timothy to join him on his journeys (see Acts 16).

Paul's primary purpose for writing 1 Timothy is stated clearly:

> Although I hope to come to you soon, I am writing you these instructions so that, if I am delayed, you will know how people ought to conduct themselves in God's household, which is the church of the living God, the pillar and foundation of truth (1 Tim. 3:14-15).

Paul's concern is that people know how to conduct themselves in the church — not in a physical building, but in the "household" of believers (God's household). The conduct of Christians is essential because we, the community of believers, are the pillar and foundation of the truth. Our conduct should convey that truth.

Paul's basic concern in this letter is lifestyle. One word sums up the characteristics of Christian conduct: GODLINESS. What is godliness?

_____

_____

_____

_____

GODLINESS IS ROOTED IN SOUND DOCTRINE.

As we've seen throughout Paul's ministry, false teachings abound in his culture. One of Paul's primary objectives in writing this letter is to warn Timothy about these teachings that are contrary to sound doctrine (1:10) and to urge him to combat these right away. The heresies in Ephesus seem to have been a combination of an early form of Gnosticism (cf. Colossians and 1 John), decadent Judaism, and false asceticism (see 1 Timothy 1:4-5, 6-7, 19; 4:1, 7; and 6:3-4, 10, 20-21).

Almost every time Paul mentions a heresy or false doctrine, he associates with it the impure actions or attitudes or the wandering from the faith that inevitably results. The godliness we are to possess as Christians is rooted in sound doctrine and in understanding who God is, what He requires from His people, and what He has provided for us through Christ. How did Paul instruct Timothy about his responsibility in this area?

_____

_____

_____

_____

_____

Paul's concern here is for the conduct of God's people — their godliness — but he continually addresses the importance of sound doctrine in maintaining a God-pleasing lifestyle (chapters 1, 4, 6). Godliness is rooted in sound doctrine.

GODLINESS IS REFINED BY SINCERE WORSHIP

A. PRAYER

Paul begins to show the necessity of prayer in refining our godliness by showing that through prayer we learn what pleases God and what His will is (2:1-8). It is only through prayer that we become co-laborers in the ministry of God, "who wants all men to be saved and to come to a knowledge of the truth" (2:4).

Why is it significant that Paul urged that prayers, requests, intercessions and thanksgiving be made for everyone?

_____

_____

_____

_____

_____

B. PROPRIETY

"Propriety" is conforming to prevailing customs. Often in the New Testament, we see a great concern for the Christian's witness. Women and slaves, especially, are to waive their rights and conform to societal standards willingly, in order to maintain a godly witness. Godliness is actually refined by this humbling submission to the will of God and by centering on Him and His purposes instead of self.

In what areas does Paul address propriety?

_____

_____

_____

_____

_____

GODLINESS IS REPRESENTED BY SELECTED LEADERSHIP.

In chapter 3, Paul gives Timothy some of the qualifications of deacons and overseers. He is not as concerned here with their duties as he is with their lifestyles and character. The leaders in the church always are expected to exemplify what they are called to teach. Paul's purpose in this letter is to share how people are to conduct themselves in God's household (3:15) and that godliness is to be represented by the selected leadership.

List some of the qualifications Paul gives for service as leaders:

_____

_____

_____

_____

_____

GODLINESS IS REALIZED IN SERVANT MINISTRY.

God hasn't called the church to be just the protectors and defenders of doctrine, or just to seek self-edification. He also has called the church to be willing servants, ministering to the needs of others. Godliness has its full realization in servant ministry, and that always involves meeting the needs of others. In chapter 5, Paul gives us just two examples:

A. WIDOWS

_____

_____

_____

B. ELDERS

_____

_____

_____

Paul's whole letter has been building up to this — how godliness can be realized in servant ministry. Godliness is much more than Christian character; it touches every area of our lives until it spills over and begins to touch the lives of others.

Paul had to know that his days were numbered. Timothy was a dear friend, and the Ephesian church also was dear to him. Paul wanted them to know how they should conduct themselves as God's church. They were the pillar and foundation of truth, and their lifestyles should reinforce that truth. They were to be a people characterized by godliness that was rooted in sound doctrine, refined by sincere worship (prayer and propriety), represented by selected leadership, and realized in servant ministry. This still is the code of conduct for the church: GODLINESS.

For personal reflection:

1. Do you think genuine godliness is possible for the average Christian? Do you consider yourself to be a godly person? Explain.

2. Do you find it difficult to pray for unlovable people? Why or why not?

3. How would you rate yourself in the areas of modesty and submission? In what ways do you find it hard to limit your rights?

4. Based on this lesson, what would you say is the number one qualification for church leaders at all levels?

5. What are some specific ways you can put your godliness into action?

For the next lesson . . .

Read all of 2 Timothy.
- 2 Timothy 1:1-18
- 2 Timothy 2:1-13
- 2 Timothy 2:14-26
- 2 Timothy 3:1-9
- 2 Timothy 3:10-17
- 2 Timothy 4:1-8
- 2 Timothy 4:9-22

2 TIMOTHY

Second Timothy contains Paul's last recorded words prior to his death. After his release, around A.D. 62, Paul embarked on a fourth missionary journey (not recorded in Acts) during which he visited Asia Minor, Crete, Greece, and possibly even Spain. It was during these travels that he wrote 1 Timothy and Titus. But, somewhere around A.D. 67 or 68, Paul is again imprisoned in Rome (this time under the wicked Emperor Nero), where Paul wrote 2 Timothy.

How was this second imprisonment different from the first?

_____

_____

_____

_____

No doubt, Paul spends much time remembering all the milestones in his thirty-year ministry and praying for friends, co-workers and the church. Between 2 Timothy 1:3 and 2:14, Paul uses the words "remember," "remind" or "recall" (all having the same root) six times. He has been reflecting, remembering his ministry.

What were some of the things Paul remembered, and what did he want Timothy to remember?

_____

_____

_____

_____

It is difficult to imagine the loneliness and abandonment Paul must feel at this point in his ministry. But how remarkable is the Apostle Paul. In this final letter to his dear friend and co-worker, we see no self-pity, no bitterness, no regrets. Paul remembers the heartaches and the persecution, but he is not consumed by them.

On the contrary, this letter resounds with confidence and assurance. With head held high, Paul marches resolutely forward, shouting, "It was worth it!" We look at Paul in amazement. How can he endure not only the physical suffering, but also the emotional suffering of being abandoned and rejected — even by those who have worked with him — and knowing that death is knocking at his door? His secret is interspersed throughout this Epistle. Paul has . . .

CONFIDENCE IN THE PROVISION OF THE GOSPEL

Paul has an absolute confidence in the truth of the gospel and the necessity of the gospel for salvation. He knows that, apart from Christ, sinful man is lost, separated from God, and without hope. He knows with absolute certainty that he holds in his hands the key to life, restoration to God, and holiness. He has confidence in the provision of the gospel, knowing that it can change lives, heal hearts and bring abundant life, both now and forever. This is the primary reason why Paul can endure. His faith in Christ, as the only means of salvation, never wavers.

CONFIDENCE IN THE POWER OF GOD'S WORD

Paul realizes that he is only a messenger of the gospel — that the real power lies in the Word of God. Though Paul is sure that he will soon face death, he is equally sure that God's Word will never die.

What does Paul reveal to us about the Word of God?

_____

_____

_____

_____

Remember Paul's first letter to the church at Corinth? Over and over he explained that human words of wisdom were foolish, but that God's Word was powerful. Paul's confidence in this fact is never shaken. He knows that God's Word cannot be destroyed or defeated, no matter what happens to him personally. God's Word will endure. "So is my word that goes out from my mouth; it will not return to me empty, but will accomplish what I desire and achieve the purpose for which I sent it" (Isaiah 55:11).

Paul's ministry has been a ministry of the Word. And even though he now has been abandoned and faces death, though heresies threaten the church (2 Tim. 2:17-18), and though it may appear that his life is ending in failure, Paul is not downhearted or discouraged, because he has confidence in the power of the Word of God.

CONFIDENCE IN THE PRESERVATION OF THE CHURCH

Paul knows that God still is actively involved in the life of the church — that God is working in and through the church and is giving them the strength to endure (1:12).

Why was Paul able to face death with confidence and courage (2:11-12; 4:7-8, 18)?

_____

_____

_____

_____

Paul has a deep concern for Timothy and for the entire church. Paul knows he'll be in God's heavenly kingdom soon, and he's probably concerned about the impact his death will have on the church and on Timothy. He wants to encourage them to endure, because the prize is worth any price.

Not only does this letter reveal to us the secret of Paul's endurance during these times, but it also gives to Timothy (and to us) some practical admonitions for enduring and for reaching the goal. Paul tells us how we can be preserved as a church:

A. BE FAITHFUL (chapter 1)

Timothy is to be faithful to sound doctrine and faithful in guarding what has been entrusted to him. He is to be faithful, not wavering — faithful to the truth, faithful in using his gifts, and faithful in guarding those under his care.

B. BE STRONG (2:1-13)

Paul tells Timothy to be strong (2:1). "Strong," in this case, actually means "empowered." The same root is also used in 2 Timothy 1:7, 8 and 4:17.

When Paul tells Timothy to "be strong," Paul knows that it is not something Timothy can do in his own power. The only way Timothy can join in suffering without timidity and have strength in the toughest circumstances is to be empowered by the Spirit of God. Ephesians 1:19 tells us that God has incomparably great power for us who believe. But there is a key to appropriating that power.

What three illustrations does Paul offer in 2 Timothy 2:3-6?

_____

_____

_____

_____

_____

Timothy must be strong — empowered — in order to endure to the end. But Paul illustrates that the only way to have true power in this life is to please God by our lives, to obey God in everything, and to see God through everything.

C. BE HOLY (2:14-26)

Here, Paul refutes early teachings which espoused a spiritual resurrection, but not a physical one. How does Paul characterize the life of holiness in these verses?

_____

_____

_____

_____

In the midst of these instructions to be holy, Paul tells us that despite heresy and opposition, "God's solid foundation stands firm" (2:19). Paul shares these admonitions concerning a righteous and holy life because he is still concerned with the preservation of the church. He has confidence that the true church is a solid foundation that stands firm. God's true church is secure, because they're living lives of holiness.

The key to maintaining the holiness God requires is knowing and applying God's Word (2:15; 2:25-26). Paul knows that the only way the church can stand firm in holiness is to be grounded in the Word of God, fully understanding it and knowing how to use it. Then they will be equipped to combat heresy and will be prepared to do any good work. They will be holy.

D. BE WARNED (chapter 3)

Paul wants Timothy to understand what lies ahead; he wants Timothy to be watchful and forewarned about the persecution to come. Nothing can be quite as unsettling to one's faith as persecution — especially if he mistakenly thinks that being a Christian will shield him from all tribulation. And for this reason, Paul wants Timothy to be warned: "There will be terrible times in the last days" (3:1b).

List some of the characteristics of people during these terrible times that are listed in 2 Timothy 3:2-9:

_____

_____

_____

_____

_____

So, Paul warns Timothy to "have nothing to do with them" (3:5). Paul also warns Timothy (3:12) that persecution awaits everyone who seeks to live a godly life. Paul is concerned about the preservation of the church, and being aware of what is to come helps us to persevere and to endure. We must expect opposition and persecution.

What enables us to endure during times of opposition and persecution?

_____

_____

_____

_____

_____

E. BE PREPARED (chapter 4)

False teachers will come, and people will no longer put up with sound doctrine. To face this opposition successfully, Timothy must be prepared — ready in any situation to speak the needed word of correction, rebuke or encouragement.

Paul is ultimately concerned with the preservation of the church. The church at Ephesus has been entrusted to Timothy's care. If the church is to survive, Timothy must not be timid; he must be faithful, strong, holy, warned and prepared. He must work hard and discharge all the duties of his ministry.

Most of us have wondered at one time or another how we would react if we were facing certain death. Would we be full of fear, anger, or faith? Paul practiced what he preached; he was a living example of what he proclaimed. It was because Paul was faithful, empowered, holy, warned, and prepared that he was able to face his death with confidence and courage instead of with fear and bitterness.

The words of 2 Timothy are the last words Timothy received from Paul. But what wonderful words of encouragement Timothy had as a remembrance! To the very end, Paul was concerned about believers, that they continue in Christ and remain faithful, receiving the reward awaiting them in God's kingdom. God's grace would be sufficient.

For personal reflection:

1) Do you ever find yourself getting discouraged when you face trials and hardships? If so, what do you do?

2) Are you living to please God and to obey Him and see Him in all circumstances? Why is this the ONLY way to experience power?

3) Paul emphasizes the power and authority of the Word of God. How much time do you spend each day reading and meditating on the Bible? What incentive is there to do more?

For the next lesson . . .

Read all of Titus and Philemon.
- Titus 1:1-4
- Titus 1:5-16
- Titus 2:1-15
- Titus 3:1-11
- Titus 3:12-15
- Philemon 1-7
- Philemon 8-25

Paul's Fourth Missionary Journey

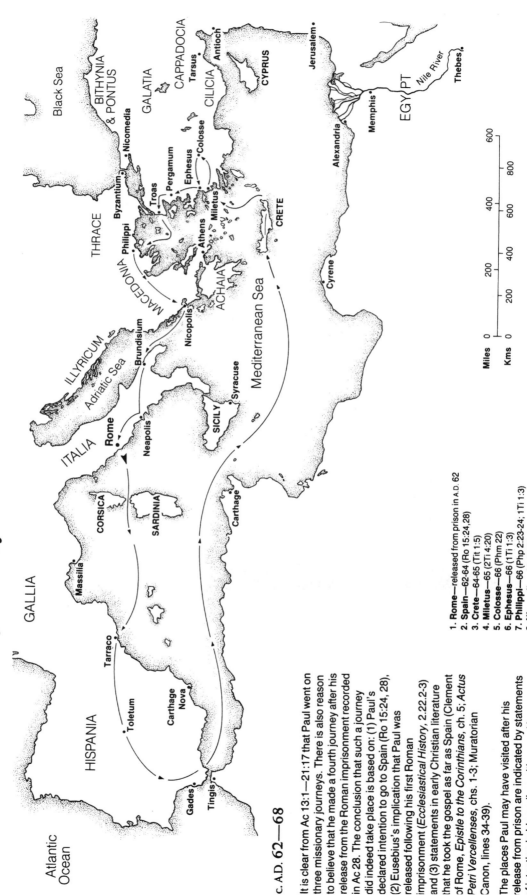

c. A.D. 62—68

It is clear from Ac 13:1—21:17 that Paul went on three missionary journeys. There is also reason to believe that he made a fourth journey after his release from the Roman imprisonment recorded in Ac 28. The conclusion that such a journey did indeed take place is based on: (1) Paul's declared intention to go to Spain (Ro 15:24, 28), (2) Eusebius's implication that Paul was released following his first Roman imprisonment (*Ecclesiastical History*, 2.22.2-3) and (3) statements in early Christian literature that he took the gospel as far as Spain (Clement of Rome, *Epistle to the Corinthians*, 2.22.2-3; *Actus Petri Vercellenses*, chs. 1-3; Muratorian Canon, lines 34-39).

The places Paul may have visited after his release from prison are indicated by statements of intention in his earlier writings and by subsequent mention in the Pastoral Letters. The order of his travel cannot be determined with certainty, but the itinerary at the right seems likely.

1. **Rome**—released from prison in A.D. 62
2. **Spain**—62-64 (Ro 15:24,28)
3. **Crete**—64-65 (Tit 1:5)
4. **Miletus**—65 (2Ti 4:20)
5. **Colosse**—66 (Phm 22)
6. **Ephesus**—66 (1Ti 1:3)
7. **Philippi**—66 (Php 2:23-24; 1Ti 1:3)
8. **Nicopolis**—66-67 (Tit 3:12)
9. **Rome**—67
10. Martyrdom—67/68

TITUS & PHILEMON

Paul's friend, Titus, is mentioned nowhere in the book of Acts, but Paul refers to him thirteen times in his letters, making it clear that Titus was a highly valued and trusted associate, one of Paul's closest companions.

What are some of the facts we learn about Titus?

_____

_____

_____

_____

_____

_____

Following Paul's first Roman imprisonment (see Acts 28), he embarked on a fourth missionary journey, during which he and Titus worked together briefly on the island of Crete. When Paul left, he commissioned Titus to remain in Crete, "that you might straighten out what was left unfinished and appoint elders in every town, as I directed you" (Titus 1:5b).

The dishonesty, gluttony and laziness of the Cretans were proverbial (1:12). Good works are the keynote of this letter, a major concern for a people characterized by laziness, untruthfulness and immorality. But Paul does more than simply list the good works they are expected to do. He gives to Titus almost an entire strategy for establishing the Cretan church in doing what is good.

THE FOUNDATION OF GOOD WORKS

Throughout this short letter, Paul carefully places classic summaries of Christian doctrine, each punctuating his assertion that good works are a logical outcome of a relationship with Christ (1:1-3; 2:11-14; 3:4-8). Paul continually emphasizes the intricate balance between faith and good works — how our lifestyles are evidence of our saving knowledge of the truth.

In all of Paul's writings, he refers to Jesus or God as "Savior" only twelve times, and six of these are in Titus (1:3, 4; 2:10, 13; 3:4, 6). Paul's purpose is to draw our attention to the saving act of Christ that frees us from sin's dominion and allows us to live the righteous life that God requires.

Paul wants the Cretan Christians to understand that "doing what is good" is a necessary corollary to salvation. It is not the *means to* salvation, but it is the *result of* salvation. The foundation of good works is the finished work of Christ, our Savior, when He gave His life as an atonement for our sin. A firm grasp of Christ's work (sound doctrine) compels us to live a holy life, eager to do what is good and to please God.

THE FURTHERANCE OF GOOD WORKS

Why was it necessary for the leadership to model good works (1:7-9)?

_____

_____

_____

_____

_____

The furtherance of good works begins with leadership. Titus 1:10-16 shows the stark contrast between godly leaders and the rebellious deceivers who propagate false doctrines. Paul says that nothing is pure to them, because their minds and consciences are corrupted. Notice their example: "They claim to know God, but by their actions they deny him. They are detestable, disobedient and unfit for doing anything good" (1:16).

In chapter 2, Paul is emphatic in his instructions to Titus that he teach everyone under his care to live lives of good works. Exemplary leadership is necessary for the furtherance of good works, but teaching and training God's people is imperative. Paul knows that if a godly lifestyle ever will be furthered in the ministry in Crete, it will come about only through firm training and teaching. Titus will have to encourage and rebuke with authority, standing on the foundation of the Word of God.

THE FRUITFULNESS OF GOOD WORKS

Why was Paul so concerned that the Cretans display lives of good works and godliness (chapter 3)?

_____

_____

_____

_____

_____

A powerful witness is one fruit of good works, but there is also personal fruit to be reaped from good works. What do Titus 3:8 and 3:14 tell us about the fruitfulness of good works?

_____

_____

_____

_____

_____

_____

_____

God wants us to live full, productive, worthwhile lives. Good works contribute to fruitful, profitable lives. Paul wants Titus to teach those entrusted to him to live lives devoted to doing good, not just because it is the evidence of their salvation, but because Paul wants what's best for them. He wants them to experience productive and fruitful lives as they serve their God and Savior, Jesus Christ. The fruitfulness of good works will be evidenced in their witness as well as their walk.

Titus' task is very difficult, but he's proven himself successful and capable in difficult circumstances before. Paul's letter to his faithful friend and co-laborer serves as an encouragement and offers an outline for accomplishing their goal — to "straighten out what was left unfinished . . ." (1:5) — by (1) understanding and teaching the foundation of good works, (2) seeing to the furtherance of good works by appointing exemplary leaders and teaching a practical lifestyle, and (3) realizing the fruitfulness of good works (witness and walk).

The letter to **PHILEMON** gives a perfect example of putting faith in Christ into action by doing what is good. This letter was written at the same time as the letter to the Colossians, during Paul's first imprisonment in Rome (c. A.D. 60). Philemon was a prominent member of the Colossian church, which met in his home.

What was Paul writing to Philemon about?

_____

_____

_____

_____

_____

_____

Why didn't Paul just condemn the evils of slavery and command Philemon to do what was right?

_____

_____

_____

_____

_____

Before he even mentions Onesimus, Paul lets Philemon know that he has the authority in Christ to order Philemon to do what he ought, but, instead, Paul appeals on the basis of love.
How is this letter an illustration of Christ's love for mankind?

_____

_____

_____

_____

_____

The furtherance of good works is actually the aim of the letter — to teach Philemon (a leader), in a tactful and subtle way, the lifestyle that is the result of a relationship with Christ. Even though this is a personal letter, it is addressed also to Philemon's family and to the church that meets in their home. It is Paul's desire that this be an opportunity for the entire church to learn about this transition from bondage to brotherhood and the social ramifications that will accompany it.

Paul wants this situation to have an impact on the Colossian church as a whole, so that there will be a furtherance of good works, exemplified first in Philemon, a leader in the church.
How is the fruitfulness of good works seen throughout this letter?

_____

_____

_____

_____

_____

In the letter to Titus, we saw instructions from Paul for Titus' ministry in Crete. This is followed by Paul's letter to Philemon, written about five years earlier, but beautifully exemplifying the principles taught in Titus. It is a personal appeal, a letter of subtle instruction, where we see Paul practicing beforehand what he preaches to Titus. His method has been tried and tested.

For personal reflection:

1) Do you agree or disagree that good works are a logical outcome of a relationship with Christ?

2) Do you ever find it difficult to do what God wants you to do? Why do you think this is so? What are the benefits of obedience?

3) Paul had to approach Philemon about a most delicate situation. How can Paul's example help us when we need to correct or rebuke others?

For the next lesson . . .

Read all of Hebrews, or at least the following:

- Hebrews 1:1-4; 2:1–4:13
- Hebrews 4:14–6:12
- Hebrews 7:1–8:7; 8:13
- Hebrews 9:1–10:4; 10:19-31
- Hebrews 11:1-40
- Hebrews 12:1-29
- Hebrews 13:1-25

HEBREWS

The author, date and recipients of the book of Hebrews might be a mystery, but what isn't a mystery is the overwhelming significance of the book. Hebrews is one of the most exciting books in the whole New Testament. In these thirteen chapters, the intricate connection between the Old and New Testaments is spelled out carefully for us.

What was the purpose of all the Old Testament ceremonial laws?

_____

_____

_____

_____

_____

During the first century, there seems to have been much confusion, particularly among Jewish Christians, as to the role of Judaistic ceremony within Christianity. Centuries of tradition were hard to abandon. This book was written to a group of Jewish Christians, possibly even former priests, who were wavering between continuing with Christianity or reverting to Judaism. Why were they tempted to return to Judaism?

_____

_____

_____

_____

_____

The author gives five warnings of the consequences of rejecting the completed work of Christ for the inferior Judaism. What are they?

1. 2:1-4 _____

2. 3:7–4:13 _____

3. 5:11–6:20 _____

4. 10:19-39 _____

5. 12:14-29 _____

Numerous times the author uses the words "better," "superior," and "perfect" to describe Christ's person, priesthood, provision, etc. The Old Testament types (e.g. rituals, worship, sacrifices) are constantly referred to as "shadows." Christ supersedes the Old Testament ritual. He is the culmination of it all, the final climax toward which everything has pointed. In every way, He is superior to what has been embraced in Judaism.

THE SUPERIORITY OF THE PERSON OF CHRIST

In the first seven chapters, the author shows with absolute certainty the unchallenged superiority of the person of Christ. Christ is superior to the prophets (1:1); the angels (1:4-14; 2:5 ff.); Moses (3:2-6); Joshua (4:8); and Aaron and his priesthood (4:14–5:10). The comparisons between these and Christ are significant, because each of these has held a position of great importance in the religion of the Jews. These have comprised the framework of Jewish worship. It is important that the readers understand that Christ is vastly superior to all of these. In every way He is superior, because of His NATURE:

A. HIS DEITY

_____

_____

_____

B. HIS HUMANITY

_____

_____

_____

What is significant about Jesus' priesthood? In what ways was it similar to that of Melchizedek?

_____

_____

_____

_____

_____

In every way, Christ's priesthood is superior to the Levitical priesthood because of who He is. It was necessary for Christ to come under a different order of priesthood — a better one — because of the absolute inadequacy of the former (7:11-12, 18-19).

THE SUPERIORITY OF THE WORK OF CHRIST

A. A BETTER COVENANT

Whereas the Levitical priests were the mediators between God and man under the old covenant, "Jesus has become the guarantee of a better covenant" (7:22b).

Why was a new covenant necessary?

_____

_____

_____

_____

_____

To those thinking of reverting back to the provisions of the old covenant, the author shows that the old covenant is no longer in effect. The new covenant supersedes it and makes it obsolete. But the new covenant is superior to the old, because it gives us the power to live the life God requires, and it restores the fellowship with God that was broken at the Fall.

B. A BETTER SACRIFICE

How does Christ's sacrifice contrast with the Levitical sacrifices of the Old Testament?

_____

_____

_____

_____

_____

In a sense, the blood of animals never could be an adequate substitute for the blood required of a man, because animal sacrifices are so finite — needing to be offered constantly — and we are made in the image of God. But Christ, as a sinless man — 100% humanity — could fully offer himself as the substitute for man's sin. And as the Son of God — 100% deity — He could give himself once and for all for the sins of every person for all time, obtaining eternal redemption (9:12).

At the time the book of Hebrews was written, the priests were still performing their ritual sacrifices endlessly, in a futile attempt to atone for the sins of man. But Christ was the perfect sacrifice that brought all the sacrifices of the past to an end, because His sacrifice was superior to them all. Christ's work is infinitely superior — "It is finished!"

THE SUPERIORITY OF THE LIFE IN CHRIST

The Christian life is characterized here by one prevailing element — faith. Looking for salvation through the ceremonial law alone did not necessitate faith. The tendency of many Jews was to "go through the motions" of sacrificial ritual and know that they had followed the rules which would result in salvation. This is why ritual and ceremony always have been so attractive and were probably a contributing factor in these Jewish Christians' desire to revert to Judaism.

But the life in Christ is superior, because it is a life of faith. Chapter 11, the "hall of fame" for the faithful, gives us examples from the Old Testament, showing that the life of faith always has been required. These heroes of the faith were confident of the reward. They all trusted God to turn their present troubles into ultimate victory. Why are these examples given in chapter 11?

_____

_____

_____

_____

_____

_____

_____

Christ is the "author and perfecter of our faith" (12:2). And it is faith in Him that enables us to persevere and to live a holy life. Chapters 12 and 13 are replete with practical applications of the Christian life, a life superior to any other. What kind of life does faith enable us to live?

— A life of love for others (13:1-7)

— A life of courage (13:9-14)

— A life of praise to God (13:15-21)

God never intended for Judaism and Christianity to exist side by side, presenting two ways of salvation. To Jewish Christians who were sitting on the fence between Judaism and Christianity, the author of Hebrews spells out the dire consequences of returning to the former, obsolete form of worship. The entire Old Testament — with all its ceremonies, rituals and regulations — was intended to point Israel to Christ, that they might fully understand the work of Christ. After learning, or realizing, the superiority of the work accomplished through Christ, it is hard to imagine that anyone would choose to abandon the perfect sacrifice and mediator in favor of a futile, imperfect, unending sacrificial system.

To those fearful of persecution for following Christ, the author says, "It's worth it!" For those disappointed because of the lack of ritual and tradition in this new form of worship, the author points out that the glory of worship is not in the *means* of worship, but in the *object* of worship. The glory of the Temple worship system never could approach the glory of Jesus Christ. He is superior!

For personal reflection:

1) Why do you think so many people today are drawn to ritual, tradition and liturgy in worship? What place do you think such worship has in today's culture?

2) How does the book of Hebrews help you to understand better why God instituted the ceremonial law?

3) How has Christ's sacrifice affected your life? In what ways are you living a life of faith?

For the next lesson . . .

Read all of James.
- James 1:1-18
- James 1:19-27
- James 2:1-25
- James 3:1-12
- James 3:13–4:12
- James 4:13–5:6
- James 5:7-20

JAMES

The author of this book introduces himself simply as "James, a servant of God and of the Lord Jesus Christ" (1:1a). It always has been recognized that the Apostle James died too early to have written this letter — he was martyred in A.D. 44. Most agree now that the author of this letter was James, the half-brother of Jesus, the son of Joseph and Mary. Here is what we know about James:

— He was an unbeliever prior to the Resurrection (John 7:5; Mark 3:21);

— Jesus appeared to him following the Resurrection (1 Corinthians 15:7);

— According to Galatians 1:19 and 2:9, and Acts 12:17, James became a leader of the Jewish-Christian church at Jerusalem. He presided over the Council of Jerusalem recorded in Acts 15, which dealt with the freedom of Gentile Christians from the law. In fact, it was James who delivered the address outlining the express areas of the law which the Gentile Christian should be required to keep in order to avoid being a stumbling block (see Acts 15:13-21).

It's notable that in James' Epistle he refers or alludes to the Old Testament 22 times in 108 verses, and there are also 15 allusions to the Sermon on the Mount. As a leader in the Jerusalem church writing to Jews, we would expect much reference to the Old Testament, the only Scripture they had. But Christ's teaching in the Sermon on the Mount was the fulfillment of the law. James ties the two together uniquely to show his Jewish brothers (Christians) that they still have a "law" to obey — the "perfect law."

Although we cannot be sure, some scholars suggest that, because there is no mention in this letter of the events of the Jerusalem Council, the book of James may have been written prior to A.D. 50, which would make it the earliest of all the New Testament writings, with the possible exception of Galatians. It was written at a time when the church was still almost entirely Jewish. This is why James addresses his letter "to the twelve tribes scattered among the nations" (1:16). This "pastor from afar" penned his letter to his scattered flock to teach, rebuke, and encourage them to continue to live a life of faith — not just intellectual assent, but honest, life-changing faith.

How do James and Paul differ in their use of the word "faith"?

_____

_____

_____

_____

THE PERFECTION OF FAITH (1:2-18; 2:14-25)

A. BY WHAT WE ENDURE

God never has promised Christians immunity from trials and tribulations. And none know this better than James' readers, who probably were present at the stoning of Stephen and now are undergoing great persecution themselves. James says that trials actually play a vital role in the development of Christian character.

How can trials perfect our faith?

_____

_____

_____

_____

_____

_____

B. BY WHAT WE DO

James explains how hypocritical it is to "talk the talk," but not to "walk the walk" (2:14-25). A faith without obedience and consecration to God is really no faith at all. James gives the examples of Abraham and Rahab, whose actions proved their faith and led to their blessing and deliverance. One verse in this passage (2:14-25) helps us to understand how all this fits in: "You see that his faith and his actions were working together, and his faith was made COMPLETE by what he did" (2:22, emphasis added).

What we do completes — makes whole and brings to maturity — our faith. If our faith in Christ is lacking obedience to His Word, it is incomplete, immature and imperfect.

THE PRODUCT OF FAITH (1:19–2:13; chapters 3–5)

Remember, the focus of this letter is not on works, but on genuine faith that results in works. James is concerned that his readers' faith be mature and complete. Obedience always increases our faith, though we usually want it to happen the other way around. We say, "Give me more faith, and I will be more obedient." But God says, "Be more obedient, and I will increase your faith." James gives practical admonitions for living the Christian life, showing us that how we live is the product of our faith.

How does James 1:19 summarize the entire letter?

_____

_____

_____

_____

_____

How should our faith be evidenced . . .

A. . . . TOWARD OTHERS? (1:27; 2:1-17)

_____

_____

_____

_____

If we have true faith, the product will be mercy, compassion, and active involvement in meeting the needs of the poor. In every way, our faith should affect our attitudes and actions towards others.

B. . . . TOWARD SELF? (chapter 3; 4:13-16)

_____

_____

_____

_____

C. . . . TOWARD GOD? (chapters 4–5)

_____

_____

_____

_____

THE POWER OF FAITH

Faith in Jesus Christ gives us the capacity to endure, frees us from sin, and allows us to obey and to overcome temptation. Because of this, we understand the infinite value God places on every individual, which allows us to show mercy and love toward all, and inspires us to work with them for our perfection. We also may conquer what seems unconquerable — the tongue — and may have supernatural wisdom and the power to say no to the world and yes to God.

James tells us that the prayer offered in faith makes the sick person well. (Yet even here, the power of faith is appropriated by what we do — praying and anointing with oil.) James says that confession of sin brings healing, both physical and spiritual. Elijah was used to doing the miraculous through prayer. He was a man "just like us," but with great faith. There is a tremendous resource of power in prayer, and it is the result of faith. That same power is available to us.

Fourteen times, James uses the verb or noun (both with the same root) for "judge": we will "be judged by the law that gives freedom" (2:12); teachers "will be judged more strictly" (3:1); Jesus is the "Judge"

(4:12; 5:9); we will "fall under judgment" (5:12) if our integrity is found to be wanting (having to swear in order for someone to believe the truth of our statements). Why do you think James emphasizes this idea of judgment?

_____

_____

_____

_____

_____

_____

The message of this letter is timeless. We will be judged. Our Christian conduct, today as always, should be above reproach. As Christians, our lives should be touched by our faith in every aspect.

For personal reflection:

1) Think back over your life as a Christian. Have your greatest times of growth been during easy times or during difficult trials? Explain.

2) Are you quick to listen, slow to speak and slow to become angry? If not, how can you become that way?

3) How conscious are you of the needs of those around you? In what ways does your faith affect what you do with your time and resources?

4) Pray that God would give you a singleness of heart and that your friendship would be with Him instead of with the world. Pray also that God would increase your faith as you determine to obey Him in every area of your life.

For the next lesson . . .

Read all of 1 and 2 Peter, or at least the following:
- 1 Peter 1:3-9; 1:13–2:12
- 1 Peter 2:13–3:9; 3:13-16
- 1 Peter 4:1-19
- 1 Peter 5:1-13
- 2 Peter 1:3-21
- 2 Peter 2:1-22
- 2 Peter 3:1-18

1 & 2 PETER

W̲ho was the author of these two letters, and what do we know about him?

_____

_____

_____

Although Peter is described in the book of Acts as being primarily an Apostle to the Jews, it is evident that Peter's two letters were written (at least) to Gentiles (1 Pet. 2:10; 4:3). Both letters were written to encourage and exhort Christians in the midst of trying times. First Peter shows the response of the church to hostility from without, and 2 Peter, the response to heresy from within.

RESPONSE TO HOSTILITY FROM WITHOUT (1 Peter)

SUFFERING is the main theme which runs through 1 Peter. Though the outbreak of persecution under Nero had not been fully realized yet, Christians in various places were undergoing persecution of sorts from zealous Jews and pagan contemporaries. Peter knew that the hostility they were encountering at this time was only a foretaste of what was to come, and he sought to prepare them and to teach them the proper response to hostility.

A. SALVATION (1:1-12)

The foundation and hope of the Christian life is salvation (1:3-4, 9, 10-12). First Peter begins with salvation, because it is impossible to stand firm in times of persecution, great or small, without a saving relationship with Jesus Christ and an understanding of that salvation. Final salvation will be culminated when Christ is revealed (1:5, 7). The salvation we now possess is not a salvation from the trials of life, but from the power and consequences of sin.

B. SEPARATION (1:13–2:12)

Why did Peter refer to his readers as strangers or aliens?

_____

_____

_____

_____

_____

To survive persecution and hostility, God's people have to realize that their home is not here. We do not live like the world because we do not belong to this world. We are a separate and holy people who do not conform to the law of a sinful world, but who follow the law of a holy God. Peter's readers need to remember this very high calling in order to stand firm.

C. SUBMISSION

This is the key response to hostility. In the Greek, forms of the word "submission" are used some sixteen times in 1 Peter. Christians must learn to be submissive to authority, not because the authority itself is always commendable, but because beiing submissive refines our Christian character.

How do we know that submission doesn't mean unquestioned or unqualified compliance?

_____

_____

_____

_____

_____

These Christians to whom Peter writes, who are scattered throughout northern and western Turkey, are facing trials and soon will face great persecution. They will have to be firm in their standards, yet submissive to authorities — not reckless, violent or subversive.

D. SUFFERING

Peter finally gets to the heart of his message and addresses Christian suffering (3:8). It is only as we live a life of salvation, separation, and submission that we are able to stand under suffering.

How is 1 Peter 3:15 a key to withstanding suffering?

_____

_____

_____

_____

_____

Peter points to the return of Christ as the foundation of hope for Christians undergoing suffering (1:5, 7, 13; 2:12; 4:7, 13). The only way to withstand suffering is to keep our eyes fixed on Jesus and His glory to be revealed. When our focus is on Christ, it keeps everything else in life in perspective; we know the end is in sight. Our goal is not a trouble-free life, but eternal life in Christ.

E. SERVICE

Peter encourages these Christians in their service (4:7-11). Suffering should not consume them. They should be clear-minded and self-controlled, loving one another, offering hospitality, and using their spiritual gifts to serve one another so that God may be praised. Peter encourages elders to be shepherds of God's flock (5:2), serving willingly as overseers, "eager to serve."

Satan often uses trials and suffering to try to undermine our faith and destroy us. But the resounding call is to stand firm (5:9, 12). God will see us through (5:10). As a roaring lion, the Devil may attack us from without by open hostility, but 2 Corinthians 11:14 tells us that he also "masquerades as an angel of light." Sometimes Satan's attacks are more deceptive and besiege us from within the church through false teachings. This is the focus of **2 PETER.**

RESPONSE TO HERESY FROM WITHIN (2 Peter)

The key word in 2 Peter is KNOWLEDGE. Forms of the word occur some sixteen times, because it is the knowledge of God and of His Word that alert us to false doctrines and fruitless lifestyles. A proper knowledge of God will lead to three responses:

A. CULTIVATION OF CHRISTIAN CHARACTER

What virtues does Peter tell his readers to add to their faith?

_____

_____

_____

_____

_____

_____

The closer we walk to God in obedience and submission, truly desiring to cultivate our Christian character, the more intimately we will know God. And it is that knowledge that will keep us from falling away when we are bombarded with deceptive philosophies.

B. CONDEMNATION OF FALSE TEACHERS (2:1-18)

Even though these false teachers would advocate a promiscuous lifestyle, peddling made-up stories and exploiting their "converts," they still would pose a threat to the immature Christians who were just escaping the error of the world. That's why Peter is so concerned about their growth in the knowledge of Jesus Christ. A little truth mixed with error can be devastating.

But Peter reminds us of the fate of these false teachers (2:4-10): if God didn't spare the angels when they sinned, or the people in Noah's day before the flood, or the inhabitants of Sodom and Gomorrah, He will not spare these false teachers either, but will hold them for the day of judgment.

C. CONFIDENCE IN THE LORD'S RETURN

Peter warns these Christians of false teachings yet to come, when scoffers will deny that God will intervene in history. Why does God seem to be so slow in returning?

_____

_____

_____

_____

_____

Our confidence in the Lord's return should motivate us to be pure in the way we live now (3:11-12, 14).

Heretics always have and always will attempt to undermine the true church. We must be students of God's Word in order to know what is true. And no matter how bleak the world situation, we must never let the world shake our confidence in the promises of God. He has promised that a day of judgment is coming and that a new heaven and new earth will be created. The knowledge of this enables us to endure and inspires us to obey and to live holy and godly lives.

These two letters from Peter show the Christian's response to hostility from without and to heresy from within. Together, Peter's epistles form a Christian survival guide. It is possible not to fall, but only with a saving relationship with Christ, which is evidenced by an obedient, holy life, growing in the knowledge of Christ. It is adequate preparation _before_ the battle begins that ensures the victory. We, just like Peter's readers, must be prepared.

For personal reflection:

1) In what ways have you had to suffer persecution and suffering for your faith in Christ?

2) Why is it so important to cultivate a godly, holy life? Are you trying to do that? If so, what resources are you drawing upon?

3) What "false teachers" have you encountered? According to Peter, how are you to deal with them?

For the next lesson . . .

Read all of 1, 2, 3 John and Jude, or at least the following:

- ■ 1 John 1:5–2:11
- ■ 1 John 2:15-17; 3:1-24
- ■ 1 John 4:1-21
- ■ 1 John 5:1-21
- ■ 2 John 4-11
- ■ 3 John 2-12
- ■ Jude 1-25

1, 2, 3 JOHN & JUDE

It is without question that John, "the disciple whom Jesus loved," is the author of the three Epistles that bear his name. What are some of the similarities between John's gospel and his letters?

_____

_____

_____

_____

_____

_____

You may remember that John's gospel was written much later than the other Gospels, probably A.D. 85 to 90, and it was intended to supplement what Christians already knew about Christ through the apostolic teachings and the other Gospel accounts. John's gospel portrayed Jesus as the Son of God, making it readily apparent that He was equal with God the Father. The deity of Christ was central.

Some believe that John's first epistle was a letter written as a sermon and was intended to accompany his gospel. The two books certainly complement one another in purpose. The Gospel of John was written to unbelievers, that they might BELIEVE that Jesus Christ is the Son of God, and by believing might have life (see John 20:31). First John was written to those who already believed so they would be certain that they did have that life (see 1 John 5:13). In keeping with these purposes, the Gospel of John contained "signs" to evoke faith, and the Epistle of 1 John is replete with tests by which to judge that faith.

What was the historical situation at the time in which 1 John was written, and what influence did it have on what John wrote?

_____

_____

_____

_____

_____

_____

What were the predominant teachings of the Gnostics, especially of Cerinthus, who lived in Ephesus while John did?

_____

_____

_____

_____

Some commentators believe that each time John uses the phrases "if we claim," "if we say," "the one who says," etc., he is referring to gnostic teachings or practices, which makes it easier to account for the tone of the letter. John is writing to his "dear children" who already know the truth (2:21), and yet his words seem to be a harsh rebuke of sin among them. But, understanding the circumstances which threaten them helps us to see 1 John for what it is: a warning for these precious saints in John's care. His first concern is not so much to refute the false teachers as it is to protect his readers and to establish them in their Christian faith and life.

COMMIT TO THE FAITH

Notice John's warnings in 1 John 2:24, 26 and 3:7. John's primary concern is that his readers be committed to the faith. They are to be steadfast and firm, fully committed to Jesus Christ.

One of the striking characteristics of 1 John is its use of contrasts. Everything is either black or white to John; there is no gray. You are walking either in light or in darkness. You either have Christ or you don't. John doesn't want them to be confused. He wants them to KNOW what it means to be a Christian and to have the assurance that they are indeed saved. In fact, John uses forms of the two Greek words for "know" forty-two times in this letter. John's great emphasis is on the difference between the genuine Christian and the false, and how to discern between the two. And he gives three basic tests, which are interspersed throughout the letter, by which to determine the authenticity of their faith:

A. THE DOCTRINAL TEST

_____

_____

B. THE MORAL TEST

_____

_____

C. THE SOCIAL TEST

_____

_____

These three tests should be applied whenever we are unsure of those who are trying to teach us about Christ. But we also should apply them to ourselves. Christians are characterized by faith in the truth, holiness in conduct, and love for the brethren. All three of these tests must be passed. Gnosticism in Ephesus failed all three!

What reassurance for these Christians to have a test by which to judge false teachers and by which to be certain of their own relationship with Christ. John's concern is that they KNOW these things, not just intellectually, but also experientially — that they COMMIT TO THE FAITH, because the reward would be life (5:12).

CONTINUE IN THE FAITH

SECOND AND THIRD JOHN also were written c. A.D. 90 by the Apostle John. Though they are the shortest of the New Testament letters, they give us insight into the circumstances of the first-century church.

Both deal with the subject of showing hospitality to traveling missionaries. As the missionary fervor of the early church grew, itinerant missionaries increasingly became dependent on the generosity of fellow Christians for lodging and meals when they taught in a certain town. But this hospitality was open to abuse, since false teachers, posing as Christians, also would expect such courtesies. Second and Third John address this aspect of hospitality, as well as the themes we saw in 1 John:

— 2 John

_____

_____

_____

_____

— 3 John

_____

_____

_____

_____

Second and Third John show for us the precepts of 1 John put into practice. They show us how to CONTINUE in the faith by not advancing the cause of false teachers and by working together for the truth through showing love and hospitality to the brethren. In each letter, John encourages his readers to CONTINUE (2 John 8-9; 3 John 3).

CONTEND FOR THE FAITH

Now we come to the final General Epistle. The book of **JUDE** was written by Jude, the younger half-brother of Jesus and the brother of James, around A.D. 80, some ten years earlier than John's epistles. The infiltration of false doctrines is a very grievous problem in the early church. Jude describes these false teachers as "godless men who changed the grace of God into a license for immorality and deny Jesus Christ . . ." (Jude 4). According to Jude, what is the fate of these false teachers?

_____

_____

_____

_____

_____

_____

Understanding the fate of those who teach false doctrines, as well as the fate of those who believe them, makes Jude's appeal all the more imperative: "I felt I had to write and urge you to CONTEND FOR THE FAITH that was once for all entrusted to the saints" (v. 3b, emphasis added).

Many of us are willing to commit to the faith and continue in the faith, but Jude reminds us that we are also to *contend for* the faith. It is our duty to fight against sin, heresy, corruption and division, and to rescue those on the verge of destruction.

This concludes our study of all the Epistles. These letters, from Romans to Jude, were written to teach us how to live the Christian life, explaining how theology and lifestyle go hand in hand. God's plan for the Christian life has been unfolded.

For personal reflection:

1) Of the three tests to determine the genuineness of faith, which do you think is the most difficult to pass? Why?

2) How should we go about "contending" for the faith? Does that mean we should fight over doctrinal and moral issues?

3) Do you have the witness of the Spirit that you are a child of God? If so, pray for the grace to continue in the faith. If not, then "pray through" for the personal assurance of salvation as attested by the Holy Spirit.

For the next lesson . . .

Read Revelation 1–5.
- Revelation 1:1-8
- Revelation 1:9-20
- Revelation 2:1-17
- Revelation 2:18–3:6
- Revelation 3:7-22
- Revelation 4:1-11
- Revelation 5:1-14

REVELATION
(PART 1)

Part of the difficulty with this book lies in John's descriptions of strange visions and unimaginable scenes. How unusual that the title, "Revelation," or "Apocalypse" (from the first word in the text), means "a disclosure or unveiling." This book wasn't intended to hide the events of the future, but to make them clear and understandable.

There are at least four viewpoints from which to interpret the book of Revelation:

_____

_____

_____

_____

_____

_____

Here are some principles to keep in mind throughout this study:

1. **Much of Revelation is symbolic.**
2. **Visions in Revelation are not necessarily in chronological order.**
3. **Revelation is a continuation of God's plan of redemption.**
4. **Much of Revelation was understandable to the original readers.**

As with any book of the Bible, the first concern is always to determine its meaning to the original readers. Revelation is addressed "To the seven churches in the province of Asia" (1:4), which are listed in Revelation 1:11 as Ephesus, Smyrna, Pergamum, Thyatira, Sardis, Philadelphia and Laodicea. These were real churches facing real problems, and they were in need of the message of this book. No matter how relevant Revelation is to us today, it was intended first for these seven churches, who must have understood much of its symbolism.

Here is the historical background. The time is around A.D. 95, when the wicked emperor Domitian is nearing the end of his reign. The Roman government is beginning to enforce its long-held cult of emperor worship. Domitian is the first emperor to demand homage while he is still alive. The Christians' unwillingness to acknowledge Caesar as Lord instead of Christ leads to their widespread persecution. We know from this book that John has been exiled to Patmos and that some Christians have been martyred (2:13), while others are imprisoned. Hostility is increasing.

This book was written to encourage Christians to stand firm because God was in control, no matter how things seemed. This is the message the early church would have gleaned readily from Revelation. John uses the word "throne" forty-seven times in Revelation (a word used only sixty-two times in the entire New Testament), showing that God's throne is above every throne, even Domitian's. In Revelation 1:5, John reassures the church that Christ is "the ruler of the kings of the earth." They should not compromise, but should keep pressing on to win the prize.

A VISION OF A STRUGGLING CHURCH

After a voice tells John to write down on a scroll all that he has seen and to send it to the seven churches, John turns and sees seven golden lampstands, which verse 20 tells us are the seven churches. John is all too familiar with the plight of these churches. But the glory of his vision is that Christ is among the churches. He is in their midst; they are not alone. In each of the letters to these churches in chapters 2 and 3, Christ says, "I know your deeds" (or similar words) a total of ten times. Jesus is acquainted intimately with every aspect of these churches, because He is in their midst.

Summarize the messages to these seven churches.

_____

_____

_____

_____

_____

_____

_____

Each of these churches has been struggling in its own way — either from external persecution and slander, or from internal compromise or indifference. But the message is clear: Christ has not abandoned them. John sees Christ among the churches, and Christ himself still calls each of the erring churches to repent (2:5, 16, 21; 3:3, 19). They are not beyond restoration. To each church, Christ sets forth the promise and reward for faithfulness.

What was the prerequisite for overcoming?

_____

_____

_____

_____

_____

Notice that each of the promises is made on an individual basis — to "HIM/HE who overcomes." The final comment to each church is, "HE who has an ear, let HIM hear what the Spirit says to the churches" (2:7, 11, 17, 29; 3:6, 13, 22, emphasis added). These are real admonitions to specific churches, but they serve as warnings to us as individuals. Our salvation is independent of the "temperature" or steadfastness of the particular church we attend. There is a *personal* responsibility to overcome and to gain the prize.

And this is what Christ turns our attention to at the end of each letter — each of us must listen to what the Spirit says to all these churches. We must examine ourselves. Suffering from a lack of love or from persecution, poverty, affliction, doctrinal and moral compromise, mediocrity, and apathy all can affect individuals as well as churches. The seven churches may not be representative of churches throughout history, but of individual struggles throughout history. The church may be struggling, but we as individuals have the choice to stand firm and/or repent. We can overcome. In Christ, we *shall* overcome!

A VISION OF A SOVEREIGN GOD

How does John describe Christ in chapter 2?

_____

_____

_____

_____

_____

After the bleak look at the struggling church, John puts everything into perspective as we enter chapter 4. The picture of the struggling church fades to that of the glorious throne of God as John is invited to heaven to see the divine perspective: God is ultimately in control of everything that is happening; He is sovereign. He is Lord of all.

A VISION OF A SEALED SCROLL

Chapter 5 is actually the introduction to, and precedent for, chapters 6 through 20. With this chapter, John begins to see events which must take place in the future (although he often darts between past, present and future events, viewing them from different perspectives). He sees a scroll in the right hand of the one who sits on the throne.

What was written on the scroll, and why was no man able to open it?

_____

_____

_____

_____

Our greatest frustration as human beings is our complete inability either to foreknow or to control human destiny. There is a sense of helplessness as we struggle through life. Some in John's day even may have been thinking that Rome held their destiny and the destiny of the world in its hand.

But here we see that God holds man's destiny in His hand. And there is only one who is counted worthy to open the scroll, only one who can reveal what is to come and can set these things in motion — Jesus Christ, the Lamb of God.

Why was the Lamb able to open the scroll?

_____

_____

_____

_____

_____

What does John see that symbolizes our prayers, and why would this be significant to his readers?

_____

_____

_____

_____

John keeps everything in perspective through the sharing of his visions. The promise is heralded from the outset in Revelation 5:10: Those purchased by the Lamb will "reign on the earth." There will be ultimate vindication and triumph for the people of God. Remember John's audience. They have been struggling and suffering at the hands of the Roman emperor. Persecution and martyrdom threaten them. But Christ has secured the victory for them. In the end, it is the church who will reign, not Rome. All of the destiny of the world is held in Christ's hand, not the emperor's. In the next lesson, we'll see the destiny of the world unfolded as the Lamb opens the seals.

Of what is the book of Revelation ultimately a revelation?

_____

_____

_____

_____

For John's contemporaries who were withstanding intense pressures to worship the emperor, or who may have been wavering in the face of persecution, John's "Revelation" points to Jesus Christ, who hasn't abandoned them, who promises eternal life to those who overcome, who is in control over all creation, and who holds in His hand the destiny of the world.

For personal reflection:

1) Of the various methods of interpretation of Revelation, with which are you most familiar?

2) Why is it important to keep this book in historical context?

3) Do you ever feel as if you're struggling all alone and that the world is "winning"? What do you do with that feeling?

4) What encouragement do you find for your own life in the first five chapters of Revelation?

For the next lesson . . .

Read Revelation 6–19, or at least the following:

- Revelation 6:1–7:4; 7:13-17
- Revelation 8:1–9:21
- Revelation 10:1-7; 11:1-19
- Revelation 12:1-17; 14:1-20
- Revelation 15:1–16:21
- Revelation 17:1-17
- Revelation 18:1-4; 19:6-21

The Seven Churches of Revelation

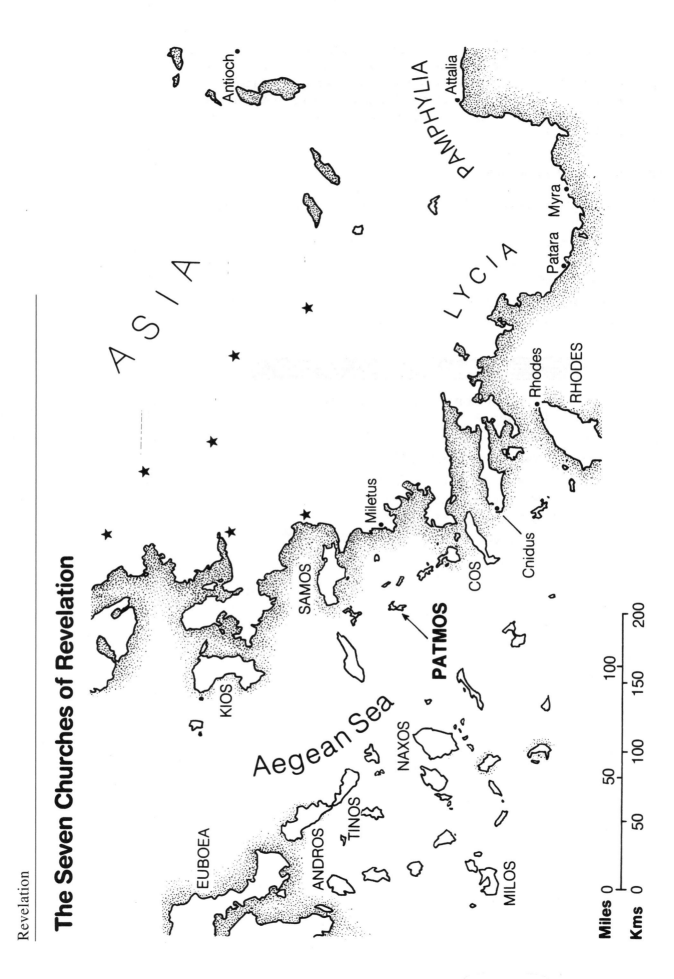

REVELATION
(PART 2)

Chapters 6 through 19 of Revelation unfold for John and for us the destiny of mankind revealed through the opening of the seven seals. Notice the repetition of events in these chapters:

   1. The fall of Babylon

_____

_____

   2. Cosmic disturbances and the upheaval of the earth

_____

_____

   3. God's triumph over evil and the gathering of His people for reward, with judgment for the wicked

_____

_____

Each of these passages describes the same events. Instead of these visions being in chronological order and following each other in time, they all are actually ending with the same cataclysmic events. Each vision takes us to the end of time, to the Day of the Lord prophesied about in the Old and New Testaments. Each successive vision steps back into the preceding vision to elaborate on or to elucidate certain aspects of it, as if John is looking from a different perspective or is focusing on a different angle. One possible way of understanding the chronology of these visions is diagrammed at the end of the lesson.

How all these events fit together is not as important as the final outcome. No matter from what perspective John views the events of human destiny, the results are always the same. Let's look again at the final events of the seals, trumpets and bowls:

   — The last trumpet

_____

_____

_____

— The harvest of the earth

_____

_____

_____

— The wedding supper of the lamb

_____

_____

_____

All through the Old Testament, the final Day of the Lord was associated with signs in the heavens, earthquakes, mountains being leveled, islands fleeing, etc. (see Joel 2:10, 30-31; Ezekiel 32:7; Isaiah 13:10; 24:23; 34:4; 50:3; and Jeremiah 4:24-26). This is what we see occurring at the end of each of John's series of visions.

What did Jesus have to say about the Day of the Lord?

_____

_____

_____

_____

_____

_____

_____

You'll also recall that in Paul's letters to the Thessalonians he was addressing some misunderstandings concerning this same event. What were Paul's conclusions as to when Christ would return (see 1 Thessalonians 5:1-2 and 2 Thessalonians 2:1-4)?

_____

_____

_____

_____

_____

_____

Why is it important to understand the order of events at the end of time?

_____

_____

_____

_____

_____

_____

GOD SECURES VICTORY FOR THE FAITHFUL.

Throughout the New Testament, we've seen that it is considered an honor to be counted worthy to suffer for Christ. First Peter 4:13 actually tells us to rejoice that we participate in the sufferings of Christ. The glorious message of the book of Revelation is that our victory is secured whether we live or die, whether we are loved by the world or are persecuted by it. Throughout the book of Revelation, John keeps focusing our attention on those who have been martyred and on their victory in spite of death. A voice even tells him, "Blessed are the dead who die in the Lord from now on. . . . they will rest from their labor, for their deeds will follow them" (14:13).

Will believers suffer in the Great Tribulation? Perhaps. Will they be defeated? No! This is the glorious message, the blessed hope of every Christian. Teaching that we will not have to experience what we read about here, even in a measure, leads only to a false assurance and a lack of preparation for what is to come. Revelation was given not only to PREPARE us and to alert us so that we will be ready (both spiritually and physically), but also to REMIND us that God has secured victory for the faithful — in spite of persecution and even death.

When the six seals are opened, what happens?

_____

_____

_____

_____

_____

GOD SEALS HIS PEOPLE IN TRIBULATION

An angel says, "Do not harm the land or sea or the trees until we put a seal on the forehead of the servants of God" (7:3). And so, 144,000 are sealed — a symbol of ownership, authentication and protection.

To whom does the 144,000 refer, and what evidence is there to support this conclusion?

_____

_____

_____

_____

_____

After seeing the devastation of the last days, John is given a picture of the faithful, who are sealed by God — not to protect them totally from every sorrow at this time of tribulation, but to protect them spiritually and to preserve them through it. Many will die physically, just as they did, in fact, in John's day. But death itself is not defeat.

So, John sees the victory of the martyrs who stand before the throne praising Christ for salvation (7:9-17). They never will hunger, thirst or sorrow again (7:16-17). The message is clear: Death for the Christian is not defeat. It is victory! We are sealed; God will bring us through, victorious!

GOD SETS LIMITS ON DESTRUCTION.

What are the results of the sounding of the seven trumpets?

_____

_____

_____

_____

What is the significance of the fraction, "one-third," that is used over and over in chapters 8 and 9?

_____

_____

_____

_____

_____

Between the sixth and seventh trumpets is an interlude describing the "two witnesses." Some believe that these are Elijah and Moses, who will return to the earth and prophesy during the tribulation period. Indeed, much of the description of these witnesses is reminiscent of these two great Old Testament prophets — power to turn water to blood, to strike the earth with plagues, and to shut up the heavens so that it will not rain.

Others believe that the "two witnesses" refer to the books of the Law and the Prophets embodied in Moses and Elijah, or to the Old and New Testaments, law and grace, or Enoch and Elijah (both of whom were "translated").

Keeping in mind John's emphasis throughout the book on the preservation of the church and the victory of martyrs, how else might this passage be interpreted?

_____

_____

_____

_____

_____

What are the seven signs John sees, and to what do they refer?

_____

_____

_____

_____

_____

In keeping with his emphasis, John points out to us again in chapter 14 that judgment will come to the wicked, that the church will be redeemed from the earth (14:3), and that all those who die from now on will be blessed (14:13). And so we reach the climax again with the harvest of the earth (14:14-20).

GOD SENDS HIS WRATH ON THE WICKED.

After reading all this, it's easy to begin to think that evil forces are really in control and that justice will never prevail. But John sees seven angels with the bowls of God's wrath in chapters 15 and 16. Notice that he also sees those who have been victorious over the beast — not by defying death, but by refusing to worship him (15:2). With these bowls, the wrath of God is completed (15:1).

How are these judgments similar to the plagues on Egypt, and why would that be comforting to those undergoing persecution?

_____

_____

_____

_____

_____

Revelation 19:11-21 records the final battle, when Christ comes with the armies of heaven (19:14), strikes down the nations, and treads the winepress (see 14:20) of the fury of God's wrath. The Beast and the False Prophet are thrown alive into the lake of fire, and the rest of the wicked are killed. God's wrath is being completed.

The encouragement of Revelation to us is this: Christ will be victorious, and He will come with certain judgment. Only the wicked will suffer His wrath and will be thrown into the lake of fire. The sequence of John's visions underscores the fact that we will be victorious with Christ. No matter how John looks at the events of history, no matter how detailed his view, the end result is always the same: The battle is the Lord's, and He is the certain victor!

For personal reflection:

1) In what ways do you find the events described in Revelation frightening? Can you see now that it is actually a book of encouragement?

2) What is your personal opinion concerning the Rapture and the Great Tribulation? Why is it important not to get overly dogmatic about the order of events?

3) Why would a loving God allow His children to experience such trying times? Do you think God would really let us be persecuted? Explain.

For the next lesson . . .

Read Revelation 20–22.
- Revelation 20:1-6
- Revelation 20:7-10
- Revelation 20:11-15
- Revelation 21:1-8
- Revelation 21:9-27
- Revelation 22:1-6
- Revelation 22:7-21

Sequence of Events in Revelation

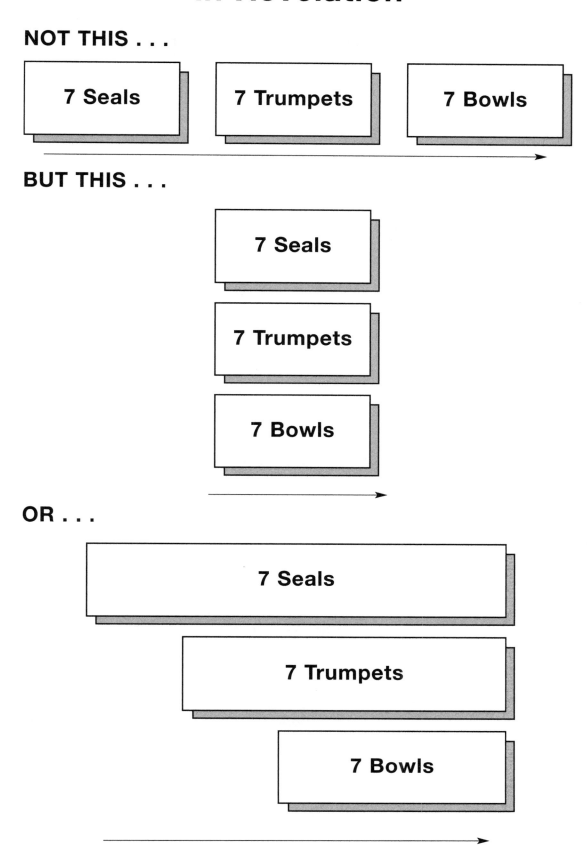

NOT THIS . . .

7 Seals   7 Trumpets   7 Bowls

BUT THIS . . .

7 Seals

7 Trumpets

7 Bowls

OR . . .

7 Seals

7 Trumpets

7 Bowls

REVELATION
(PART 3)

You can see from our studies so far on the book of Revelation what a comforting message this would have been for the church in John's day. It helped them to realize that they were just a small part of the grand struggle between God and the forces of evil — the enmity of Genesis 3:15. But now they could be assured of the outcome: Christ would win. On every page of Revelation, we see this encouragement.

What is the significance of the references to the Temple in Revelation?

_____

_____

_____

_____

_____

_____

As significant as this book is to the historical situation of the first-century church and, for that matter, the church of every age that undergoes persecution, we must recognize that the events it describes detail for us the final conflict at the end of time. Revelation goes far beyond its first-century setting to describe a time of unparalleled tribulation on the earth and the ultimate outcome of the struggle between good and evil.

THE REIGN OF CHRIST AND FINAL RETRIBUTION

What events are recorded in chapters 20 through 22?

_____

_____

_____

_____

_____

These events have been subject to more diverse interpretations than even the rapture of the church. Though there are numerous divergences among proponents of each interpretation, they fall into three basic categories:

1. Amillennialism:

_____

_____

_____

_____

_____

2. Postmillennialism:

_____

_____

_____

_____

_____

3. Premillennialism:

_____

_____

_____

_____

_____

Why are there so many interpretations?

_____

_____

_____

_____

_____

List some of the considerations in interpreting the millenium:

1. Satan is bound for one thousand years, and then is released to deceive the nations.

_____

_____

_____

_____

2. Is this an earthly, political reign or a heavenly, spiritual one?

_____

_____

_____

_____

3. Those who reign with Christ are the souls of those who have been martyred.

_____

_____

_____

_____

4. The Great White Throne Judgment occurs after the one thousand years.

_____

_____

_____

_____

5. John sees a new heaven and a new earth.

_____

_____

_____

John's focus in these chapters, though, is not Satan, but the fate of the martyrs. In John's day, many have been killed for their faith in Christ. John shows us that those who have died are far from defeated, and actually are now reigning with Christ and are seated on thrones. He can see their souls.

The fact that John doesn't mention the other dead in Christ does not mean they aren't there. His focus is on those who have been slain for their testimony, which would appear to the world to be ultimate defeat. John is revealing to us the present reality: The souls who died are reigning with Christ right now. John shows us that they have received the promises recorded in the letters to the churches in chapters 2 and 3.

Jesus has overcome the world and death and is seated at the right hand of God. So, too, those who overcome — who are faithful even to the point of death — also will be seated on thrones. They can't be hurt by the second death (which implies that they've already experienced the first death). They have overcome.

THE REDEEMED OF CHRIST AND FINAL REWARD

Chapters 21 and 22 describe the dawning of the Day of God (cf. 2 Peter 3:12). John's description interestingly includes elements of Jerusalem, the Temple, and the Garden of Eden. He sees a new heaven and earth. The old order of things has passed away. Everything is made new and is restored perfectly to God's original intention.

Much of John's description centers on the New Jerusalem, which he sees coming down out of heaven from God. What are some of the possible interpretations of the Heavenly city?

_____

_____

_____

_____

_____

_____

Chapter 22 describes the reward of the redeemed. We see, flowing from the throne, the River of Life, the water promised to all who thirst and will come to Christ (22:17). We also see the Tree of Life, which has been promised to those who overcome (2:7). And Christ's servants will reign with Him forever (22:5). This is the climax of God's plan of redemption. All of Scripture has been pointing to this day. It is the final restoration of everything destroyed by the Fall:

* In Genesis 1 through 3, we read that God made a perfect earth, which was soon marred by sin. Satan was introduced, Adam and Eve disobeyed, the ground was cursed, death and sorrow became a reality, and the first man and woman were banished from the garden and were denied access to the Tree of Life. Fellowship and communion with God were broken.

* Revelation 20 through 23 reveals the consummation of God's plan of redemption, the promise of restoration that began in Genesis 3:15. God creates a new heaven and earth, and nothing impure ever can enter it (Rev. 21:27); there is no longer any curse (22:3); death, sorrow and pain are forever gone (21:4); we are given access to the Tree of Life (22:14); and God and Christ will dwell with us for eternity. Everything lost in the Fall now is restored perfectly and is completed with the return of Christ. This is redemption in its fullest sense.

God's plan of redemption, from beginning to end, is thoroughly set out for us in the Bible. The blessed hope of every Christian is the redemption disclosed here.

We will end our study with the seven blessings in the book of Revelation, which apply to the whole of God's Word and God's people:

> Blessed is the one who reads the words of this prophecy, and blessed are those who hear it and take to heart what is written in it, because the time is near (Rev. 1:3).

> Blessed are the dead who die in the Lord from now on (Rev. 14:13).

> Behold I come like a thief! Blessed is he who stays awake and keeps his clothes with him (Rev. 16:15). [Be prepared!]

> Blessed are those who are invited to the wedding supper of the Lamb! (Rev. 19:9).

> Blessed and holy are those who have part in the first resurrection (Rev. 20:6).

> Behold, I am coming soon! Blessed is he who keeps the words of the prophecy in this book (Rev. 22:7).

> Blessed are those who wash their robes, that they may have the right to the tree of life and may go through the gates into the city (Rev. 22:14).

A glorious inheritance awaits those who overcome. The appeal is given to every individual: "The Spirit and the bride say, 'Come!' And let HIM who hears say, 'Come!' WHOEVER is thirsty, let HIM come; and WHOEVER wishes, let HIM take the free gift of the water of life" (22:17, emphasis added). This is the invitation to every one of us — to come to Christ and accept His free gift of eternal life. Then we can make our prayer that of Revelation 22:20: "He who testifies to these things says, 'Yes, I am coming soon.' Amen. Come, Lord Jesus."

The Lord's redeemed indeed have "a hope and a future" (Jeremiah 29:11).

For personal reflection:

1) Do you think we need to thoroughly understand everything in the book of Revelation in order to gain encouragement from it? Why or why not?

2) Do you tend to think of death as defeat or victory? How has this study affected your attitude toward death? Explain.

3) As you look back over your study through the entire Bible, can you see how everything fits together to form one great plan of salvation? How does it make you feel to know that God has provided so fully for your restoration and reward?

For future study . . .

Don't stop studying the Bible. Make a plan to continue the good reading habits you have begun. Pray regularly about what you read, and allow God to bring the truth to light in your heart and mind. No single study can cover everything — the Bible is inexhaustible! Keep up the good work, remembering that we will reap a harvest if we don't give up. You've only just begun!

NEW TESTAMENT STUDY QUESTIONS

1. What significant political, religious and social developments occurred during the four-hundred-year intertestamental period, and how did they pave the way for Christ and the spread of Christianity?

2. How do the four Gospels complement one another in their description of Jesus Christ?

3. What is the key theme of the book of Acts, and how does that influence Luke's arrangement of the historical information found there?

4. What was the historical situation of the Roman church at the time Paul wrote Romans? How is it evidenced in Paul's emphases in this book?

5. What were some of Paul's underlying motives for many of the teachings in his letters, especially 1 Corinthians?

6. What do we learn about the character of Paul from 2 Corinthians?

7. How does the book of Ephesians influence our understanding of the intent and integrity of the church?

8. What is the significance of Paul's focus on joy in Philippians?

9. Describe the heresy threatening the church in the latter half of the first century, and show from Colossians and 1 John how it was refuted.

10. What prompted Paul's letters to the Thessalonians, and how does his purpose dictate his major themes?

11. When and to whom were the pastoral Epistles written? Explain the significance of Paul's emphases on sound doctrine and the truth found in them.

12. How does Hebrews affect our understanding of the status of the Jews (both as a religion and as a people) in the kingdom of God? How does the book tie together the Old and New Testaments (the covenants)?

13. Explain why James is really a book of faith, and not just of works. How do you reconcile the teachings of James and Paul on justification?

14. According to 1 and 2 Peter, what is the Christian response to hostility and heresy?

15. What three tests do we find in 1 John that help us to be certain of our own salvation and by which we can test the spirits?

16. What was the historical situation at the time of the Revelation given to John, and what comfort would the book have brought to Christians at that time?

17. Of what is the book of Revelation a revelation? Explain. How does Revelation offer hope and a future for the faithful Christian?

SELECTED BIBLIOGRAPHY

Alexander, David and Pat, Ed. *Eerdmans' Handbook to the Bible*. Grand Rapids: Wm. B. Eerdmans Publishing Co., 1973.

Barker, Kenneth, et. al., Ed. *The NIV Study Bible*. Grand Rapids: Zondervan Publishing House, 1985.

Biederwolf, William E. *The Second Coming Bible Commentary*. Grand Rapids: Baker Book House, 1985 (orig. 1924).

Douglas, J.D. et. al., Ed. *The Illustrated Bible Dictionary,* 3 vols. Wheaton: Tyndale House Publishers, 1980.

Gundry, Robert H. *The Church and the Tribulation: A Biblical Examination of Post Tribulationism*. Grand Rapids: Zondervan Publishing House, 1973.

Harper, Albert F., et. al., Ed. *The Wesley Bible*. Nashville: Thomas Nelson Publishers, 1990.

Henry, Matthew. *A Commentary of the Whole Bible,* 6 vols. Old Tappan, NJ: Fleming H. Revell Co.

Higle, Tommy C. *Journey Through the Bible*. Marietta, OK: Tommy Higle Ministries, 1980.

Ladd, George Eldon. *The Blessed Hope*. Grand Rapids: Wm. B. Eerdmans Publishing Co., 1956.

Ladd, George Eldon. *A Commentary on the Revelation of John*. Grand Rapids: Wm. B. Eerdmans Publishing Co., 1972.

MacPherson, Dave. *The Incredible Cover-Up*. Central Point, Oregon: Omega Publications, 1975.

McKeever, James, Ed. *End-Times News Digest*. Medford, OR: Omega Ministries, 1989.

Mears, Henrietta C. *What the Bible is All About*. Ventura, CA: Regal Books, 1953, 1983.

Rosenthal, Marvin. *The Pre-Wrath Rapture of the Church*. Nashville: Thomas Nelson Publishers, 1990.

Ryrie, Charles Caldwell. *The Ryrie Study Bible*. Chicago: Moody Press, 1976, 1978.

Stringfellow, Alan B. *Through the Bible in One Year*. Tulsa: Virgil W. Hensley, Inc., 1978.

Tenney, Merrill C. *John: The Gospel of Belief*. Grand Rapids: Wm. B. Eerdmans Publishing Co., 1948, 1976.

The Tyndale New Testament Commentaries. Grand Rapids: Wm. B. Eerdmans Publishing Co., 1958, 1982.

Wilkinson, Bruce and Kenneth Boa. *Talk Through the Bible*. Nashville: Thomas Nelson Publishers, 1983.

Yamauchi, Edwin. *Harper's World of the New Testament*. San Francisco: Harper & Row, 1981.